Windows 2000 Quality of Service

David Iseminger

MACMILLAN
TECHNICAL
PUBLISHING
U·S·A

Windows 2000 Quality of Service

By David Iseminger

International Standard Book Number: 1-57870-115-5

Library of Congress Catalog Card Number: 99-62128

03 02 01 00 99   7 6 5 4 3 2 1

Interpretation of the printing code: The rightmost double-digit number is the year of the book's printing; the rightmost single-digit number is the number of the book's printing. For example, the printing code 99-1 shows that the first printing of the book occurred in 1999.

Composed in MCPdigital by Macmillan Computer Publishing

Printed in the United States of America

Trademark Acknowledgments

Warning and Disclaimer

Publisher
David Dwyer

Executive Editor
Linda Ratts Engelman

Managing Editors
Patrick Kanouse
Gina Brown

Acquisitions Editor
Karen Wachs

Development Editor
Lisa M. Thibault

Project Editor
Nancy Sixsmith

Indexer
Lisa Stumpf

Proofreader
Elise Walter

Acquisitions Coordinator
Jennifer Garrett

Manufacturing Coordinator
Chris Moos

Book Designer
Louisa Klucznik

Cover Designer
Aren Howell

Production Team Supervisor
Tricia Flodder

Production
Liz Johnston

About the Author

The *Windows NT/2000 Network Architect and Developer Series* is a set of guides that meets the needs of the growing community of technical-level Windows NT/2000 users. Each title in the series focuses on a single aspect or part of the Windows NT/2000 technology and provides networking professionals with detailed proven solutions to their problems.

David Iseminger is an individual consultant at Microsoft, and has worked on Windows NT and Windows 2000 (since Windows NT 3.5) as a networking and router performance analyst, telecommunications specialist, and performance tool developer. These days, he writes a handful of books a year (nonfiction computer books and novels). He also works with Microsoft's Developer Documentation Group as a programming writer, creating and maintaining many of the Platform SDK's established and emerging networking technologies, including Quality of Service. Check out David's Web site at www.iseminger.com for more information.

As the traffic on networks continues to increase, the strain on the network infrastructure and available resources has also grown. In response to this increased demand, Microsoft is building a set of components into Windows 2000 for network bandwidth management called Quality of Service. *Windows 2000 Quality of Service* is a critical guide to these emerging technologies. This authoritative reference includes the following:

- Expert real-world insight into QOS by the author of Microsoft's Windows NT/2000 QOS technology programming documentation
- Detailed coverage of QOS implementation, including client, subnet, router, and WAN implementation mechanisms
- Critical information on application-, network-, and policy-driven QOS and how to unite them
- Information about how to use and exploit QOS in programs
- Authoritative information on the open QOS technology standards, and how Microsoft has implemented them in Windows 2000

If you engineer or administer Windows NT networks, *Windows 2000 Quality of Service* is an essential resource to help you implement Quality of Service components in your Windows 2000 network. This comprehensive reference will help you do the following:

- Install, configure and enable QOS on your Windows 2000 platform
- Specify the way bandwidth will be utilized on a network by defining traffic control patterns for different types of network traffic
- Plan and design your Windows 2000 system with QOS in mind
- Program applications to take advantage of QOS components

About the Technical Reviewers

These reviewers contributed their considerable practical, hands-on expertise to the entire development process for *Windows 2000 Quality of Service*. As the book was being written, these folks reviewed all the material for technical content, organization, and flow. Their feedback is critical to ensuring that *Windows 2000 Quality of Service* fits our readers' needs for the highest quality technical information.

Eural Authement is a Senior Network Engineer for Microsoft's Global Networking. His focus currently is on designing and implementing Quality of Service (QOS) for Microsoft's worldwide IP/ATM network. Before joining Microsoft, Authement was a director in Bay Networks' Strategic Planning Group. In prior roles, he was a senior network consultant and professional services manager for Bay Networks. Since 1990, his specialty has been designing IP networks for Internet service providers and large corporations using OSPF and BGP, and fine-tuning OSPF over complex topologies such as Frame Relay and ATM networks. His largest design and implementation project was to migrate a 1,000-router network to OSPF from RIP, and design a 15,000-router network using OSPF and RIP2. Authement has been teaching OSPF since 1993 to Bay customers and through NetWorld+Interop. He has a B.S. in electrical engineering from the University of Southwestern Louisiana with a specialty in telecommunications.

Tim Moore of Microsoft also gave excellent technical feedback.

Acknowledgments

First of all, a special thank you goes out to Tim Moore of Microsoft Corporation, whose input was invaluable, breadth of QOS knowledge expansive, and approachability second to none. This book is, without question, better because of his technical input and insights; any shortfalls found herein are certainly mine.

Appreciation is also extended to Kirsten Iseminger, who put up with less deck-building, dirt-shoveling, car washing, and project completing during the course of this book's writing. I know...the list has been simply deferred—it has not disappeared.

Thanks to the crew at MTP—Linda Engelman, Lisa Thibault, Jennifer Garrett, Karen Wachs, and Nancy Sixsmith—for all things book-creation-oriented. Of course, it goes without saying (but shouldn't) that all agent-related acknowledgments and thanks go out to Margot Maley, agent extraordinaire.

And last, but not least, thanks to the readers—the IT professionals, administrators, and programmers dealing with the squirmy technology of QOS—for making the work that goes into these projects worthwhile.

Contents at a Glance

Table of Contents

Introduction

The paper office is shrinking—giving way to small offices, mid-sized businesses, and corporate environments. Data is kept on the network, sent through the network, saved on servers scattered across the network, and retrieved from data stores over that same network. While freeing us from the monotony of hand-organized filing cabinets and penned memos, the digital age is also demanding more from us, requiring double or triple the productivity in the same hour...achieved through our slave surrogate, the computer.

As much as we depend on the computer, it, in turn, depends on the network. Only a few years ago, networks were novelties used to share peripherals or to make "light" queries to some huge water-cooled computer that sat in the center of a glass-encased mosque. Today, the network has matured into a data traffic freeway, whose usage seems to know no bounds. Such increased use of the network has certainly upped the productivity of users, but, unfortunately, it must be squeezed through the same network interface (often a shared 10Mbps network tap). But, as we know, technology waits for nothing and no one, including overburdened network infrastructures.

Although this universal and now dependent use of the network didn't happen overnight, the volume of the data we want to send has increased dramatically...and almost overnight. It's the same network that it was last week—its bandwidth hasn't magically increased with our transmission appetite—yet, we now want the same network to transmit streaming audio and video from CNN's Web site while simultaneously downloading a 20MB software patch. Not such a tall order until you consider that 30 other people on your shared Ethernet subnet are doing similar work and contending for network access. If we could simply turn away and go on with our work, doing our jobs without the use of the computer or the network, our problem would be easily solved. But we depend on the computer to do almost everything, so the issue must be addressed.

Quality of Service addresses the issue from a software perspective (rather than a hardware perspective—such as providing 1000Mbps Gigabit Ethernet taps to every desktop). The computer and its connected network are sometimes called the great equalizer: a forum in which all people (and data) are created equal. This level playing field, though perhaps empowering, is the root of the problem because not all uses of this empowering network are necessarily of equal importance in the grand scheme of business activity. Mission-critical SQL queries can be more important than downloading the newest browser, your IP telephone is more sensitive to latency than an FTP download, and backbone router resources could be better spent servicing important data instead of secondary or less-important data (however your organization defines "important" and "secondary"). Mission-critical applications, streaming audio and/or video applications, and even user-based utilization decisions could benefit from some means of differentiating between "important" and "less-important" data. Such differentiation, such preferential treatment of data, and such user- or group-based favoritism is what Quality of Service technology in Windows 2000 is all about.

Network transmissions will continue to increase in volume, and, realistically, hardware-based solutions simply won't always be able to keep pace. This is not because fast networking technologies aren't available, but because new hardware-based network technologies are expensive to deploy. Imagine upgrading your switches or routers every time a new processor hits the market. If your company can afford that, hire me; I have a special billing rate just for you. For the rest of us, the data we want to transmit over the network increases faster than "free-for-all" network transmissions can handle, creating a need for some other kind of solution. There needs to be a way of getting better and smarter use out of the network—a way of giving network-resource preference to data deemed more important.

Fortunately, there is… now. With the collective computer industry's nurturing of Quality of Service, coupled with the Quality of Service support found in Windows 2000, you can get smarter use of your existing network with the deployment of Windows 2000 Quality of Service.

Why this Book Is for You

Quality of Service is a confusing technology. It's complex—perhaps one of the most complex subjects in today's network environment. This book takes the confusion out of Quality of Service (or at least helps to do so), and provides integrators and programmers with enough information to start making Quality of Service part of their routines.

This book also makes sense of the complexity that's part and parcel of Quality of Service. It presents it in a way that enables a firm grasp on the technology as a whole, as well as giving detailed information to those who want to get granular about their control of its components. This book also integrates real-life recommendations for deployment of the technology and its requisite components, not just heady theoretical discussions and explanations. Real life is where you'll be using Quality of Service, so it makes sense to include real-life recommendations and examples.

And perhaps one of the most important reasons that this book is for you is its approach: No monotone lectures or unintelligible incantations. Instead, discussions are tailored toward making the subject of Quality of Service engaging and interesting, rather than a substitute for Nyquil.

How this Book Is Structured

One of the most important aspects of approaching Quality of Service is structure. Quality of Service has its hand in every device across the network, and it's most comfortable—at least in a primal instinct sort of way—in a technical-discussion state of chaos. To avoid such chaos, the book has been divided into sections that will guide you through Quality of Service while building an understanding of the technology.

Part I, "Quality of Service Introduced," provides definitions and information about the industry-wide concept of Quality of Service and what the concept means for the network. It then explains how Quality of Service has been implemented in Windows 2000, offering information that ties industry standard (and traditional) Quality of Service terms with the Windows 2000 implementation of QOS. The discussion then includes Windows 2000 Quality of Service components, introducing how Quality of Service is achieved within Windows 2000.

Part II, "Quality of Service in Detail," gets down to the implementation and functional details that make Quality of Service in Windows 2000 a reality. Part II goes through the structured discussion of each Windows 2000 Quality of Service component in detail, starting with application-driven components, then network-driven components, and finally policy-driven components. Part II concludes with a chapter that brings the three Quality of Service component "groups" into perspective, reminding us that Quality of Service is a cohesive technology and explaining how all three groups really interact to create the end-to-end Windows 2000 Quality of Service solution.

Part III, "QOS in the Real World," departs from the theoretical world and moves into the real world, where deployment and programmatic integration of technology actually take place. Part III begins with the practical side of Quality of Service: how to get it, how it is installed in Windows 2000, and how it is installed on clients.

Traffic Overload and the Plight of the Network Device

Technology speeds into our lives at an alarming pace, bringing new uses and unconsidered capabilities to the computer environment that seem to keep us steadily on our toes. But don't be misled; we demand such technologies and drive that pace. We want added functionality, improved performance, and ever-renewed features that startle us with realism and wow us with increased business applications. And we want them brought right to our desktop. How do such features get to us? Increasingly, they get to us from the network, and the network is getting crowded.

It isn't just multimedia applications and video transmissions that are filling network bandwidth, either. Applications that were once 25MB in size are now 125MB, and the files they create seem to be doubling in size with each new release. Software downloads from central installation sites on the network create network traffic; and, as development and release cycles of core business applications (let alone Web browsers) shrink, the network activity associated with their installations increases. The most heavily hit devices under these increasingly burdened circumstances are the network devices sitting between our computers and the resources we want to use (network devices such as switches, routers, and WAN links). We continue adding to their burden but expect them to ferry our data efficiently, and we become frustrated when we experience delays. Much like a freeway system designed for half as many vehicles as it needs to service, soon everyone is slowed down...even those with a higher priority for use. And, much like a freeway system, adding more bandwidth (freeway lanes) means sharing those resources again with everyone. At best, it creates relief that can be measured in months; at worst, it affects only an incrementally "less-congested" situation. Also similar to freeways, network infrastructure improvements carry additional negatives: They are expensive and sometimes disruptive.

A smarter approach is in order. There is a better way of addressing congestion problems and oversubscription to existing resources. This has already happened on freeways in most metropolitan areas. High Occupancy Vehicle (HOV) lanes offer priority to those commuters who ride together; large companies mitigate "bursty" freeway congestion by "shaping" the way traffic enters freeway systems (by staggering shift quitting times); metered on-ramps act as traffic cues when rush hour is in effect; and express lanes offer directional gates for traffic flow, essentially creating a policy to allow preferred (carpool) traffic access to reserved freeway lanes (bandwidth). With such freeway resource management, freeway use becomes smarter, and traffic flows more smoothly than it would in a "free-for-all." Although such management doesn't mean an end to adding more lanes, it adds a new lease to the life of existing freeways. It provides a cost-effective approach that extends the effectiveness of existing freeways and improves the overall efficiency. Even when new lanes are added, such mechanisms maintain efficient use of new resources and keep the infrastructure in the best shape it can be in.

As you may have guessed, network infrastructures aren't too different from freeway systems. They get congested, and there's more and more traffic wanting to use the same resources. But there are no HOV lanes, metered on-ramps, or express lanes. Although Quality of Service, offers solutions similar to all of these and more, it takes some work to understand how Quality of Service goes about doing so. Before the first on-ramp light can be installed, a firm grasp of Quality of Service and its multitude of components is required.

Part I

Quality of Service Introduced

1 **Defining Quality of Service**

2 **Quality of Service Technical Issues**

3 **Quality of Service Implementation in Windows 2000**

4 **Quality of Service Components in Windows 2000**

Knowing the basics of a technology is a must for anyone who wants to learn more about its details. In short, there must be a foundation of knowledge built before the structure and detail work of a given technology can be properly discussed, explained, or furnished with specifics. In Part I, "Quality of Service Introduced," the concepts of Quality of Service are provided, from both an industry-wide perspective and a Windows 2000 perspective.

This part explains the concepts necessary to enable detailed discussions of the way Quality of Service is implemented in Windows 2000. It also provides the necessary background to understand Quality of Service implications for non-Windows implementations and devices, and how Quality of Service can affect the entire networked world.

Defining Quality of Service

Before too much work can be done on the explanation of Quality of Service, there must be an establishment of terms and a consensus of meaning. To avoid ambiguity and to foster the best explanation of Quality of Service possible, this chapter explains and defines Quality of Service, gives some background on its inception, and discusses the factors that have generated the real need for Quality of Service in today's network environment.

The Plight of the Network

Listen to any IT analyst, any Internet service provider, or any person responsible for network functionality in the data network environment today—you'll almost certainly hear complaints about network availability, network bandwidth, or network transmission quality. Network congestion and its complement of side-effects are common ailments in today's networking environment. This is the result of more and more users, who make more extensive use of the network for more diverse reasons every day. Networks are getting more and more congested, and the outlook for the foreseeable future is unquestionable: more usage, more network growth.

Is the network slow? Is the network bandwidth acceptable, but the packet latency too unpredictable or too high—resulting in glitchy real-time applications whose poor performance makes them too cumbersome to use? Is there too much frivolous, non-business activity happening on the network, taking up valuable network bandwidth that's no longer available for business-critical networking? Perhaps it's none of these in particular—just a matter of inconsistencies across the network, with its availability and transmission quality going from excellent to a snail's pace in unpredictable cycles. Unpredictability can be especially vexing when you're trying to plan business activities around availability—because ensuring a certain level of acceptable, predictable, and available network quality can determine whether business activities over that network are going to sink or succeed.

The stopgap solution for this unbridled network usage growth almost always comes in one of the following forms:

- More bandwidth
- Specialized network segments for particular subsets of users
- Higher-performing network devices
- Better network equipment drivers

Although there are other categories (such as new segments and new routers, multiple access points, load balancing, and the like), the solutions almost always share a common thread: more bandwidth, not better use of the existing network. Don't blame the administrators, network architects, or IT implementers—they haven't had any alternatives. Until now.

Today's stopgap solutions are somewhat akin to throwing money at the problem. Buy more routers; balance the load; or upgrade to Fast Ethernet, FDDI, ATM, or Gigabit Ethernet. Get better switches, install the latest drivers, and hope that performance improvements will be enough. Implement policies against corporate network use for non-business activities and have the Corporate Game Police look over the employees' shoulders as they work.

Are these solutions? Yes. Are they good solutions? They're probably the best solutions to the problems faced by today's network integrators and administrators, with the exception of the Game Police. But wouldn't it be better if you could somehow guarantee network performance? Better yet, wouldn't it be nice if you could somehow differentiate between "important data" and "less important data," and give priority access to the network for "important data" based on some criteria? You can... now. Quality of Service can do all these things and more; it is the long-term solution that can alleviate the need for many of the stopgap solutions.

But what is QOS? Is it a concept? A theory? Is it a technology or a group of technologies? Is it hardware-based or software-based? Is it a standard, a recommendation, or neither? Is it the first step to an entirely new generation of computing applications and paradigms? The answer to these questions inherits the ambiguity that generally hovers over QOS discussions. The answer to these questions is commonly: Yes, or 17... Take your choice. Each of those answers is equally meaningful, helpful, and explanatory when it comes to such QOS questions. I think a better answer is required.

What is Quality of Service?

Quality of Service is a theoretical technology that proposes to make smarter use of the existing network by implementing reservations and service quality provisions for differentiated subsets of data. There are two types of QOS: the first has its roots in providing prescribed service quality; the second is geared more toward providing a handful of classes of service, or priority levels, to transmitted data. These "ideas" behind QOS are perhaps the only straightforward aspect of QOS, and the ideas can be further defined in a couple of simple statements: for the first type of QOS, the idea is to provide deterministic network service. By *deterministic*, I mean predictable, preordained, prearranged, systematic, and expected network service. The second type of QOS is used to bump network service priority up or down for subsets of data, and thereby provide differentiated service quality for different subsets of data.

Note

To put it in salad terms, the first definition of QOS is like ordering a salad that has 1.5 ounces of salad dressing in a separate ceramic container, one-half of a head of romaine lettuce (torn, not cut), three diced carrots, shredded cabbage, and one three-inch ring of onions included. It is tossed by hand and served seven minutes before the main course, and no later than 300 seconds after the order is placed. The second definition of QOS is like ordering a dinner salad with the dressing on the side, with all the garnish vegetables included as an appetizer. You're going to get roughly the same thing, but the second salad is much easier to prepare and deliver. ♦

QOS, then, is the concept of creating more predictability and manageability with our network resources. With QOS, we should be able to reserve and predict network resources across the network for specified, differentiated subsets of data. Such predictability should include the amount of bandwidth required, perhaps the amount of latency that's acceptable, and maybe the optimum size of the packet we want to submit. We also want to be able to manage and administer with QOS, including specifying how all of that reserving and predicting is taking place, so that we perhaps can apply permission policies to those who have the right to make such reservations. In two words, we want *predictability* and *manageability*.

Note

Regardless of which type of QOS you describe, another way of defining it is to say that with QOS, you want to be able to classify and differentiate between data—and thereby assign priority, transmission characteristics, or policies to such data based on things such as network conditions, user permissions, available bandwidth, and data type. But just as importantly—and arguably more importantly to network administrators and chief technology officers—with QOS, you also want to be able to manage these resources.♦

Let me give you an example. Let's say you have some sort of mission-critical application that your company—a telephone-based sales order business—uses to place customer orders and make queries. Let's also say that the company is large, and that (like many companies these days) the network is used for all sorts of things. On a particular day, Mary is preparing to upgrade her Windows NT Workstation machine from Windows NT 4.0 to Windows 2000, and will also be installing the latest version of Microsoft Office. Mary's subnet includes a number of people who are taking calls and submitting orders, and they are on a 10MB Ethernet subnet. So, Mary starts her installation of Windows NT Workstation. All of a sudden, unbeknownst to her, two other people on her subnet have also chosen this particular day and time to upgrade their machines. Jim, one of the sales representatives, is online, talking to a customer who's getting ready to place a $100,000 order. He has his screen ready, he's about to take the customer's information and place the order, when all of a sudden his mission-critical ordering application slows to almost nothing. He can't place the order. He can't finish the order. Meanwhile, Mary has gone off to the coffeepot and is talking with Bill and Jackie—both of whom are also upgrading their machines—and eating a donut (multitasking, that is). Jim loses the $100,000 sale because he can't complete the order. What's the moral of the story? The network bandwidth was being eaten up by relatively unimportant activity—the upgrade process for three users—while a mission-critical application was starved of bandwidth.

Everyone's network access was actually degraded because of the upgrades going on, but there were different effects of such a degradation. To Mary, the long upgrade process simply meant that she got to eat two donuts instead of one; to Jim, it meant that his $100,000 deal went down the tubes, and the commission he was going to use to buy a DVD player went with it. All of this could have been remedied by QOS. If the priority of the mission-critical application had been higher than the download process, Jim would have been able to finish the sale because his network packets would have reserved a certain amount of bandwidth, and therefore would have gotten through the network in a timely fashion. With QOS, Jim would have completed the sale and gotten the DVD player, and Mary still would have been able to eat two donuts. Everyone would have been happy.

Don't be fooled by the simplicity of this example. Although it sounds like an easy enough thing to up the priority of one person's application over another's, it isn't very simple at all. There was the reservation of bandwidth that had to transpire, the specification of a certain level of service quality (perhaps latency requirements, though not necessarily), and (just as important) the implementation of management and policy information into the affected network devices to support such service quality parameters. In the example, the management end of it would have been someone (management, presumably) setting the priority of the mission-critical application higher than standard transmissions. The predictability included the amount of bandwidth that Jim's mission-critical application needed to be able to perform its tasks. The manageability included specifying that Jim (or the application) had the proper permissions to reserve the bandwidth, and also included the increased priority level assigned to that data—again, predictability and manageability.

All these requirements are easier asked for than done. Easier theorized, pontificated, and conjectured than put into practice. In fact, there are some who have said that implementing QOS is simply too complex to successfully achieve. Granted, any attempt at the implementation of QOS is as complex, technical, and controversial as its idea is simple, but it can be implemented successfully—you wouldn't be reading this book if it couldn't. Implementation of QOS has been achieved. In fact, it's been around in one form or another for over twenty years.

The History of Quality of Service

QOS isn't a new concept. In fact, there's been QOS in isolated spots for— believe it or not—more than twenty years. But a lot of things have changed since then, and the basic thrust behind QOS and the scope of its implementation have broadened significantly.

In the 1970s, network designers wanted a way to classify the importance of certain subsets of data as they crossed what was a revolutionary concept of lowering the cost of networking over wide geographical areas by creating a shared, standardized network. Until then, networks were implemented based on one vendor's proprietary transmission medium—such as Digital or IBM. If you had a computer made by one vendor that needed to communicate with a computer made by another vendor, the process of doing so was long and expensive, if available at all. This shared network, and the standardized access to computers from different vendors, was the *X.25 network*, and it still exists today. The significance to our discussion, however, is that the X.25 specification had QOS parameters built into it, in order to differentiate between different packet streams and thereby allow the X.25 network provider to assign increased priority to qualifying packets.

Don't think that QOS has been dormant since then, though. Frame Relay also has QOS parameters built into it in its CIR, CBR, and EBR (committed information rate, committed burst rate, and excess burst rate) settings— essentially setting bandwidth transmission values on the Frame Relay link. There is also a bit setting that can be programmed for a Frame Relay interface that allows a certain drop priority to be assigned to packets.

And what about the latest in WAN and LAN technologies? As you might have guessed, ATM (Asynchronous Transfer Mode) also has QOS parameters built into the protocol, and in fact, it has extensive QOS parameters.

So there's a bit of a common denominator here—these are all primarily WAN technologies that have had QOS parameters and capabilities built into them for awhile. You might be asking, "If they can implement QOS in the WAN, why is it so difficult or complex to do so in the regular old LAN?" The answer has to do with network isolation. WANs are fairly isolated, and what I didn't mention before is that the QOS parameters that these WAN technologies provided only affected the packet or frame's or cell's transmission *within the WAN*. That is, once the transmission got out of the WAN network, the quality of that transmission was no longer guaranteed.

For example, suppose that you're back in Los Angeles, trying to get some video feed from the server in Texas. Let's further say that the WAN connection that your Los Angeles network has to Texas is ATM. You're actually traversing three networks to get to the video server in Texas: your local network, the ATM network, and then the Texas local area network. If your ATM connection between Los Angeles and Texas is configured to supply a certain QOS (we'll say that it's going to guarantee that cell delivery will cross the ATM network within a certain latency value), then that QOS is valid only within the ATM network. Getting to the WAN link on your local network in Los Angeles, and then getting from the ATM link in the Texas office to the video server, has no QOS guarantee in the ATM QOS scenario. What does this mean? It means that if either the Los Angeles LAN or Texas LAN is particularly congested, you could still experience poor transmission. The cells would still be making it across the ATM network within the specified QOS levels, but the lack of QOS guarantees basically negates the service quality being provided by the ATM network on either end of the connection.

QOS for a network, then (or perhaps all-encompassing QOS), must provide end-to-end network service quality. That's more than a WAN network that provides tight latency tolerance. That means involving the network, including clients, switches, and routers, as well as the WAN. That's a pretty big shopping list, and quite frankly, it is asking for a lot.

Why the migration of QOS from the WAN to the entire (WAN-included) network? Because attributes that used to be associated more with the WAN have, with the exponential growth of network usage and Internet connectivity, infiltrated the local network—attributes such as expensive upgrade costs, ever-increasing bandwidth need, precious resources, service delivery guarantee needs, and increased dependence on interconnectivity. Also, the effort and complexity associated with getting different segments of the network—such as the router, the WAN connection, and the Frame Relay connection on the other side of the connection—prohibited the capability for such different segments to communicate and translate service quality requirements.

Perhaps most importantly, QOS has infiltrated the network because we're finding more uses for what has classically been used only for "data data," as opposed to voice-data or video-data. Uses such as telephony, streaming audio, or even video services are becoming more viable as bandwidth capabilities and clients' processing power/application availability arrive at multimedia-functional levels. In essence, what used to be the *computer network* as recently as a few years ago is now becoming an information superstructure that can integrate multiple information services: voice, video, and data.

Interpreting the Meaning of Quality of Service

Going back to the previous definitions of QOS, what does "provide deterministic network service" mean, exactly? It means a lot of things, and it sometimes means different things to different people. You can call it *predictability*. You can call it *a classification of network service*. Unfortunately, the very concept of QOS can also mean different things to different people, which only contributes to the confusion that sometimes accompanies QOS discussions. Such differences in opinion, explanation, or definition (choose whichever word you like, depending on how strongly you believe in yours) is understandable and expected in a technology whose implementation is in such infancy. To some, a certain implementation is much better than another—perhaps it provides more functionality that is absolutely necessary to justify calling it "QOS." But to someone else, QOS may mean something entirely different, perhaps because she believes that QOS will only become a reality if its functionality is pruned to reasonable levels. Who is right? If one person is right, is the other person wrong?

Those questions are difficult to answer. It's like the old phenomenology dichotomy of perception and reality, which my University of Washington phenomenology professor so poorly put forth. In QOS terms, the dichotomy translates to something like this: What your perception of QOS is and what my perception of QOS is may be different, and the true definition of QOS can only depend on one... right? So that means that your perception is incorrect and mine is correct, (or vice versa). In this case, the answer is... not necessarily.

Differing definitions of QOS will probably exist for quite some time. For our definition—which happens to be based on the Windows NT implementation of QOS—the definition remains something like the following:

> The differentiation of network service quality that is provided to certain subsets of data, and the provision of predictable or classified network service levels across a given network.

There will likely be dissension about this explanation, perhaps outright accusations of blasphemy, but I'm sticking with it. And with regards to the Windows 2000 implementation of QOS, it's right on track, especially when coupled with the predictability and manageability ideal.

All this predictability, classification, and manageability is a tall order in almost anyone's book—and especially difficult when we consider that a good deal of the network is completely unpredictable and chaotic by nature (such as Ethernet's CSMA/CD design). First come, first-served is essentially the antithesis of QOS, and it runs rampant across networks all over the world, especially including the Internet.

This brings us to the next point, which has to do with understanding QOS: there's a lot of low-level, network functionality going on within the QOS arena, which makes its understanding somewhat difficult to most of the computer-using people in the world.

Knowledge of the Network

QOS is mired in technology. There's no avoiding it because the capability to implement (or really, to even discuss) QOS really requires a significant knowledge of the network. Rather than say "go learn everything about networking," however, the discussions of QOS in this book will put things in understandable terms—not terms that I'm going to expect you to know and, if you don't, will leave you in the abyss of networking technology. In fact, the following chapter addresses the technical issues surrounding network functionality, and explains what the QOS technical requirements must do to fit into (that is, become a part of) the existing network.

However, deploying QOS does, without question, require a significant amount of knowledge about networking, protocols, and routers; and there's just no way around that. That doesn't mean that you need to learn it all before you read this book or that you need to know all the different queuing algorithms used in QOS to make it work in your organization; quite the contrary, especially with the networking and QOS explanations included in the following chapter. But it does mean that if you plan to implement QOS in your Windows 2000 environment, you'll need to clearly understand how networking works and have some detailed knowledge of why it works the way it does. In a phrase, implementation of QOS in a network is going to require knowing *how* the network works, not just *that* it works. Such understanding is what the next chapter aims to provide, but even that discussion necessarily assumes some pre-existing knowledge of the network.

Cursory familiarity with protocols and networks, then, won't quite cut it if a person really wants to understand QOS and the broad implications that

QOS has for the future of networking. There's a certain depth of familiarity that must be had to grab onto what QOS might do for an organization or, on a broader scale, for the entire communications infrastructure. Am I over-stating the importance of QOS? Time will tell, but I'm willing to bet a bucket of Seattle rainwater that its implications will be something akin to "convergence acceleration" or at least a change in the way information is distributed around the globe. Certainly, it has implications for how expensive network growth will be (whether it will be prohibitively expensive or just incrementally expensive). It also has implications for whether IP telephones will ever be mainstream or whether video such as pay-per-view sporting events will be pulled from your ISP instead of from some set-top cable box.

What does this mean for you? Why does this mean that you need to have a good working knowledge of the network to be able to implement QOS in your organization? There are a number of reasons:

- First, discussions of the way that QOS functions on Windows NT will necessarily include references to network technology. QOS is all about the network, and explanations of how it works or how to implement QOS will require a certain understanding of these underlying network technologies.

- Second, knowing how general network devices such as routers and hubs/switches operate will help because QOS requires that these devices modify how they operate to accommodate QOS provisions. This inclusion of network devices in the QOS fold means that the effects on these devices will be felt by implementations of QOS.

- Third, actually deploying a QOS in a corporate environment will certainly require extensive, broad network knowledge. Not cursory knowledge; not familiarity.

If you have a good knowledge of networks, and you are looking for the expertise and information necessary to implement QOS with Windows 2000, you're in the right place. This book will tell you what you need to know. Your contribution to this firm grasp of Windows NT QOS is going to be a reasonable knowledge of networks and network devices.

If you're looking for a working knowledge of QOS, you're also in the right place. By the time you finish this book, you'll understand what QOS is and how it's been implemented on Windows 2000, and what you need to do to take advantage of it.

If you're unsure what the difference is between a router and a hub, you should get some information on basic networking essentials, absorb it, and then pick up with Chapter 2. Otherwise, despite my effort to thoroughly explain the components and interaction of Windows 2000's QOS implemen-tation, you'll likely have a hard time knowing why a certain technology limitation has to be overcome. You'll get a lot more out of this book if you have the basics of networking down before pushing through the rest of the book. But don't get discouraged. No one was born with all of this networking knowledge—it had to be learned, from someone or somewhere, so you can learn it as well.

The point is this: QOS is complex, and it is inextricably tied to network functionality and protocols, so knowledge of such things will be necessary to put QOS functionality into a network infrastructure. The more network knowledge, the better. But then, that isn't just a QOS requirement, is it?

Leveraging Quality of Service in Business Terms

One common misconception of QOS is that it's primarily targeted at multimedia applications, such as being able to get reasonable quality out of some radio program being broadcast over the Internet. That's a misconception, and somewhat akin to saying, "Networks are valuable mainly because they let you share printers." At one time, in the 1980s when LANs were young and geared more toward workgroup environments, that was probably a fairly true statement. But we've come generations since then, and sharing printers isn't the most valuable use of networks any more. Similarly, at one time it may have been that QOS had its best use in enabling multimedia applications to function on computers. Not any more, however.

Today, we depend more on our network functionality than ever before, and in a few years, we'll all probably look back at this time and say "Man, I depend on the network ten times more now than I did back then." Businesses stop if the network goes down. Businesses gauge their loss of income in hundreds of thousands of dollars per hour when the network goes down. If you think I'm exaggerating, think back to the AOL blackout in August 1996, and remember the screaming and ranting that went on back then for people who were depending on AOL connectivity to get business-critical email out. That's nothing compared to what big business depends on today. Businesses depend on the network, and QOS has everything to do with network availability. The example offered previously in the chapter with Jim and his lost $100,000 deal because of Mary's donut time is a perfect example.

Because of the increasingly network-centric business model, QOS has its place in ensuring the mission-critical application connectivity even more than it does in multimedia. Don't get me wrong. I'm not saying that multimedia applications can't or won't benefit from QOS because they certainly will, but just not at the expense of mission-critical application functionality. I'm simply dispelling a myth, and putting QOS attention where that attention is due—on business, network availability, and application manageability and network device predictability.

Network Device Intercommunication

So, QOS is the concept that embodies our desire to predict and manage network resources, such as bandwidth and latency and other network transmission attributes. How is this kind of thing achieved? After all, there are lots of network resources in the potentially long line of devices that sit between any client and its potential network-connectivity target. Devices such as network cards, Ethernet hubs, routers, WAN links, and even more routers must all work together before we can even begin to figure out how QOS might be implemented. And on top of all that, there's software to get involved—some sort of client-side software that can invoke the whole process of getting a certain quality of service.

As you might have guessed by now, QOS has to be an end-to-end solution. If there's any one type of network device in the end-to-end solution that has no way of knowing about QOS or its parameters that you place on a certain subset of data, then you aren't really going to get the overall service quality you're looking for, are you?

Let me clarify with an example. Let's say there's a server on the central corporate site in Texas, from which you want to pull an online training video, and you're four hundred miles away in Los Angeles. In this example, if QOS worked for everything except WAN links, for example, the implementation of QOS would do you absolutely no good. Well, almost. The WAN link would have to give you at least the QOS level you were requesting from the rest of the network (for example, 120k/sec with latency at or below 120ms) for QOS to be effective. But without getting too technical at this point in the book, the bottom line is that QOS is an end-to-end solution: client to client, or client to server, or notebook to server, or IP phone to Central Office. Not part of the way, not excluding certain network devices, but end-to-end.

And therein lies a significant contributor to the complexity of QOS. All of these very diverse network devices (such as hubs, switches, routers, WAN links, and network devices), which are probably built from different vendors and run on different operating systems (if any), need to communicate with one another in order for QOS to have any chance of operating. If that's not complex, then neither is quantum mechanics.

But that's what QOS must do to implement what has come to be at least generally accepted as QOS. How that is done will be the subject of many later discussions in this book.

Why Quality of Service is Coming of Age

When the X.25 packet-forwarding network was created, it had a significant amount of overhead associated with each hop in the route between source and destination. That's because end nodes back then were not powerful machines, and they couldn't use their own processor power to ensure that transmissions through such a packet-forwarding network occurred without errors. That, in fact, is the reason why X.25 is dwindling and Frame Relay is getting so much attention. Frame Relay is quite similar to X.25, except that Frame Relay does no integrity-checking on packets as they get forwarded through Frame Relay networks. Why? Because end nodes and TCP/IP can do their own error-checking these days; there's enough processing power on the end node to do so.

To implement QOS for something as ubiquitous as the local area network, there is all sorts of cooperation that needs to go on between network devices. This cooperation requires communication, and any time there is communication, there is overhead. Five or even three years ago, the processing power of most end nodes wasn't enough to undertake such additional processing requirements. Don't get me wrong—QOS doesn't necessarily introduce a large burden on the client; in fact, quite the contrary. But the speed with which this processing must be done simply requires reasonable power on the client end of things, and that power is available today. Certainly, there are other factors, but the power of processors is a significant factor.

And it isn't just on the client where this processing has to occur. Remember, network devices at every stage between the end-to-end QOS solution must partake in this cooperative ensemble of packet delivery, and routers are certainly included. As processing power has continued to evolve at the desktop, so has the processing power and capabilities of network infrastructure devices such as the router. These devices have perhaps gained even more from the ongoing spike in processor power than the desktop has. Certainly, this additional processing power has contributed to the viability of QOS for the entire network.

Another contributing factor is *need*. The Internet and the next-generation Internet, called the *Internet2*, need QOS to bear the burden of the seemingly endless increase in growth for the use of the Internet. When customers or the industry needs a technology, it's interesting how such a need drives the technology into realization. Supply and demand, as the adage goes. But there's more to this need than a simple increase in bandwidth or guaranteed availability; more to it than using cooler, bigger graphics on Web pages because there's more bandwidth to everyone's desktop. It has to do with additional service moving over the Internet. The topic was touched on earlier in this chapter, and merits additional attention: the integration of services.

Integrated Services and Other IETF Working Groups

The idea of an information superhighway—one that provides the infrastructure necessary to provide all sorts of information—is something that has the attention of lots of people. Today, we have three networks (at least):

- Telecommunications (telephone) network
- Video network (usually your cable provider)
- Data network (which isn't necessarily universally connected)

Imagine what it would be like if all this could be provided to us in the form of one network—you could get your voicemail, phone calls, favorite radio station, videoconferences, and stock quotes through one network interface. People in the networking industry long ago imagined something very similar to that, and, as a result, the Internet Engineering Task Force (IETF) created a handful of working groups to steer the course toward such a network. These focused working groups started with Integrated Services (IntServ), and then Differentiated Services (DiffServ), as was RSVP Admission Policy (RAP). Other IETF working groups have also been created to contribute to the QOS movement, including the Multi-Protocol Label Switching (MPLS) Working Group and the QOS Routing (QOSR) Working Group. Other organizations, including 802.1 IEEE, contribute to making QOS more than an idea.

However, for the Internet to become the communications infrastructure that can deliver all of our communications needs, there has to be a fundamental shift in the existing (or future) Internet: there must be some way to guarantee network service. For example, radio transmissions are susceptible to certain delay requirements that, if not met, render their use over the Internet useless. Video and real-time applications have other important requirements, as does Voice-Over-IP, all of which have their own individual requirements—none of which are necessarily the same. In essence, in order for the Internet to be the communications infrastructure that can integrate the communication services that we need, there must be a certain quality of service that a given stream (or flow) of information must be able to depend on. This requirement for a certain service quality guarantee is a heavy contributor to the "coming of age" of QOS, and the recent acclimation of the Internet as *the* communications medium of choice has accelerated its relevance.

Someone, though, has to define the services that must be made available for this integration of services to become a reality because without such definitions, too many varied interpretations would almost certainly result in nothing ever being implemented. That someone is collectively the Integrated Services, Differentiated Services, and other QOS-related IETF working groups. The IETF Working Group basically creates an agreed-upon standards recommendation against which multiple vendors—such as router vendors and switch vendors—can develop their versions of the service. The advantage of adhering to the standard is this: proprietary solutions are expensive, cumbersome, and usually dead-ended; customers want choices, not locked-in technologies. By adhering to the recommendations and ensuring a certain level of interoperability, the technology gets to the market faster (making money for the companies who produce the equipment), and those same manufacturers can tout standards-compliance (a big selling point).

For QOS recommendations, this is especially important because running into multiple vendors' machines in an end-to-end network connection—perhaps crossing the entire Internet—is an absolute certainty. Without standards recommendations, QOS would have no hope of becoming a reality, and too many customers want QOS for manufacturers to simply turn their backs to it. This situation isn't new (indeed, it is part of the reason that the IETF exists), and the IntServ Working Group's charter is a reflection of the problems that needed to be addressed for such recommendations-creation to occur.

IntServ, therefore, was chartered to focus on three problems, which can be paraphrased in the following ways:

- First, IntServ intended to clearly define the services to be provided.
- Second, IntServ intended to specify the application-level, router-level, and subnet-level requirements for creating an integrated services model for the Internet.
- Third, IntServ intended to define a minimal set of router requirements that would ensure that the Internet would be able to support the Integrated Services model.

What the IntServ Working Group (and other IETF working groups) hopefully does is to present a way for the collection of different network devices (clients, switches, routers, WAN interfaces, and NICs) to work toward the same implementation framework. There is, thus, a way provided for routers from different vendors (or switches or WAN interfaces) to understand QOS signaling from each other. Left to its own device, each vendor would likely pursue its own implementation of QOS and inter-device communication. The likely result of such an approach would almost certainly be that QOS would remain a theory, and never reach the level of inter-device cooperation that it needs to become a reality. There are a lot of benefits that could come from a QOS-enabled network—whether that's a corporate network or the Internet itself—and such benefits are, arguably, worth the efforts being put forth by the IntServ Working Group.

But perhaps the most important element to remember is this: IntServ provides recommendations for services that should or must be offered to provide the end-to-end QOS necessary to make the integration of services over the Internet a reality, but it does not provide implementation details. This is an important fact because the theories (services) and recommendations that IntServ puts forth can elicit divisive and heated differences between camps who believe their approach to implementing IETF recommendations is best. IETF prepares recommendations and required services, and eventually these gel into recommended approaches. Until that gelling occurs, proving that your way is the best way of doing it can mean widely different opinions. Need an example of how heated the implementation of a technology can get? Java.

So, in the end, the demand for QOS and the implications of what the implementation of such service guarantees could provide for the future of all networks, including the Internet, is worth the effort of steering implementation frameworks through the use of an entity whose interests are implementation-agnostic.

But such needs, such supply and demand, and such processing power would be meaningless if there were no available software that implemented QOS. Indeed, there are all sorts of technology theories that are great ideas, but they are improbable or impractical to design or implement. The software that automatically does yard work comes to mind. However, QOS is a sharp departure from pie-in-the-sky technology ideals that could do all sorts of things for the computing and networking industries: It's available today.

Conclusions

QOS offers a way for networks (and network management) to give priority to certain data, users, or applications. With such treatment, the overburdened 10Mbps Ethernet segment can, all of a sudden, sufficiently service mission-critical applications. As remaining network resources are available, it can service less-important transmissions. It can breathe new life into networks on their deathbeds; and make an unresponsive, overburdened, or oversubscribed network resource—such as an expensive WAN interface—sufficiently responsive. It can also provide enough bandwidth to handle the necessary prioritized network traffic, perhaps avoiding expensive bandwidth or network upgrades.

Getting specific about a definition of QOS, however, can be a slippery undertaking because there are different perceptions of what QOS entails and encompasses. The company-neutral entity, the IETF, has brought the task of supplying recommendations for QOS under its umbrella of influence, and the benefits of its undertaking can be said to be geared toward furthering the future of the Internet. As a result, the concept of QOS is becoming manageable because there is a yardstick against which the interoperability and standardization of QOS can be measured. But to get a mental grip on QOS, there must be a definition we can latch onto—one onto which we can place the context of the myriad services and components of a QOS implementation. Otherwise, keeping all of the concepts that collectively call themselves *QOS* don't have the common goal toward which all of their efforts are moving. The definition we're going to use is this: QOS is a technology that provides deterministic network service in a predictable and manageable fashion.

QOS weaves itself into multiple networking technologies, so knowledge of the network is somewhat of a prerequisite to understand QOS. This is due largely to the fact that devices across the entire network must interact to create end-to-end QOS, which adds to the complexity of QOS. The next chapter investigates the goings-on of all the network devices that play a part in providing QOS, and what QOS is going to have to do, technically, to fit into this pre-existing framework.

2

Quality of Service Technical Issues

When Quality of Service changes from a shopping list theory of requirements into an actual implementation, the complexities of its details are revealed. In this chapter, we take a look at the requirements for any implementation of QOS to be considered reasonably complete, and then discuss just what is involved in any undertaking that must implement all of these requirements.

Although this chapter discusses a few items specific to QOS, it also discusses the complexities involved in fitting QOS into existing network functionality. As a matter of course, networking details are also discussed. Some of these networking details may be review for some readers, but they must be addressed in this chapter to properly explain how QOS works within the existing network framework.

Remember that QOS intends to create an end-to-end solution that provides a certain predictable and manageable level of service. In the next section, we'll look at the technical specifics of QOS requirements. Then, in the following section, the current state of affairs in most non-QOS enabled networks is explained and will provide the necessary context for addressing the technical issues surrounding the implementation of QOS as an end-to-end solution.

Applying the Quality of Service Theory

QOS has to operate within the framework of the traditional network, which is to say that QOS has to adapt to clients, LAN segments, routers, and WAN interfaces. In order to know just what kind of adaptation QOS is going to undergo to fit into the traditional network, you need to know the technical details of QOS. Chapter 1 provided the overview and theoretical information necessary to get a good feeling about what QOS is supposed to do. Now, what is needed are the technical details that define the requirements of the QOS that will deliver all of the service guarantees necessary to turn the Internet into an integrated-services superhighway or to turn your oversubscribed network into a high-performance information tool.

Quality of Service Technical Details

Getting a certain QOS guarantee out of the network, in technically boiled-down terms, means getting a certain bandwidth and/or latency delivery guarantee for packets traversing the network. Getting *differentiated service*—a more simplistic kind of QOS—means getting preferential treatment for those packets.

The bandwidth guarantee part of QOS has the following requirement to live up to: If a QOS guarantee is provided for a certain bandwidth value, packets that conform to that bandwidth value should get service across the entire network as if those packets had the wire of that bandwidth all to themselves. The latency guarantee part of QOS has this requirement: If a QOS guarantee is provided for a certain timely delivery bound (latency range), packets must traverse the network within those delivery bounds.

The preferential part of QOS has a simple premise: If the general population of packets traversing the network have a priority of, say, three (on a scale of zero to seven), your packets have a priority of something higher than three. This sounds straightforward at first, but upon further investigation, much work is necessary to provide such preferential treatment—especially when providing guarantees. The details involved in providing certain guaranteed bandwidth levels and latency parameters include lots and lots of coordination between all of the involved network devices (not to mention some sort of mechanism for getting all of these devices to conform to these guarantees). This guaranteed service includes reserving resources across the entire path between each end node involved the QOS transaction.

When the bandwidth/latency guarantee requirements are combined with the need to enlist affected network devices into the resource-reservation scheme, we end up with the following issues:

- Resources within each of the network devices that are affected by a service quality guarantee between two end nodes must be reserved (an end-to-end guarantee), based on the set of QOS requirements particular to the instigator of the QOS guarantee. In shorter terms, resources on network devices need to be reserved.

- Devices within this path must be able to recognize resource-reservation requests and must be able to offer guaranteed transmission service, based on the bounds set forth in the resource reservation request.

- Implied with the request and establishment of certain QOS parameters is the capability to police the use and granting of such service guarantees. This introduces a need for some sort of policy-based admission control system for the initiation, and certainly for the establishment of a flow of packets for which guaranteed service quality is going to be provided.

- For differentiated service, devices within the path must be capable of providing some packets with better service than others, which implies the capability of differentiating between such packets and subsequently providing different treatments for packets with differing priorities.

The process, then, is twofold. First, there is the setting up of any resource reservation that must include all network devices that sit in the path between the end nodes (every network device between this end-to-end solution). This essentially is the process of asking the following: "I would like this kind of service guarantee and would like it for x bandwidth." Although there can be other service requests, including latency requirements and the type of service guarantee, requesting a certain level of bandwidth is example enough at this point in the discussion. This first part of the process requires some mechanism by which all network devices—clients, switches, routers, WAN interfaces—can communicate. This comes largely in the form of a reservation protocol that all of these devices can understand: *Resource Reservation Protocol*, or *RSVP*. RSVP is discussed in Chapter 5, "Application-Driven QOS." This part of the process can be called the *setup process*.

Second in this twofold process is the actual transmission of data. Assuming that the reservation is in place—facilitated by the setup process—there is the matter of transmitting the data from one end of the QOS reservation to its destination. The idea is that all conforming packets (that is, packets that are within the bounds of the reservation guarantee) will receive the level of service quality guaranteed in the reservation. This is simple in theory, but difficult in implementation. The best way to illustrate why this is difficult is to provide an example situation.

Suppose that the reservation was for 1000 bps of guaranteed service. As long as the amount of data transmitted on this reservation (we'll call it a *flow,* as in a flow of packets) doesn't exceed 1000 bps, all of those packets would receive service quality commensurate with the reservation. But what if more than that amount of data is sent? What if the computer that has set up this reservation starts sending 1200 bps of data instead of the reserved 1000 bps? The quick answer is that only 1000 bytes of that data will receive the service guaranteed in the reservation. But what happens to the other 200 bps? Are they dropped? How should they be handled? The long answer details how packets that are conforming to the reservation are deemed and tagged as "conforming" packets and how some implementations of QOS would keep track of such a seemingly untrackable issue.

The nitty-gritty details will be covered in later chapters with the rest of Windows NT's QOS-implementation details. The conceptual approach to this transmission policing, however, can be explained through the approach by which such transmission policing is tracked; it's done through the *Token Bucket model.*

The Token Bucket Model

To ensure that a given application (or client, or service) adheres to QOS guarantee transmission guidelines set forth in its reservation, there has to be some procedure in place that monitors the flow of transmitted data. In addition to monitoring the flow, this procedure has to be able to keep track of how much data the client has transmitted over time. The difference between those two requirements can be represented as: "How much data can this particular flow transmit?" and "How much data has this flow transmitted over the last ten seconds?" This procedure is called the Token Bucket model.

Imagine a *Token Bucket* as a variable-sized bucket, containing tokens that a flow can trade in for the right to transmit a certain amount of data. Token Buckets come in all sorts of sizes—that is, the bucket size equates to the largest amount of data that a given flow can transmit at any one time. As a flow transmits data, the transmit-tokens in its Token Bucket are reduced accordingly. Fortunately, the Token Bucket is filled with tokens (by the entity that's policing the transmission tokens, which is generally the operating system) at a rate equivalent to the transmission reservation associated with the flow.

Because this is all somewhat nebulous, let's go to an example. Suppose that you have a QOS reservation that (in simplistic terms) allows your flow to transmit 100K/sec. Call this your *token rate.* The reservation has a maximum burst-transmission value of 250K/sec. Call this your *peak rate.* It also has a total bucket size of 350k. Call this your Token Bucket. So, you have a token rate of 100k, a peak rate of 250k (which is the most you can send in one burst), and a Token Bucket of 350k (the maximum amount of tokens that your flow can accrue). With these assumptions, you can put this particular reservation into Figure 2.1.

With this QOS reservation, your bucket will receive 100k worth of transmission tokens every second. This is the token rate, which can be loosely translated into the rate at which the Token Bucket is filled with tokens. This value is generally the rate at which you expect your flow to transmit data on an ongoing basis. Most applications have variations within the parameters of expected transmission requirements. For example, during ten seconds there may be a second or two when no data is transmitted at all. But for one second, there may be a burst of data—which brings us to the peak rate.

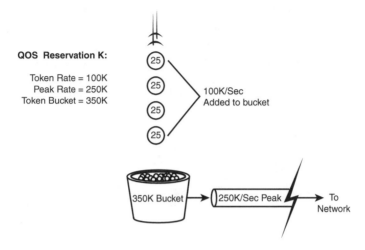

Figure 2.1   *A QOS reservation with a 100k token rate, a 250k peak rate, and a 350k Token Bucket.*

With the peak rate, in this example, the flow can transmit up to 250k during a one second period, as long as enough tokens are in the Token Bucket to sustain such a burst. The peak rate allows for occasions when a flow needs to transmit a burst of data. However, to keep tabs on this peak rate—so that the reservation can't be abused by understating its anticipated rate (100k/sec in this example) and to constantly transmit at its peak (250k/sec in this example)—there is the Token Bucket.

The Token Bucket is basically a governor of data transmitting. Although the Token Bucket gets continually filled at a specific ongoing rate (the token rate, or 100k/sec in this example), it cannot be filled higher than its maximum rate. When there aren't any available tokens in the Token Bucket, the flow is not allowed to transmit any data. In everyday terms, this keeps flows honest; it allows for an occasional burst, which is assumed to be offset over time with occasional lulls in activity, but it prevents a flow from sustained transmission at its sustained peak rate, which could "overload" the network. Figure 2.2 shows what this example reservation might look like over a ten-second interval.

To put the Token Bucket into everyday terms, you can think of the flow as a ten-year-old boy; he gets an allowance of 100 cents every day, but his pockets can hold only 500 cents. The owner of the nearby candy store happens to also be a dentist, and because she's concerned about cavities, she only allows this boy to buy 250 cents worth of candy on any given day. If the boy's name is Flow, then Flow gets an allowance of 100 cents every day, but his pockets can only carry 500 cents. This means that even if he doesn't go to the candy store for eight days straight, he can still hold only 500 cents. The 300 cents he might have received for the additional three days' savings (8 days=800 cents, but he can only hold 500 cents at a time) is lost; he can't hold it, so he doesn't get to keep it. With five days' savings (500 cents), he could go to the store two days in a row and buy 250 cents worth of candy each day. What would he be left with? 200 cents—because each of those two days he went to the store, he also received an additional 100 cents of allowance.

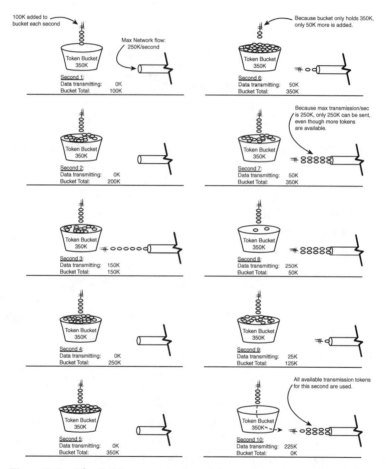

Figure 2.2   *The QOS reservation's activity over a ten-second period.*

Why Quality of Service Must Coexist within the Network

Within the framework of the traditional network, QOS must find room to operate. To do a little QOS personification, QOS must look at existing network devices and traditional network methodology and say, "How can I be implemented within this framework?" Network integrators won't redesign their networks because of some fancy new technology; corporations won't rip out all of their old cables and clients to implement even a significant increase in network capabilities.

Therefore, in order for QOS to become viable, it must *embrace and extend* the capabilities of the network. That phrase has been used before, but the idea is the same: an attempt to reinvent or fundamentally change a network generally results in failure, whereas embracing existing technologies, and then expanding on their capabilities from within the established framework can go a long way toward ensuring success.

This "embrace-and-extend" disposition is at the heart of QOS and the QOS network: expand the capabilities of the existing network while existing within the established framework, and by wiggling into existing technologies (and maybe introducing some additional technologies or protocols that don't interfere with others). In the next section, the discussion turns to just how that existing network operates, and interjects what QOS will have to do in order to function within it.

Networking 301: Quality of Service in the Traditional Network

You're probably familiar with networking and networks if you're reading this book. You know about switches, routers, LAN segments, and the like. You may know about packets and how packet-switched networks operate, and even how routers go about deciding where to forward a given packet (if you don't, don't worry. We'll cover that briefly very soon). But you may not know some of the internal goings-on in routers, how Ethernet LAN segments' access methods make QOS so difficult to implement, or even why it's a fairly big deal to map any kind of network-based QOS to a wily transmission protocol such as ATM. If you don't know these things (few people do, and those who do are generally people who spend more time with networking than is healthy), discussions about QOS will be unclear in places. There's no way to get a firm grasp on a technology when parts of its discussion are unclear.

There's a good way to remedy such possible clarity deficiencies: Discuss and explain networking in terms that are especially relevant for a thorough understanding of QOS. This section acts as a refresher or a technical networking primer (depending on the depth of your networking knowledge), so that the low-level aspects of QOS can be discussed and explained on even ground. The concepts are therefore understood by networking experts and acquaintances of networking alike.

Note

If you are well-versed in networking, this section may be old news to you, so you may choose to skim the networking information and pay more attention to QOS-specific information. ◆

We'll start simply, with an example that'll be used throughout the discussion. It will then become more complex as the discussion runs its course.

The Traditional Network View

Suppose that your computer is connected to a network, and you decide that you need to transfer a file from your computer to another node on that network, such as some file server. The file is 1MB large. How does the file get from your computer to the file server (more specifically than saying it gets there "over the network")? Here's how:

1. The file is first chopped up into little pieces on the client.

2. The chopped-up file is wrapped with addressing (and sequencing) information in order to be able to find the file server, and it is then sent across the network in the form of packets (the pieces of data that have been wrapped with addressing information).

3. When these packets arrive at the server, information in the address "wrap" allow the file server to put the chopped pieces back into the appropriate order.

4. After the addressing information is unwrapped and discarded, the 1MB file resides on the file server in the same condition as it did on the client.

Figure 2.3 puts this process into visible terms.

Now, let's say that the file server is located on another LAN segment, and that the segment happens to be three hops (routers) away. In this case, the packets that go from the client to the file server have to go through each router in the path to the file server. Each router in the path between the client and the server, in this case, must examine each packet and forward that packet to the next appropriate hop (router) based on the router's *routing table*. (A routing table logically determines the best next-hop destination, based on a packet's destination IP/IPX address.)

With three routers in the path between the client and the server, the configuration of this particular end-to-end connection would look something like Figure 2.4.

This is still a relatively straightforward situation. Next, let's say that the client and server are in different geographical regions, such as Seattle and Las Vegas. Under such circumstances, the wide area network (WAN) comes into play. For more information on WANs, refer to the section "Networking Across the WAN Interface" later in the chapter.

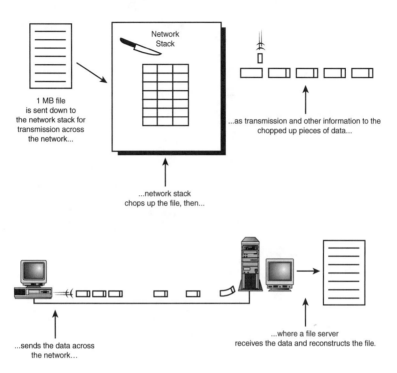

1 MB file
is sent down to
the network stack for
transmission across
the network...

Network
Stack

...as transmission and other information to the
chopped up pieces of data...

...network stack
chops up the file, then...

...sends the data across
the network...

...where a file server
receives the data and reconstructs the file.

Figure 2.3   *A 1MB file getting chopped up, wrapped with information, and then sent across the network onto a file server.*

For fun, let's say that the Seattle network is connected to the Internet through an unchannelized T1 Frame Relay interface and that the Las Vegas network is connected to the Internet through a 25Mbps ATM link. To be consistent, suppose that there are still three routers in the path between the client that's in Seattle and the server that's in Las Vegas; two in Seattle, one in Las Vegas. What happens to our flow of packets now?

As before, the 1MB file is chopped up into smaller pieces and sent across the Seattle network toward the Frame Relay interface (we'll call it the *WAN interface* from here forward). This is again because the packets' destination IP address—the address of the Las Vegas file server—allows routers along the path to forward them to the most appropriate next hop. When the packets get to the WAN interface—the T1 Frame Relay interface for Seattle's Internet connection—the packets are actually chopped up again. This is because the T1 has certain Layer 2 (L2) signaling that it uses to transmit data across its interface.

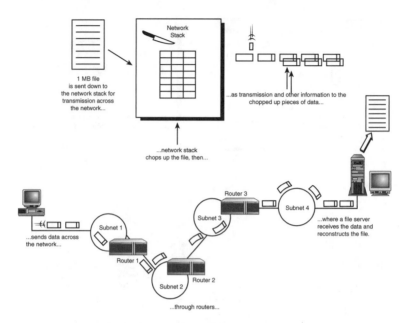

Figure 2.4   *The 1MB file is sent between a client and a server, where three routers sit in the path between the client and server.*

Note

Most of this chopping-up of the data isn't of much concern to the user or even to the integrator, but as the technical details of QOS are explained, you'll remember this fact and see why some QOS things are done the way they are. ◆

The chopped-up T1 frames are then reconstructed on the other end of the T1 interface, and then sent out over the Internet in whatever signaling format the Internet backbones are using. Then (actually having gone through a bunch of routers on the Internet; a fact we're ignoring for now), the packets get to the 25Mbps ATM interface that connects the Internet to the Las Vegas network. The packets are again chopped up into 53-byte ATM cells, so that they can be sent over the Las Vegas network's ATM connection.

At the ATM interface in Las Vegas, the ATM cells are turned back into packets that can traverse the Las Vegas WAN, and those packets are sent across the network toward the file server. They then go through one last router before being broadcast onto the Ethernet segment on which the file server resides. Because the file server is listening on its Ethernet segment, it knows that the data is intended for it, and copies it into its network stack and starts reconstructing the file. And, of course, at the file server, the packets are stripped of all their headers as they pass back up through the network stack, where the data is placed back into the order it was in on the client, and the 1MB file is perfectly reconstructed.

Figure 2.5 gives us a graphical representation of what this ordeal might look like.

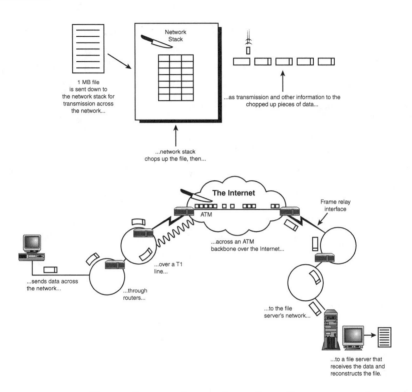

Figure 2.5   *A 1MB file transfer going from a client, through two routers, through a T1 and across the Internet, and then through an ATM interface and back across another LAN to its target file server.*

When all of these network devices, clients, WAN interfaces, signaling technologies, and LAN segment switches are thrown into the equation, a little bit of complexity is introduced into the process. Keep in mind, too, that this is simply an overview of the process that transpires when data is sent from one end-point to another.

In QOS, however, overviews don't cut it. In order to understand QOS, we need to know the specifics of what's going on in each of these network devices, and how these devices communicate with the next device in the network path.

Networking in the Client

The client, in this section, is meant to represent each end device. In this example, we're going to presume that the first end device is a Windows NT Workstation computer (the client side of this discussion's example), and the second end device is a Windows NT Server computer (the file server in this example).

The user who is sitting in front of the client computer is the instigator of this connection, and the computer itself just carries out the user's requests. This paradigm can be used throughout the client's process of sending the file—a request that is carried out through services that exist lower in the stack.

What's a Stack?

A stack *is actually a collection of services that, as a whole, represent the overall network capabilities of a given client. The term came from the fact that most visual representations of these network services came in the form of a bunch of boxes stacked on top of each other. Explanations of the International Standards Organization (ISO) Open System Interconnect (OSI) Model, with its seven layers stacked on top of each other, surely contributed to the coining of the phrase. The term stack is most often used to represent the collection of services that create network connectivity. This term is often also referred to as the network stack or just the stack.* ◆

In this example, suppose that the user was running an application in which a file transfer request could be made by clicking a certain button. That button is then translated into a request for a file transfer that is passed on down to the network provider, which then determines that a connection must be established with the file transfer's target computer. The network provider then instigates this connection, placing the file transfer on hold until the connection can be established.

With the transfer on hold, the network provider initiates services provided by the layers below it to initiate a connection. The network provider doesn't necessarily know how to establish this connection, and doesn't really care how it gets done, because there's a service designed specifically for doing such things. In this case, the network provider requests that a connection-creation service (perhaps Winsock) establish a connection with the target file server. This connection-creation service receives some information from the network provider, and then goes through the process of sending a few administrative packets out to the target server to establish the connection. Once the connection is established, the connection-creation service informs the network provider of the successful connection, along with some pertinent information about the path itself. The connection is also logged into a sort of electronic clipboard (so that the network can keep track of which packets belong to which connection... after all, this might not be the only active connection). Once this process is complete, the file transfer associated with the connection can begin, and because of the way networks function, packets get sent out onto the network as fast as possible, saturating the network interface if at all possible.

When the transfer begins, information about the source and destination address, as well as a significant amount of other information, is included in the header that is added to the data as it gets sent out to the network. This is similar to the ordeal that you have to go through to send anything fragile through the mail. You have the actual item you want to send, but in order to get it there, you have to wrap it in paper, put bubble wrap around all of that, stuff some box with newspaper, put the package in the box, address the box, and then get an appropriate stamp (depending on whether you're sending it US mail, UPS, or FedEx). You can then actually send the package. By the time you're done with all that packing, you've added a fair amount of payload to this little item. Without the packaging, address, and correct postage, the item won't get routed to its destination in good (unbroken) shape. A similar concept applies to the network, although if the network item (packet) is broken or lost, it's simply transmitted. Just like that fragile item that has to be unwrapped from its layers of packaging, the recipient of the fragile item has to go through the same steps to actually get to the item; but in the opposite direction (*un*wrapping and *un*stuffing).

Quality of Service in the Client

Networking in the client is a complex process in itself, and the packet is barely onto the Network Interface Card (NIC). The next step—getting across the LAN segment—is only slightly less complex.

The client must be able to instigate the QOS mechanism and must be able to respond to the decisions of such requests in an appropriate manner. The client must also be able to make request modifications for QOS parameters, and put such requests into formats that the other network devices in the chain can understand. The client must also be able to modify its transmission characteristics (in other words, control the timeline with which it puts packets on the wire) in order to implement the Traffic Control feature of QOS. Traffic Control controls the way a QOS client places data on the network (generally implemented on the QOS client), and it is also generally the QOS component that enforces the Token Bucket model of data transmission.

The client must also be able to manage the algorithms surrounding the maintenance of the Token Bucket model implementation so that the proper amount of data is transmitted, based on reservation guarantees. Implied in all of this "request" process is the capability of some decision-making body to determine whether a QOS request should or should not be granted. The client, then, has to be able to properly identify itself within the framework of these requests; without such identification, the premise of granting QOS provisions based on some differentiating factor (identity) becomes meaningless.

Networking Over the LAN Segment

Once the packet is ready to be sent out onto the segment, there's another header that gets slapped onto it—the Ethernet frame header (assuming that you're on an Ethernet segment).

Why Ethernet?

Today (and for the foreseeable future), Ethernet is the reigning king of the desktop. Even though Token Ring touts new technology that will increase its throughput and ATM has desktop solutions that can bring ATM to desktop speeds, the simple fact of the matter is that Ethernet is the most widely deployed and arguably the most cost-effective solution. There's more room for discussion on this subject and there are times when extenuating circumstances make another topology a better choice, but for the vast majority, Ethernet is the desktop technology of choice. QOS only proposes (as a result of its technology, not its intent) to cement that fact further. ◆

An Ethernet frame header is slapped onto the packet as it prepares to go out onto the Ethernet segment, or the *wire* as it's often called. If the packet's destination is a computer on the same segment, the frame will be placed onto the segment, its intended recipient will recognize that it is the packet's intended destination, and it will then copy the frame into its network stack to "receive" the frame.

This is where NICs' MAC addresses come into play. Every client on the segment keeps a table, called an *ARP table*, which contains a mapping of the IP address and MAC address of each node on the local segment. If the IP address of the intended recipient matches one of the IP addresses in the ARP table, the frame is transmitted onto the local segment. If the IP address is not on the local segment, the packet is forwarded to the default gateway—the IP address of the router (which also has a corresponding ARP table entry) that's attached to the segment.

But because of Ethernet's fundamental signaling characteristics, Ethernet frames (which are the packets that have Ethernet information added to them) are placed on the wire in a completely chaotic, unruly fashion. The technology used to put frames onto an Ethernet segment is *CSMA/CD (Carrier Sense Multiple Access/Collision Detect)*. In essence, a NIC checks the wire to see whether anyone else is using it. If not, it grabs hold of the wire and sends its data. Fortunately, many LANs use Ethernet switches these days, which provide an isolated wire to each node connected to the switch, thus effectively increasing the availability of the Ethernet medium by avoiding congestion of the overall wire. However, such CSMA/CD transmission characteristics still hold for each individual node on the switch, so the chance for collision with a switch (versus a hub, which shares the same access to the wire among all nodes) still exists on each individual connection to the switch.

Granted, Ethernet transmits its packets extremely quickly, but this doesn't change the fact that its transmission efficiency—which is somewhere between thirty and forty percent of the actual wire speed in shared Ethernet environments—is dismal. Dismal as it is, it's still relatively inexpensive, and it's easy to implement and support. But for the sake of our discussion, the important fact to keep in mind is that Ethernet's chaotic nature makes regulating this first (or last) gateway to the client extremely challenging. Contributing to this challenge is the fact that networks, by their very design and nature, send packets onto the wire in as bunched-up a fashion as possible—a veritable rush hour on the Ethernet wire every time a significant amount of data is being transferred from any given client. This overload of packets can mean that a switch, or hub (the central unit into which all end nodes in an Ethernet segment are connected) drops packets as a result of having too much data coming at once. There is no decision mechanism built into switches that allows them to determine that one Ethernet frame is more "important" than another. All data on the chaotic Ethernet segment is therefore treated the same way. Or more precisely, all data is equally subject to being dropped during periods of segment congestion.

Quality of Service Over the LAN Segment

When a data transmission is targeting a network node that isn't on the same segment, the packets are sent to the default gateway. This is usually a router that's connected to the segment, and once the packet reaches the router, an entirely different set of issues must be addressed.

Getting QOS implemented over the LAN segment—or over multiple segments, as the case with an IP subnet that incorporates multiple LAN segments would present—is tricky. As mentioned earlier in this chapter, QOS has to work within the framework of the existing network, and Ethernet doesn't lend itself to such predictability or structured access management. Therefore, the issue of QOS over the LAN segment has to take a different approach to resource reservation and allocation, such as voluntary (cooperative) access management. This means that some sort of access management entity must be sitting on the LAN segment, with a service available to clients in which admission of packets onto the LAN segment is managed.

This concept requires a sort of LAN segment manager; one that has a priori knowledge of the LAN segment's available bandwidth, and can thereby reserve some or all of that bandwidth for QOS reservations.

With this kind of management-entity arrangement, LAN segment (or subnet) bandwidth can be managed or allocated, so that when bandwidth resources begin to run low (according to expected bandwidth usage, not the actual physical monitoring of the wire), client reservation requests can be rejected. Actually, if Ethernet switches were to incorporate such LAN segment management into the switch itself, the capability to monitor bandwidth could be done by actually monitoring the wire itself, introducing a high degree of bandwidth-management accuracy.

The obvious presumption of a subnet bandwidth manager—with regard to attempting to regulate the availability of a first-come, first-served access medium such as Ethernet—is that clients must first make a reservation request. If rejected, they much comply with that rejection and not "send the data out anyway."

Networking through the Router

The router is the intersection of the network. At the router, there are often many different routes that a packet can take, but due to logic built into routing protocols, routers are able to interrogate the header of each packet and determine the best route onto which to send each packet. This header interrogation occurs for every packet. To get an idea of just how many packets that is, consider the following. If the smallest interval between packets is used on a 100Mbps Ethernet segment, 1,518 full-sized packets can pass through a 100Mbps interface every second. If that sounds like a fair amount (it isn't really), then consider what happens when the size of the packet is reduced: In a 64-byte Ethernet packet, more than 150,000 packets can pass through a 100Mbps interface each second. That's a lot of packets, and all of those packets have to be interrogated by the router.

When a router starts to become congested, packets can't be processed as quickly as they come in on a given interface. So, rather than getting the packet routed to its next hop as quickly as the router can interrogate the header information (and make a routing decision), the packet is put into a queue. If you've ever been in a hurry at a train station or some other place where lots of lines form, you're familiar with this kind of situation. There may be twelve turnstiles with people lined up twenty feet back to get through them, and everyone must wait his turn to get through. Generally speaking, you are in much more of a hurry than anyone else in line, and whatever trip you're taking is much more important than anyone else's.

Still, you don't get to wave some card and say "I have priority here," and then jump to the front of the line. Many routers today suffer from that same problem. Figure 2.6 illustrates this very problem.

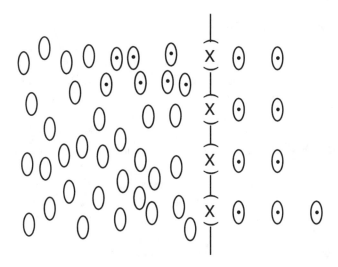

Figure 2.6   *The concept of queues, in which gates and slow turnstiles stifle throughput.*

As routers get more and more congested, their queues fill up until there is no longer any room to put packets into the queue (buffer), at which time packets begin to be dropped. Routers determine the best way to route packets—based on routing protocols such as OSPF, RIP, and RIP II—and have logic schemes or protocols for managing other routing activities. For example, you can have a router with the OSPF routing protocol enabled, and also have another kind of protocol, such as SNMP, installed on the router to carry out management activities. The point is that there is often more than one protocol running on a given router at any given time, performing a different function. For more information on OSPF, RIP, and RIP II, check out *OSPF Network Design Solutions*, published by MTP/Cisco Press.

Because routers are the intersections and even the "glue" that stitches networks together, their resources can be considered to be fairly precious. You can't get from one LAN segment to another—or across the network, for that matter—without going through at least one router. When routers become congested and their queues fill up, everyone waits... Even the most important data sit in the queue with other less important information, waiting for their turn to get through the turnstiles and onto the next hop along the network path toward their destination.

Most networks these days aren't isolated to their local network; the Internet is too compelling to be isolated. And when a network is hooked up to the Internet—or to any other geographically diverse network—packets will eventually cross a WAN interface.

Quality of Service through the Router

For routers to provide a certain service quality to individual packets, there must be some way *within* the router to differentiate between, to time the deliveries of, and to queue packets based on their QOS parameters. Such coordination almost certainly means a different set of queues for packets, based on their relative priority, as well as some method or algorithm that ensures that packets with a higher priority get more attentive treatment than average, or best-effort, packets—without completely ignoring the best-effort traffic.

Also, the router must be able to understand the QOS request coming from the client. So, between the client and the router there must be some means of communicating a certain (bounded) set of information—such as a protocol that both the client and the router can understand. This set of information constitutes the QOS parameters; therefore, there must be some sort of coordination between the client, the router, and any other network device that is responsible for data transmission in the path between the end nodes. That coordination must include a way for QOS parameters that are set within the client to be mapped to QOS provisions in the router (such as bandwidth, delay requirements, burst allowances, and others). They must then be mapped to other affected network devices, such as the WAN interface.

Networking Across the WAN Interface

As far as the user is concerned, the WAN interface is invisible; packets get from their LAN to some distant LAN as if magically shuttled over that distance without ever changing their contents. As far as the packet itself is concerned, however, there are plenty of changes that it undergoes as it crosses the WAN.

Note

As a quick definition, a WAN only differs from a local area network (LAN) in its geographical disposition. LANs are generally considered to be networks that reside in a close geographical region, such as a building, whereas a WAN generally consists of two or more LANs that are connected by some sort of telecommunications interface (such as a T1). This differentiation is growing less and less definitive as networks are becoming less and less isolated, and are becoming more interconnected. Rather than LANs and WANs, we are beginning to see "the network," in which the Internet is the backbone. ◆

Transmitting data across a WAN interface has some fundamentally different characteristics from transmitting data across a standard LAN. When a packet arrives at a WAN interface—whether it be a T1 interface or an ATM interface— the packet itself has to conform to the signaling characteristics that are specific to the WAN interface. This almost always results in the packet getting further chopped into pieces that the WAN interface can fit into its transmission "slots." Much like the chopping up of the 1MB file that's done at the client when it sends the file across the network (see "The Traditional Network View" section earlier in this chapter), the WAN link chops up the packet and sends it across its link. At the other side, the chopped-up pieces are reconstructed into the original unchopped packet, which can then be sent onward toward its destination. Figure 2.7 illustrates this process.

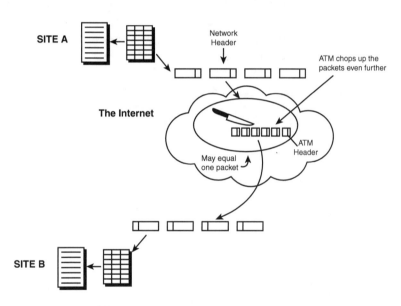

Figure 2.7 *Getting a file across a WAN and the chopping of the data that must occur along the way.*

You can imagine this WAN interface, which often comes in the form of a *WAN cloud*, as a network within the larger network. Its devices and transmission mechanisms are inconsequential to the overall network process because, in the end, the packets get to the other side of the WAN link in the same form they were in before. But for more technical discussions, the fact that WAN interfaces apply further segmentation and reassembly of packets is of significant interest because this "WAN network within the larger network" can also become congested and provide further cause for concern to those interested in guaranteeing some sort of service quality.

One fact to keep in mind about networking considerations on the WAN interface is this: WAN technologies apply their own extended segmentation and repackaging to traditional network data packets as they are sent across the Telecommunications network. Because the Telecommunications network can be subject to the same kind of congestion traditional data that networks endure, a means of differentiating between subsets of data and ensuring that transmission priority can be placed on important data must be mapped to the WAN interface. This concern, or issue, is called *L2 signaling*—after the fact that WAN transmission characteristics operate within Layer 2 of the ISO OSI model.

Quality of Service across the WAN Interface
Similar to the router, the WAN interface must be able to understand the QOS requests being made from the client, interpreted by the router, and passed on to the WAN interface (or, if necessary, passed directly from the client). This requirement necessarily means that the WAN interface, too, must understand the communication method employed in conveying QOS requests, and can interpret and act upon such requests.

But for the WAN interface, there is an additional layer of QOS provisioning that has to take place. Although the WAN interface has to be able to reserve a certain part of its bandwidth for those reservation requests that it accepts, it must take reservations from one network (the "data network") and map those reservation parameters to the other network to which it is attached (the "telecommunications network"). This mapping process increases the complexity of QOS at the WAN interface because the mapping of such service quality parameters may not necessarily be one-to-one.

The Overall Network Conclusions

As data is transmitted across the network, it gets processed by a number of different network devices before ever reaching the destination. To the user, the file seems to simply appear on the distant server. To the network administrator, the network utilization is affected, but little more. To the integrator or planner of QOS guarantees, however, the process becomes much more complex. There is queuing going on, packet dropping, latencies potentially introduced, and other such quality-killing activities to be dealt with. And everywhere, with each device touching the packets, there is the risk of important data becoming just part of the overall packet mob and treated accordingly.

To further complicate matters, some of these network devices perform necessary segmentation and reassembly of the packets, which puts the data again at risk of congestion and poor transmission quality within the sometimes-opaque Telecommunications network. Although such WAN issues may be less of a concern to those who have negotiated levels of service quality with their Telecommunications carrier, an end-to-end QOS solution that includes the LAN and WAN link is more of a challenge. It is especially difficult when trying to coordinate LAN-based QOS characteristics to WAN QOS settings. The WAN devices aren't alone in this complexity; as the next section describes, the characteristics of all of these network devices need to be carefully scrutinized when designing, implementing, and understanding the way QOS pulls all these devices together.

Quality of Service Conclusions

To get QOS across the network, the client has to have the necessary software components that allow it to make a service request. Then, all of those network devices along the data transmission path must be able to interpret the request, make decisions on the request, and actually implement the service guarantee. Perhaps the largest challenge in such a scenario is getting all of the devices to be able to understand a common langauge, or protocol, so that this communication can occur across the entire network. If that is the greatest challenge, then actually implementing the bandwidth reservations and service guarantees within all of the diverse network devices comes in as a close second.

The diversity of the network has always been a challenge for any network infrastructure; getting these diverse network devices to provide what could be a called a "common service," or at least a "cooperative service," adds another dimension to the challenge. Operating systems, switches, routers, WAN interfaces, and even some sort of industry-standard protocol that they all can understand must come together and cooperate for QOS to attempt to offer what is core to QOS technology: the reservation of bandwidth and transmission guarantees, and the management of such reservations.

3

Quality of Service Implementation in Windows 2000

Quality of Service technical requirements must somehow fit into a functional framework—a facilitator of sorts that implements the QOS shopping list. As we discussed in the last two chapters, such an implementation is not necessarily an easy task; a significant amount of cooperation has to occur between devices that aren't inherently prone to cooperation—or even communications—at such levels. Despite all of that, Windows 2000 implements QOS within the operating system. This chapter discusses how it is done.

How Quality of Service Fits into Windows 2000

In Windows 2000, Quality of Service functionality is available as a basic part of the product, and it is easily enabled by simply adding the QOS packet scheduler component during network setup. More information on installation and deployment of QOS for Windows 2000 deployments is provided in Chapter 9, "QOS in Windows 2000." When a Windows client is QOS-enabled (that is, the QOS component option is installed on the client), QOS capability is available, but its mechanisms are only invoked when QOS service is invoked.

To get its mechanisms started, there needs to be only an application or client that invokes its services. Although there's more complexity involved in getting QOS to *function across the network* than simply flipping a software switch, the point is that QOS, like networking was a few NT versions ago, is built seamlessly into the operating system (rather than being included as an afterthought). For the integrator or consumer of QOS, that means fewer installation, compatibility, and seamlessness concerns to deal with.

For Windows 2000 QOS to be seamless across an entire network, however, its seamless integration must also have other characteristics that enable it to work together with other devices on the network. Such characteristics include agnosticism to the transport media (it has such agnosticism) and QOS capability that is available to any application or service on the machine (it can have that, as well).

These requirements add up to the same idea: to provide differentiated and/or deterministic and manageable transmission facilities within the Windows 2000 framework. There is one very significant piece of information, however, that makes this undertaking such a challenge: not all network devices that participate in the network run Windows. Such an observation—that Windows 2000 isn't running on all the devices included in the network path—should elicit an important question, along the lines of the following: "If Windows 2000 isn't running on all those network devices, but it proposes to be able to provision QOS across the network, how can QOS really be achieved?" As discussed frequently in these first few chapters, QOS requires an end-to-end solution (there are merits to having QOS capabilities across some or most of the network as well, but that's covered in Chapter 10, "QOS for the Integrator and Administrator"). So, if Windows 2000 doesn't run on all devices in the end-to-end path, what good is getting Windows 2000 QOS capabilities built into the client going to do anyone?

Good question. The quick answer is that Windows 2000 has thought through this challenge and come up with a solution. The longer and more detailed answer has everything to do with the *methods* surrounding the Windows 2000 QOS implementation and how those methods create a cooperative, QOS-cohesive network from the multiple levels of device independence that exist across the network. In other words, it's the mechanisms that QOS uses to implement QOS that makes the end-to-end solution possible.

Windows 2000 QOS Implementation Mechanisms

Getting away from theory-based QOS discussions is similar to working on an engine without getting dirty—it's not usually conducive to effectiveness or efficiency. There are still some higher-view explanations about the way Windows 2000 implements QOS to discuss before boring into the nitty-gritty details. These explanations will help to get the understanding of QOS bolted down.

This section describes the way QOS has been implemented in each of the pertinent areas of the network. These are the same topics that were discussed in Chapter 2, in which the QOS requirements for functioning in the existing networking framework were explained. After this section, we move into Windows 2000 implementation specifics. Without discussing the implementation specifics first, though, the reasoning behind QOS implementation won't be clear, and your understanding of QOS in Windows 2000 will suffer. Understanding QOS details can be suffering enough; providing the right perspective on Windows 2000's implementation—through an understanding of the methodology behind its mechanisms—can assuage it considerably.

In any end-to-end transmission, there is a certain set of activities that go on. Think of a simple TCP/IP session: there is the invocation of the transmission, the establishment of an identifiable line of communication, the involved carriers of the transmission, and the actual transmission (across all involved parties) of the information (see Figure 3.1).

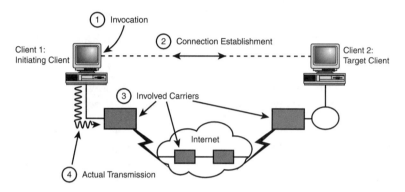

Figure 3.1   *The steps involved in an end-to-end solution.*

The implementation of QOS in Windows 2000 has to do all of these things, but in much greater granular detail and under much more complex communication requirements. However, the basics of establishing and maintaining a QOS-provisioned transmission are exactly what you see in Figure 3.1, plain and simple. So keep this illustration in mind as we move through the mechanisms. Through all the included complexity, and under all of the necessary communications mechanisms and service-mapping requirements, QOS implementation requirements can be reduced to this basic idea.

In the following sections, we'll merge the requirements of QOS theory and the realities of its existing network-framework constraints, with what any operating system must do in order to get an implementation of QOS built into its core architecture. We'll do this by first translating QOS theory and real-world requirements into a list of requirements. Then, we'll discuss the operating system goals of such requirements as they apply to the particular part of the network that's in question. Finally, we'll see how the requirements—and the specific goals derived from such requirements—are achieved in Windows 2000.

QOS in the Client

The first step in the end-to-end communication process is to handle the invocation of a QOS-enabled transmission. There has to be a request for the transmission somewhere (unless you want to create a static, always-up reservation guarantee—which is only suitable in limited situations), which needs to be processed, handled, and passed on to the next step in the process. This is perhaps one of the most complex places in the QOS scheme of things.

Requirements: Allow for any application to invoke a QOS request. Enable a modular approach to provisioning different aspects of QOS (such as reservation requests versus traffic control versus policy enforcement). Allow seamless integration with the existing network stack.

Goals: Be invisible to the end user. Allow individual aspects of QOS to be implemented or provisioned independently of others (reservation requests versus traffic control versus policy enforcement). Use open standards and thereby provide for interoperability with non-Windows 2000 devices. Provide for an application that can act on behalf of non-QOS-aware applications.

Implementation Design: Modular services and service providers, each of which can be invoked through mechanisms independent of the others. Abstract these services within the network stack so that a common programmatic interface above and below can be used.

With these requirements, goals, and its actual implementation design, the end result is a QOS client that looks something like Figure 3.2.

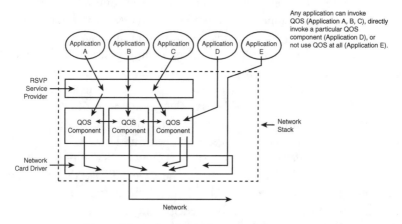

Figure 3.2 *The QOS client implementation.*

QOS Client Requirements

Allowing any application to request or invoke a QOS request makes dynamic reservation requests necessary and, subsequently, makes necessary the dynamic removal of such reservations. This ensures that network resources won't be requested, requested, requested, and eventually used up because only requests and no removal of reservations occurred. Dynamic requests are also necessary because there's no way to determine what the different applications will require in terms of reservations. Thus, the approach of static QOS reservations is doubly (at least) inappropriate. Allowing any application to request or invoke a QOS request also requires some sort of standard interface to its services, as well as application independence. In short, allowing any application to make QOS requests requires the Windows 2000 implementation of QOS to have a generic interface by which requests are made, and it requires standardized responses to such requests (limiting the responses that such applications will need to handle).

The modular approach requirement for implementing QOS into the operating system isn't new or unusual in Windows 2000; the requirement actually fits well within the Windows 2000 development approach. By giving individual components responsibility for providing subsets of QOS functionality—such as one for invoking QOS, another for handling traffic control, and another for handling policy issues—the abstraction and efficiency of individual components is increased.

To put this in real-world terms, imagine that a computer was one indivisible manufacturing unit: the speakers, monitor, keyboard, CPU, CD-ROM, and so on were all built into one piece of plastic and silicon. With such a monolithic (rather than modular) approach to manufacturing the computer, the capability of the manufacturer or the user to add the newest CD-ROM or a faster CPU would be nullified, as would the capability to update or upgrade speakers or the monitor. Not only would the CD-ROM be inefficient and overpriced, there would also be additional overhead associated with ensuring that everything worked as one big unit. Also, if one piece were changed or broken, the entire unit would have to be rebuilt. Rather than having standardized interfaces so different manufacturers could specialize in building speakers, one manufacturer would have to be able to do it all. As a result, the room for innovation and extended capabilities for individual components (services) would be stifled.

Seamless integration with the existing network stack—which falls right in line with the overall QOS requirement to work within the existing network framework—requires the use of a pre-existing mechanism. Perhaps such a pre-existing mechanism could be expanded upon, extended, or otherwise enhanced, but the mechanism cannot be an entirely new approach to networking or QOS is doomed to fail before it gets started. That's both a real-world and a psychological reality. Therefore, QOS must use some already-in-place mechanism to invoke its services, perhaps expanding and extending those services in some way, but not reinventing them or requiring new ways of interfacing with old (existing) networking activities.

All of these requirements must be part of the client solution, or else the solution will fail to meet its objectives. There are other similar requirements that could be argued into this list, but these are the basic requirements.

Now, on to what these requirements are expected to achieve.

QOS Client Goals

Being invisible to the end-user means that no additional complexity is introduced to the computing experience. This may sound like a sales pitch, but it isn't. It's a reflection of the increasing use of computers and the availability of average users to deal with the deluge of existing information. If you think it entails a bit of work to understand how QOS works, multiply that by ten, and you have the amount of work necessary for someone unfamiliar with computers to type and print a simple letter. You'll know how true this statement is if you ever tried to help parents or friends get "up and running" on their new computers. QOS is simply too complex for average users—it's already complex enough for sophisticated administrators.

Being invisible to the end-user, however, means that the responsibility for QOS capabilities is going to rest with the application developer. That means that QOS has to be readily available (and not too arcane) to the developer, and it should be simple enough in programmatic terms to make QOS-enabling an application a worthwhile undertaking.

> **Note**
>
> *There is an important exception to this programmer-responsibility approach, which we'll investigate at the end of this section.* ◆

The goal of allowing individual aspects of QOS to be provisioned independently of others requires that these components (such as traffic control or policy) have their own interfaces, which *can* be implemented by those who wish to do so. Compare this to putting in underground sprinklers. You can have someone provide the service for you (a sprinkler specialist) to orchestrate the necessary design, sprinkler heads, trenching, laying of pipe, equipment automation, and labor to get the job done. Or you could do the necessary research to take a stab at design, sprinkler head choosing, labor, and all the other facets of putting in sprinklers yourself. Which is easier? The former. Which is more work? The latter. But which provides more granular control over just how the sprinkler system is put in? The latter again, but it presumes that you know what you're doing or that you're willing to put in the necessary effort to get there.

Using open standards to facilitate interoperability with non-Windows 2000 devices means that there isn't a hard-lined requirement to conform to the way Windows 2000 is implementing QOS in order to interoperate and interact with other QOS-required devices on the network. Translation: Using open standards elicits less animosity and encourages extended acceptance of an implementation, which is the goal of any technology looking for industry-wide availability. It also leverages any momentum that existing open standards have by being able to tout that Windows 2000 uses open standards and offers a solution today. The inclination for others to say, "That's the way to do it" is much stronger than if proprietary solutions are attempting to be dictated (which would likely result in others saying "There's a better, more open way to do it"). *Open standards* means known interfaces that allow a common interface point, behind which (in their own devices) vendors can do whatever they want, as long as they conform to the common interface point. Use of open standards encourages development and interoperability, and that's good for (their) consumers, which makes it a win-win-win (Windows 2000—network devices—Windows 2000 and network device customers) situation.

Providing a moderator application enables users who are running applications that aren't QOS-enabled to still take advantage of Windows 2000's QOS capabilities. A *moderator application* (also called a *provisioning application*) is an application that runs in the background and makes requests for QOS guarantees on behalf of applications that can't make the requests themselves. This allows a QOS-enabled network to take advantage of QOS, without requiring every application running on the network to be immediately QOS-aware.

QOS Client Implementation Design

Windows 2000 has taken these derived requirements and their associated goals, and created a handful of services that address QOS requirements and goals within the client (that is, within the Windows 2000 Professional or Windows 2000 Server machine).

Within Windows 2000, there are individual service providers that handle requests or services that fall under their umbrellas of responsibility. The division of responsibility for certain aspects of QOS achieves the modular design. These services include the RSVP Service Provider (RSVP SP); Traffic Control (TC), which is further divided and discussed in Chapter 5; the Local Policy Module (LPM); and others. By creating services and service providers, Windows 2000 can take advantage of the benefits of modular design and inherit its benefits. Such benefits include the capability to invoke any of these services without the need to go through the "overseer" service (the RSVP SP), and to provide for a granular—and perhaps specialized—application of their services.

Abstraction of these services within the network stack, which then lends itself to using a common programmatic interface above and below them (in the stack), achieves a different goal in the process. First things first—abstraction of these services is done by implementing Windows 2000 QOS calls through the use of an existing network programming interface: Windows Sockets 2. Technically, Windows Sockets (Winsock) 2 had provisions for QOS built into it; there was only one thing missing—an implementation. Now that Windows 2000 has an implementation of QOS available within the network stack, the Winsock programming interface (also known as *sockets*) can be used to make QOS reservation requests. As alluded to, this also covers another important tenet in the "QOS shopping list" must-haves: work within the existing network framework. Winsock and sockets have been around for awhile and are well established.

By tying Windows 2000 QOS to the Winsock programming interface—or at least by implementing its basic services through Winsock—Windows 2000 QOS can leverage developers' existing programming knowledge of Winsock to get QOS-enabled applications built (or existing applications easily modified to be QOS-enabled). By using sockets, QOS also achieves another important requirement: it creates a mechanism by which the end-to-end connection can be established. By definition, a *connected socket* is a unique connection between two sockets-compatible computers. Adding QOS capabilities to that connection simply extends the sockets' functionality and role, without having to create an entirely new mechanism.

Each service provider also includes programmatic interfaces (*Application Programmer Interfaces*, or *APIs*) for those who are interested in more granular control over QOS specifics. However, the "overseer" service provider (the RSVP SP) can handle most QOS requests and, on behalf of requesting applications, interact with the other services, as necessary to secure a QOS reservation—all within an abstracted, industry-standard request mechanism framework.

QOS in the client, then, uses a group of services and service providers to implement QOS in Windows 2000, and does so within the pre-existing networking framework. Existing services—such as Windows Sockets—are leveraged and actually extended to provide QOS functionality in the client. For more granular control, services and service providers expose their own APIs. QOS in the client works within the existing networking framework and simply extends the existing service capabilities. As you see in Figure 3.3, the somewhat generic representation of QOS in the client begins to take shape and take on some specific names.

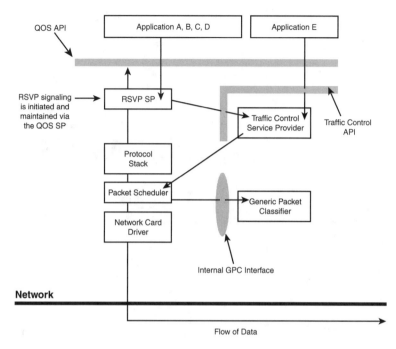

Figure 3.3 *The Windows 2000 QOS implementation.*

QOS Over the LAN Segment

We've established how Windows 2000 QOS is implemented in the client, but the first stop on the way across the network in an end-to-end solution is probably the most difficult section of the network over which to provide any kind of service guarantee. We've already discussed why the LAN segment is such a difficult part of the network to address in Chapter 2, citing Ethernet's CSMA/CD engineering as the major contributing factor. Despite this difficulty, without getting some sort of guarantee over the LAN segment, QOS and the Windows 2000 QOS implementation are undone as soon as they get out of the client's network card.

Requirements: Enable a way of differentiating Ethernet frames and, with such differentiation, apply priority to frames that merit increased priority.

Goals: Bring a manageable, deterministic (or at least differentiated) solution to the inherent unruliness of Ethernet segments.

Implementation Design: Policy-based admission control services that moderate reservations across the LAN segment.

With these in mind, the QOS-enabled LAN segment looks something like Figure 3.4.

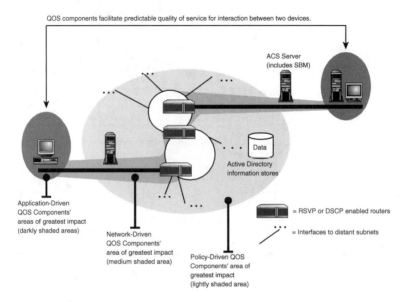

Figure 3.4   *Implementation of Windows 2000 QOS across a QOS-enabled LAN segment.*

QOS LAN Segment Requirements

Differentiating between Ethernet frames necessitates that information about an Ethernet frame be available in the only part of the packet that the Ethernet switch is interested in: the Ethernet header. The placement of such information requires that the operating system or the driver for the network interface card (NIC) places information into the Ethernet header, which is the L1 header. Figure 3.5 illustrates the Ethernet header's place in the packet.

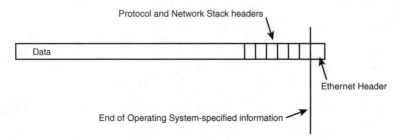

Figure 3.5   *The Ethernet header, sitting on the end of the packet, is all that the Ethernet switch acts upon.*

In order for QOS to be implemented on the Ethernet LAN segment, some sort of QOS-imparting information must be placed in the Ethernet header. Such a requirement means that either the operating system (Windows 2000, in this case) or the network card driver must interact with the Ethernet header before the packet gets placed onto the LAN segment. Before inter-action, however, the goal of such interaction must be clearly defined.

QOS LAN Segment Goals

Bringing manageability, and differentiated or deterministic behavior to the Ethernet segment means interfacing with the Ethernet header. The operating system can and has, in the past, interacted with the NIC as it puts Ethernet headers on outgoing packets—although perhaps with some sort of cost to resources, such as CPU cycles. Ethernet switches and hubs look only at Ethernet headers—they ignore the rest of the frame. Remember that QOS has to function within the existing network framework. That is to say, there can't be a significant departure from existing network technology if QOS will be successful. Any change in the LAN segment implies a significant departure from existing network technology, so it is not a good solution.

With all this information considered, the operating system (Windows 2000) must either take on responsibility for Ethernet header modification itself, or it must interact and cooperate with the NIC to achieve the goal of setting priority on the LAN segment. Manageability and deterministic or differentiated activity means that this interface must somehow be set and managed from the operating system (or a flag sent to a QOS-enabled NIC driver). Setting such QOS-related information in the Ethernet header is only half the equation, however. For QOS capabilities to work across the LAN segment, the operating system has to be able to set some sort of priority within the Ethernet frame, *and* the Ethernet switch has to be able to read such priority and act upon it. That means cooperation between the Ethernet switch and the NIC/operating system pair.

In addition to this setting of priority within the Ethernet frame header, there is another important aspect of this equation that must be considered—determining how permission to increase the priority of said Ethernet headers is granted or revoked. The goal of being manageable necessitates such admission control—without it, any NIC could boost its priority and make the setting of such priority ineffectual.

QOS LAN Segment Implementation Design

Windows 2000 implements LAN segment priority by supporting an industry-standard Ethernet header priority-tagging scheme called *802.1p*, in conjunc-tion with a policy-based admission control service aptly called *QOS ACS*. A quick explanation of QOS ACS is provided here to aid the explanation of QOS on the LAN segment. (QOS ACS is explained in detail in Chapter 7, "Policy-Driven QOS".)

There are two implementations of QOS ACS: ACS/SBM and ACS/RRAS. *ACS/SBM* includes an implementation of the Integrated Services idea of a Subnet Bandwidth Manager (SBM). ACS/SBM, a service that runs on a Windows 2000 Server, is responsible for handling admission requests, including requests pertaining to LAN segment transmission priority. The ACS/RRAS implementation of ACS handles bandwidth usage requests associated with routing interfaces that are connected to and serviced by a Windows 2000 RRAS Server.

The important point to keep in mind about ACS is that participation is voluntary; the QOS-enabled client must request priority reservations with the QOS ACS for the QOS ACS service to work the way it is intended. This may sound like a hole in the service, but it isn't—applications that go through the trouble of implementing QOS (with 802.1p capabilities a possible component of that overall QOS solution) will want to tout that they're compliant with Windows 2000 QOS and, thereby, with QOS ACS. Otherwise, why go through the development effort? And for those applications with more nefarious intentions—well, those aren't generally the applications that gain wide acceptance in corporate environments.

QOS is implemented across the LAN segment, and then by boosting the priority of Ethernet frames across the LAN segment with a tagging mechanism called *802.1p*. These tagged Ethernet headers are set with special priority information that the Ethernet switch reads to determine which frames are treated with more priority than others. To put this back into visual perspective, when implementation is achieved, the diagram looks like Figure 3.6.

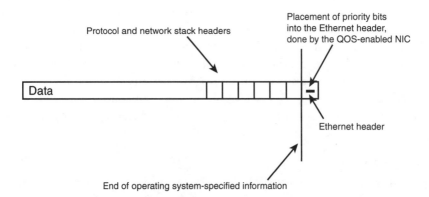

Figure 3.6 *An 802.1p-enabled network packet, with its priority information placed within the Ethernet header.*

An important point to note here is that the network device mitigating access to the actual wire—the Ethernet switch—may not be running Windows NT or Windows 2000 (I say *may* not because at least one available Ethernet switch does). Despite the fact that the switch may not be running Windows 2000, Windows 2000 is able to cooperate with standards, and work within a standardized framework to provide a LAN segment service-quality guarantee implementation as part of the overall Windows 2000 QOS solution. This happens through industry-wide cooperation and a standardized implementation mechanism. This approach extends the functionality of the network through cooperation, integration, and standards that are embraced by (or at least agreed-upon by) the majority of the networking industry.

QOS through the Router

Once the packet gets through the Ethernet switch, it's often destined to go through a router.

In order to achieve end-to-end QOS, Windows 2000 QOS must be able to communicate and reserve its bandwidth and other network resource requirements to the router.

Requirements: Establish and maintain a communication medium to transmit and update Windows 2000 QOS client reservation requirements to all routers in the path between each QOS end node.

Goals: Use industry-standard communication protocols to communicate with QOS-enabled routers.

Implementation details: Use RSVP messages to communicate and maintain resource reservations in routers along the path between end nodes.

With the QOS requirements, goals and implementation details for the router, the interaction between Windows 2000 QOS and the router must look something like Figure 3.7.

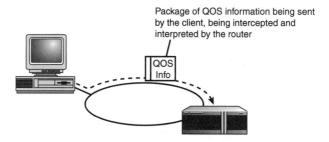

Package of QOS information being sent by the client, being intercepted and interpreted by the router

QOS Info

Figure 3.7 *Interaction between the Windows 2000 QOS client and the router.*

QOS Router Requirements

In order to establish and maintain communication between the router and the Windows 2000 QOS client—which is necessary to transmit and update client reservation requirements—there must be some common communication medium that the Windows 2000 QOS client and the router share. Although all clients send packets that go through routers, there is no inherent communication going on between the router and the client. Rather, the router is looking at each packet individually (not caring which client or machine it came from), and then sending it on to the next appropriate hop. That means that somehow, before these packets are sent on to the next hop in their destination, the Windows 2000 QOS client and the router must communicate. A resource reservation protocol, such as RSVP, comes to mind.

Routers do communicate with each other, using various routing protocols that each router participating in the "conversation" can understand. For example, routers that understand the OSPF (Open Shortest Path First) routing protocol (which disseminates routing table information) can use OSPF to direct packets to the routers themselves. The routers then read and interpret them in order to communicate with one another. OSPF is a routing protocol, which is to say it is a preordained method of transmitting information. The fact that it's preordained allows routers to deal with only a certain number of variables (fictitious example: the third through sixth bit in the OSPF header indicates the type of message contained in this particular OSPF packet), thereby reducing the overhead of implementing the protocol on the router. The transmission medium used for OSPF is usually IP, so OSPF has worked itself into the existing framework of network activity by using an existing protocol to ferry its communication protocol information across the network.

In order for any client implementing QOS—including Windows 2000 QOS clients—there must be some sort of communication medium, or protocol, that both the client and the router understand. The QOS reservation has to be able to get to the router somehow, and using a protocol to communicate such reservation information is the best approach... preferably a protocol that is specifically designed to reserve resources.

QOS Router Goals

Routers out there today aren't all running Windows 2000 as their OS. Many are running Cisco OSs, 3COM OSs, and all sorts of other companies' OSs, so presuming or even suggesting some sort of Windows 2000-proprietary mechanism for communicating QOS-specific information would be met with a cold reception. A better approach is to use a communication protocol that has been created as the result of a consortium of input from leaders in the router industry.

Keep in mind that QOS is hardly a Microsoft or Windows 2000 idea—it's been around for a long time, and most companies involved in the network infrastructure (router companies, switch companies, WAN device companies, and Internet interest groups) have equal interest in making it a reality. QOS is not Microsoft-centric or Windows 2000-centric. Its deployment is in the best interest of the future of the Internet as an all-encompassing communications medium, and the Windows 2000 QOS client is one (albeit big) piece in the overall picture.

Being one piece in that overall picture, however, means that Windows 2000 QOS must fit with all the other disparate pieces in that picture, including routers. Fitting together means finding a common, industry-standard common denominator by which they can communicate. Such a common communications denominator means all routers—as well as any other clients such as UNIX, Macintosh, or other operating systems that care to enable QOS—will be able to "hook in" to QOS enabling, which just furthers the industry-wide push toward ubiquitous QOS capability across the Internet. This is a good thing, in my opinion. A proprietary solution that locks customers into a certain solution are bad, whether that proprietary solution is offered by Microsoft, Sun, Novell, Cisco, or any other company. The IETF, in directing QOS recommendations (that's pronounced "standards" to those implementing said technologies), ensures that such proprietary solutions don't stifle the technology, and thereby slow or kill its deployment and acceptance in the real world.

QOS Router Implementation Details

It just so happens that the push for QOS (by the industry as a whole) produced just such a communications protocol: the *Resource Reservation Protocol*, commonly known as *RSVP*. RSVP can be used by any client or device to communicate resource-reservation requests, and the protocol itself has defined mechanisms for communicating such information. RSVP is discussed and explained in detail in Chapter 6, "Network-Driven QOS."

Windows 2000 QOS clients use RSVP to establish and maintain communications with routers (and other devices). Using RSVP satisfies Windows 2000 QOS router requirements, and also achieves the goal of using industry-standard communication media to communicate reservation requests. Figure 3.8 shows how this process works.

Again, there is something that may be obvious (too obvious to notice, perhaps), but is worth pointing out. The network device whose resources are being reserved—the router—isn't running Windows 2000. Windows 2000 is still able to cooperate with routers because it works within a standardized framework to provide the overall, end-to-end QOS solution. This approach

embodies a cooperation with existing devices and interoperability with existing, industry-wide standardized implementation mechanisms. Again, such a
cooperative and standardized approach, which extends the functionality of
the network through standards that are agreed upon by the networking
industry, makes implementing QOS within the existing framework viable.

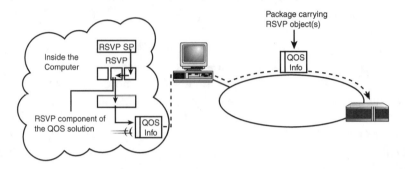

Figure 3.8   *Interaction and communication between the Windows 2000 QOS client
and the router.*

QOS Across the WAN

In any end-to-end solution today, the WAN must be considered. Geographically distributed networks are the norm these days, and the emergence of the Internet as a corporate WAN backbone only cements that fact
as the way of the network computing future. The WAN must, therefore, be
addressed when considering the Windows 2000 QOS implementation and
its end-to-end solution. The nature of the WAN and the telecommunication
network that WANs traverse, contribute to a fairly specific problem that the
WAN introduces to the QOS equation.

> **Requirements:** Enable QOS resource reservations to be made to WAN
> devices.

> **Goals:** Use existing WAN QOS provisioning techniques—leveraging native
> WAN QOS provisions—within the Windows 2000 QOS implementation
> scheme.

> **Implementation Design:** Map RSVP messaging to the WAN device and its
> Layer 1 and/or Layer 2 signaling

The WAN requirements, goals and implementation details for interaction
with Windows 2000 QOS ends up looking like Figure 3.9.

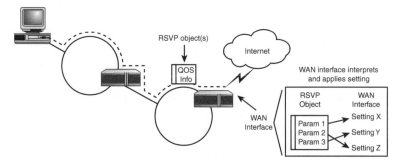

Figure 3.9   *Windows 2000 QOS client RSVP requests being "mapped" to Layer 1 and/or Layer 2 signaling in the WAN devide.*

QOS WAN Device Requirements

The requirement of getting network device reservation requests in a form that the WAN device can understand is similar to the same requirement for the router. WAN devices don't inherently communicate with the client—they investigate each packet instead. However, WAN devices differ from routers in their transmission characteristics. WAN devices take a packet and usually chop it into pieces of data that are commensurate with their particular transmission medium (for example, ATM must chop it into 48-byte pieces and add its header, whereas Frame Relay can take the entire packet), and then send it across their network.

There is a fundamental difficulty with provisioning QOS on a WAN device, and it has everything to do with the way the WAN device deals with these (generally) larger packets. WAN devices generally don't investigate the packet before it gets chopped into its smaller pieces, so communication regarding processing requirements for the packet doesn't have a prescribed means of getting to the WAN interface.

The inherent difficulty with getting QOS information from the packet to the WAN interface is that the packet is chopped up as a whole, sent across the WAN network (cloud), and then reconstructed on the other end and sent on its way. No interrogation of header information is done, nor is any interpretation of the routing information at the WAN device done (it's done by the router part of the larger WAN device). This makes for a certain degree of difficulty in getting QOS provisions to the WAN device itself. Another way of looking at this process is to put it into terms of the ISO OSI model, with its seven layers. Routing information is housed in Layer 3, whereas the WAN interface is largely functioning on Layer 1 and/or Layer 2.

Getting information that is housed in Layer 3 (L3) transmitted to a device that only looks at Layer 1 or Layer 2 (L1 and L2) can be challenging.

However, most WAN interfaces—including ATM, Frame Relay, and X.25—have built-in QOS capabilities that are generally statically set up. In other words, all data that cross a certain Virtual Channel (VC) on the WAN interface receive a certain level of service quality. This facilitates QOS guarantees within the WAN cloud, and for a certain general customer, but not on either side of the WAN cloud. So, if BigCompany has a 1.536Mbps (T1) Frame Relay connection to the Internet and has certain QOS provisions (a CIR, or Committed Information Rate) for data transmissions up to, say 768k, it means that *all* data from BigCompany up to 768k receives the QOS that's been provisioned for the link *as it crosses the WAN cloud*. Not individual flows, but *all* data. Not as an end-to-end solution, but *within the WAN cloud*. This differs significantly from the dynamic, flow-by-flow, end-to-end service quality guarantee capabilities of "data-network QOS" or in our specific implementation, Windows 2000 QOS.

The end-to-end nature of the Windows 2000 QOS solution requires that the WAN interface be able to honor reservation and transmission guarantees for individual flows.

QOS WAN Device Goals

With the requirement of getting the WAN device to guarantee service quality, there comes the necessity of getting Windows 2000 QOS service quality reservations somehow mapped to the existing WAN QOS provisions. The details of getting QOS reservation information translated into WAN device QOS provisions depend less on the device itself (though drivers would have to have the capabilities built into them, of course), and more on the transmission type. For example, ATM has a certain set of QOS-enabling provisions, as does Frame Relay, but each is implemented differently. So each transmission medium must be addressed individually in order to get Windows 2000 QOS to work over each.

QOS WAN Device Implementation Details

In order to get QOS requests translated into reservation information that the WAN interface can understand, a mapping must occur between the Windows 2000 QOS requests (achieved through RSVP requests) and native WAN QOS provisions. To put this in other terms, Windows 2000 QOS has to map its requests into terms that the WAN interface can apply to its transmission medium.

To apply this concept to the illustrations that have been included in this section, we see that the reservation requests have to somehow be translated into terms that the WAN device can understand—and more importantly, into terms that the WAN device can apply to its particular transmission medium.

Generally, once the packet gets across the WAN, the packet is sent through one or more routers on its way toward its destination (where router requirements, goals, and implementation design apply), and then likely through one or more LAN segments(in which LAN segment requirements, goals, and implementation apply) until it finally reaches the client or server it was trying to reach. So, by explaining Windows 2000 QOS mechanisms from the client to the WAN interface, the network devices that will be encountered (routers and WAN devices and LAN segments) have all been covered.

The Overall QOS Picture

Although all of the requirements, goals, and implementation designs reflect different points in the network path between end nodes, the initiation of the reservation starts with the Windows 2000 QOS client. All of the reservation request information—the details of which we'll go into in Chapter 6—originates from the client and simply gets carried to these other devices through the general mechanisms that have been covered in this chapter. Of course, there are more details to discuss in order to understand Windows 2000 QOS in detail, but it is important to remember that the Windows 2000 QOS client initiates these reservation requests. The rest of these mechanisms simply aid in getting the request to all the necessary network devices in the path between the end points in this end-to-end solution.

Another important point to remember is that the implementation of Windows QOS can be credited to Windows 2000, but not the idea of the technology. These requirements, goals, and implementation designs are the result of Windows 2000's implementation of QOS—as well as, often, a reflection of IntServ's (and DiffServ's, and other IETF Working Groups') findings and recommendations. That is to say, don't give Windows 2000 credit for coming up with all of these requirements or goals (nor all of the implementations); they reflect a body of work that's been steered, at least in theory and recommendations, by the work of IETF Working Groups. So let's give credit where credit is due. But the large, daunting task of implementing those recommendations goes to Microsoft, and more specifically to the Windows 2000 group that brought recommendations, shopping lists, and goals into a working, real-life implementation that encompassed and embraced non-Windows 2000 variables.

Now that we know the requirements, goals, and implementation designs of all of these QOS-specific requirements, let's get an overview of the Windows 2000 components that comprise its QOS solution, so that when the drilling down of details occurs, you can keep the big picture in perspective. Chapter 4, "Quality of Service Components in Windows 2000," provides just such an overview.

4

Quality of Service Components in Windows 2000

Although there are a number of components that contribute to the creation of the Windows 2000 QOS solution, not all of them are specifically implemented within the Windows 2000 environment. As discussed in the previous chapter, many network devices are included in the path between two end points; to create an end-to-end solution, these components must somehow provide QOS service guarantees. Some Windows 2000 components, then, address the required cooperation between Windows 2000 QOS and network devices, but are integral components, nonetheless.

This chapter is geared toward giving an overview of all the components involved in creating the Windows 2000 QOS solution. The idea behind this chapter stems from personal experience, in which a fundamental and perhaps overview-level explanation of the technology is lost during the detailed explanation of a technology or component. The result is that, despite all sorts of details and implementations and nuances, the entire effort is undermined because a sense of the "big picture" was never provided. I'll have none of that in this book. As proof of that promise, this chapter provides an overview of each of the components involved in Windows 2000 QOS. So, if you get mired in too many details down the road and can't quite remember what all of those detailed implementation techniques are trying to achieve, you can flip back to this chapter to get the proper perspective.

QOS Complexity and the Need for Components

Quality of Service is inherently all over the place. It's somewhat like trying to be all things to all people, or, more commonly, like pleasing all of the people all of the time. Pleasing or not, Windows 2000 QOS has its hands in every network device that sits in the network, and being able to address the technologies and nuances of each of those requires specialization in a number of areas (a major contributing factor to QOS woes). The approach that Windows 2000 has taken to this challenge is to implement *components*— services or other pieces of software that address the various and diverse requirements involved in achieving end-to-end QOS.

To facilitate the discussion of these components, they will be broken up into three groups:

- Windows 2000 QOS components in the end node
- Windows 2000 QOS components in the network
- Windows 2000 QOS components and policy enforcement

There's a certain reasoning behind such grouping, but detailed discussion of the logic behind that grouping is better left for the next chapter. Suffice it to say for now that this grouping helps bring some semblance of logic and order to the discussion…not always the attributes that come naturally to discussions of QOS.

One important concept to note is that QOS connections, or flows, are unidirectional. It means that, for example, if a Windows 2000 Professional client wants to connect to a videoconferencing server and *receive* data with a certain service guarantee, one guarantee (flow) is established. If that Windows 2000 Professional client also wants to *send* data to the videoconferencing server with a certain service guarantee, another guarantee (flow) must be established, and it will be completely independent of the other flow. Figure 4.1 illustrates this concept.

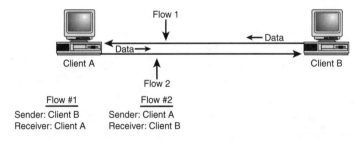

Figure 4.1   *Two independent flows are necessary to establish two-way communication between a client and a videoconference server. Either may be rejected or torn down independently of the other.*

Keep this in mind when going through the following overview; it can help to keep things straight because a client or some video server may be "client" and "server" at the same time.

QOS Components in the End Node

The *end node* is the Windows 2000 QOS client and/or some server (a video or audio server somewhere on the Internet or any other QOS-enabled network device) that initiates a QOS request. The following sections provide short explanations of these components and how each fits into the big picture.

The RSVP Service Provider

Imagine a central handler of almost all Quality of Service provisioning within Windows 2000, and you imagine the RSVP Service Provider (RSVP SP). The *RSVP SP* accepts QOS requests on behalf of applications or services that sit above it (stack-wise), and then manages the service-specific requests necessary to invoke Windows 2000 QOS components that handle individual QOS services, essentially beginning the chain of events that results in QOS provisioning for Windows 2000 clients.

The RSVP SP can be thought of as the diplomat, or the Windows 2000 QOS facilitator, which accepts QOS requests and returns QOS results to applications or services that want overall QOS capabilities for their network transmissions. The RSVP SP sits as a layer that essentially abstracts all of the nitty-gritty details that necessarily go into providing the many facets of Windows 2000 QOS, providing a central and dedicated interface with which applications/services can interact.

Why provide this kind of service? Because this approach relieves applications from having to generate (and handle) requests to all of the individual Windows 2000 QOS components. This would result in much, much more complexity and overhead for the average application's development. Also, this approach allows for a central nervous system for Windows 2000 QOS components; individual Windows 2000 QOS components are good at their areas of specialty, but they cannot provide a cohesive QOS interface on their own. The RSVP SP, on the other hand, accepts requests from an application or service, and then dissects the request and sends multiple appropriate requests (on the application/service's behalf) out to the myriad Windows 2000 QOS components. When responses come back, the RSVP SP packages these responses into a nice clean format that the application/service can understand, thus making it easy for the application to make use of Windows 2000 QOS.

Most of the other nitty-gritty detailed components that the RSVP SP is designed to abstract also have programmatic interfaces (APIs) of their own. This enables those developers who wish to get nitty-gritty about their QOS development effort to do so, essentially circumventing the RSVP SP and dealing with the components themselves. ◆

The RSVP SP is the diplomat and translator of all things to do with Windows 2000 QOS functionality. It is the effective go-between that coordinates interaction between applications/services that want QOS capabilities and the complex Windows 2000 QOS components that provide them.

The QOS API

Applications and services interact with the RSVP SP through the *QOS Application Programming Interface (API)*. This is the general-purpose (but functionally complete) interface to Windows 2000 QOS, and it is the only interface to Windows 2000 QOS that most developers will need to interface with.

Traffic Control Modules

Traffic control is exactly what its title suggests—the capability to regulate the flow of data traffic. You're probably looking for more explanation than that (I would), so the longer version of that explanation is as follows. Traffic control, through its three modules, implements Windows 2000's capability to queue, schedule, and modify the transmission of data—on the packet level—so that traffic transmitted onto the wire conforms to certain patterns, policies, and priorities.

The Role of Traffic Control in the Network

Traffic control is a major component of QOS in general, and it plays a significant role in overall Windows 2000 QOS technology. In every component, there is a defensible position that can be taken, which states that QOS revolves around (or is inextricably tied to) traffic control. Understanding traffic control, then, is integral to understanding QOS and to understanding the Windows 2000 implementation of QOS.

Keep in mind, however, that traffic control is not isolated to the Windows 2000 QOS client; indeed, traffic control is a major (if not the major) function of routers as they provision and honor QOS guarantees. Traffic control occurs in the Windows 2000 QOS client, in the LAN segment, in the router, and even in the WAN device. Traffic control is everywhere QOS is important, and its importance is the impetus behind this section.

But what is traffic control, and how does its provisioning across the entire path between the Windows 2000 QOS client and the other side of the connection play in the big scheme of things? In the short term, it means nothing less than breathing new life into the existing overburdened LAN infrastructures. But the short-term is the least interesting of traffic control's contributions to QOS and Windows 2000 QOS. Have you ever heard of IP telephony? It has everything to do with traffic control (and QOS guarantees). But what about video feeds or audio addresses? Radio over the Internet; phone calls on the computer? Controlling traffic, tagging traffic with priority, and transmitting (scheduling) based on relative priority all play major parts in the future of networking.

The implications of traffic control across a network that, increasingly, carries more and more computer data, voice data, and (as bandwidth becomes available) video data is sobering. These implications merit attention, and they demand that the profound impact they could have on us all be addressed. It's a cliché, but it could be the harbinger of the Information Age...or at least a major catalyst. That, of course, is what makes QOS technology so exciting and interesting. ◆

The idea of traffic control reflects the problem with standard networking on the network stack and NIC level. Without QOS (therefore, in standard networking environments), packets are sent out as fast as possible. (To use a term that is more commonly recognized, traffic is sent out in *bursts*.) Have a 1MB file to send? The packets will be sent to the network one after the other, as quickly as possible and with the shortest gap possible. This is a very selfish approach to the problem because when all computers do this, the result is bursty transmissions that get scrunched together, stifling the availability of the network as long as one network device is attempting to send data. Figure 4.2 illustrates this problem.

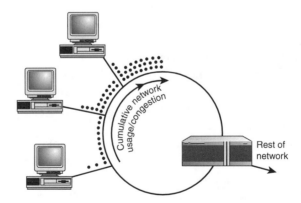

Figure 4.2   *Multiple computers sending data in the traditional fashion, resulting in bursty transmissions that immediately congest the network.*

There is a better approach, and that is to spread out the transmission of the packets somewhat, so that bursty data transmissions don't clog the network with short spikes in activity. By smoothing out the transmission, or *shaping* it, the network is better able to deal with the traffic and everyone gets a better shake at the available network bandwidth.

The first reaction to such an idea might be as follows: "So, if my NIC can't send in bursts, then shaping effectively slows transmission time by spreading out the packets." A reasonable reaction, however, when backoff algorithms (such as those used in Ethernet when collisions are detected or the wire is busy) are figured into the big picture, the effect of traffic shaping (which reduces the frequency of "busy signals" on the wire) on transmission time becomes more attractive (or at least less unattractive). To put this into perspective, Figure 4.3 illustrates the effect of traffic shaping on the network.

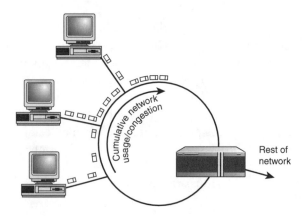

Figure 4.3   *The effect of shaping traffic on an Ethernet subnet.*

Traffic shaping, however, has benefits across the entire network, not just the subnet. Routers are less inundated with bursts of traffic and perform better, WAN interfaces are better able to handle extended reasonable loads than sporadic bursts of packets, and other network devices fare similarly better with shaped traffic.

Along with shaping traffic, there is another method of ensuring that certain traffic generated (or received), even by the same computer, receive differing levels of priority. For example, if a download of an application is happening at the same time that a query to the mission-critical SQL server is being executed, the SQL query should receive higher priority than the application download.

And finally, there must be some method of classifying which traffic should go out first and enforce other elements of Windows 2000 QOS, such as regulating a certain flow's data-transmission allowance.

These traffic-controlling functions are achieved through three primary components that make up the traffic control aspects of Windows 2000 QOS: the Generic Packet Classifier; the Packet Scheduler; and the shaping component of the Packet Scheduler, the *Packet Shaper*.

The Generic Packet Classifier

Within a network node, there may be some flows (and, therefore, certain subsets of packets) that should receive higher transmission priority than other packets. There also is a need to be able to identify which packets are associated with a given flow, and perhaps what the characteristics of that flow are. In other words, there needs to be a certain classification of packets, based on the flow with which they are associated and the relative priority that such flows may have within the Windows 2000 QOS client. The *Generic Packet Classifier* is the traffic control component that enables the classification of packets through a process of "tagging" packets with a programmatic handle, so that information about the packet and its flow can be had by other QOS components. The Generic Packet Classifier is responsible for doing such packet tagging.

The Generic Packet Classifier, then, enables the classification of packets and their priority by tagging packets with a reference that enables other QOS components (as well as any other network component in the stack, for that matter) to access the packet's prescribed QOS-based information. This allows other traffic control components to use such information to make decisions regarding their subsequent transmission onto the network.

The Packet Scheduler

The *Packet Scheduler* is comprised of three subcomponents: the Conformance Analyzer, the Packet Shaper, and the Packet Sequencer. The Conformer and the Sequencer will be discussed under the guise of the Packet Scheduler.

The Packet Scheduler can be considered the QOS enforcer; once the Generic Packet Classifier has tagged a packet with its classifying-enabled handle, the Packet Scheduler's Conformance Analyzer component can enforce data-transmission parameters for individual flows, essentially enforcing the limitations placed on a given QOS guarantee. When the Conformance Analyzer determines that a packet conforms to its flow parameters (that is, its Token Bucket parameters), it can pass the packet on to the Packet Scheduler.

The Packet Scheduler queues a packet until it is in conformance with its Token Bucket parameters; when it is in conformance, the Scheduler passes the packet off to the Packet Sequencer. The Packet Sequencer can then arrange the order and interval of packets (based on issues such as priority and burstiness, for starters) so that they can be transmitted across the network.

The Packet Scheduler effectively schedules the transmission of packets within the Windows 2000 QOS client so that all packets conform to their QOS service quality transmission constraints.

The Packet Shaper

Shaping packet transmissions is equivalent to smoothing out the peaks (bursts) associated with standard network transmissions, as discussed in the previous paragraphs. The *Packet Shaper* is the traffic-control component, responsible for mitigating packet transmissions from a Windows 2000 QOS client. Packet shaping alone can have a tremendous impact on alleviating network congestion.

The Packet Shaper smoothes bursty transmissions, thereby making steadier (and more effective) use of network resources.

The Traffic Control API

Traffic control is a big part of the overall QOS scheme. Although the RSVP SP can and will invoke appropriate traffic control measures on behalf of applications and services using the QOS API, Microsoft has made it possible to address traffic control functionality independently of the QOS API. The method of doing so is called the *Traffic Control API*.

With the Traffic Control API, developers can develop applications (or services) that can initiate and handle the traffic control capabilities of Windows 2000 QOS, and thereby gain granular and specific control over traffic control issues.

QOS Components in the Network

QOS necessarily traverses the network, which means that there must be mechanisms in place to address deterministic treatment of packets (flows) as they cross the network. There are QOS components—more accurately described as networking technologies designed to interact with QOS capabilities—that facilitate getting manageable and deterministic service guarantees honored as packets cross the network.

These technologies have been closely embraced by Windows 2000 QOS, and the standards that have evolved for these component technologies have allowed Windows 2000 QOS (and Windows 2000 itself) to interact with each technology within the Windows 2000 network stack.

802.1p

The technology behind *802.1p* (prioritized services on an 802 LAN segment, such as an Ethernet or Token Ring LAN segment), is geared toward creating a priority scheme that can be applied to the traditionally difficult-to-prioritize Ethernet segment. Indeed, even management of the subnet (Ethernet subnet, generally) is almost impossible, due to the transmission characteristics of Ethernet. However, with 802.1p technology, a three-bit flag is set in the Ethernet header to assign a relative priority to the packet, allowing a hub or switch that is 802.1p-aware to provide prioritized service to packets with relatively higher priority.

The conclusion for 802.1p, then, is that 802.1p offers a way to apply differentiated services to packets traversing an 802 subnet. However, 802.1p NICs and switches (hubs) must be deployed in order to take advantage of 802.1p technology.

The Subnet Bandwidth Manager

The *Subnet Bandwidth Manager (SBM)* is designed to take the total amount of available subnet bandwidth—say, 10MB—and manage how that bandwidth is used by various QOS-enabled clients. The SBM is implemented as part of the QOS Admission Control Service (QOS ACS). The QOS ACS is presented in the "QOS Components and Policy Enforcement" section, later in this chapter.

In conclusion, the SBM manages and regulates access to the subnet for cooperative QOS-enabled clients. Windows 2000 QOS technology incorporates SBM technology in its ACS/SBM component.

DiffServ Codepoint

Just getting priority or management over the local subnet, which is facilitated by 802.1p and the SBM, isn't enough. There must be some way of establishing a priority for IP packets as they make the jump from the local subnet to the general network path. This necessity becomes apparent if we take a moment to see what happens to a packet once it gets through its local subnet, as seen in Figure 4.4.

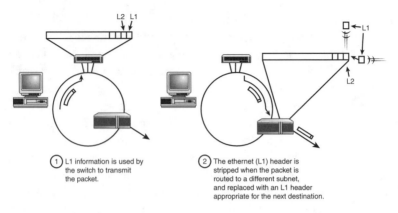

Figure 4.4   *A packet that goes from the local subnet, its Ethernet header stripped, onto other network devices as it makes its way over the network.*

Note

Note that the Layer 3 information is not stripped, and it stays with the packet on its entire journey across the network. ◆

As you can see in Figure 4.4, the Ethernet header is stripped once the packet gets through its local subnet, making any 802.1p flagging useless as it traverses the rest of the network. Most network devices outside of the local subnet, such as routers, operate on Layer 3 information like the IP header. It becomes paramount, then, to be able to apply some differentiation to Layer 3, so that network devices that act on Layer 3 information can give precedence to packets with higher priority, or at least appropriate treatment to packets whose relative priority can be differentiated from one another. This priority is applied to the IP header through the DiffServ Codepoint, or DSCP, which then allows the packet to traverse the network and maintain its priority ranking as it does so. DSCP has obviated the former approach of achieving this precedence tagging, called IP Precedence. With DSCP, IP Precedence is no longer needed.

In conclusion, DSCP is a means of marking and maintaining an IP packet's relative priority (or precedence) as it traverses the network.

L2 Signaling

Layer 2 signaling—more commonly referred to as *L2 signaling*—is a technology rooted in the fundamental differences between traditional LAN-based data transmissions and WAN transmissions. This fundamental difference is that LAN routing generally only deals with Layer 3 (such as IP), whereas WAN technologies deal with Layers 2 and 1. The problem that this addressing of different layers presents is that QOS information, which is generally included in a packet's Layer 3 header, must be translated or communicated somehow to Layer 2 upon reaching the WAN interface, so that WAN interfaces can maintain the service guarantees in the end-to-end paradigm. Many WAN technologies already have some sort of QOS capabilities built into them, but getting information from Layer 3 headers communicated to Layer 2 WAN signaling becomes the challenge.

L2 signaling, as a QOS or Windows 2000 QOS technology, addresses the challenge by translating QOS parameters and guarantee requirements so that L2 signaling (WAN transmission mediums) can implement QOS guarantees across the WAN link. By applying QOS parameters to WAN transmissions, the service guarantee is applied to the network and true end-to-end service guarantees are possible, even when a WAN interface is thrown into the path.

L2 signaling, then, is the technology that translates QOS parameters into service guarantee requirements that are understandable by WAN signaling technologies, so that the QOS guarantees can be applied to the packet as it traverses the WAN transmission medium.

QOS Components and Policy Enforcement

As a matter of observation, all of the QOS and its guarantees rest on a rather large assumption: the client has sufficient permission to request and receive its QOS guarantee. That assumption brings with it a big Pandora's box. How is such permission determined and regulated, let alone monitored?

Of course, Windows 2000 QOS (and QOS in general) wouldn't be effective without some sort of permission mechanism (or many mechanisms), so the issue of client permission is certainly addressed. If it were not, then anyone who knew enough about Windows 2000 QOS programmatic interfaces could simply flag all of their packets with the highest priority possible, and thereby get the best service possible. The rest of the poor schmucks on the network received what bandwidth was left (perhaps little or none). The effect of so many schmucks would be a technology (QOS) that landed us right back where we were before its introduction: with bogged-down networks, oversubscribed capacity, and a need for services that relied on service quality that wasn't achievable over the network. Not a rosy picture for the outcome of such a vast developmental undertaking.

Fortunately, policy enforcement regulates almost every aspect of the network when Windows 2000 QOS is implemented. I say "almost" because there are places on the network (in the non-802.1p LAN segment, namely) where cooperation from the client application is required for Windows 2000 QOS to be as effective as it can be (more on this in Chapter 7, "Policy-Driven QOS"). Don't be fooled by that little caveat, though; permissions are well enforced in Windows 2000 QOS, and the components that implement such policy enforcement are given introductions in this section.

The Admission Control Service

In order to bring some semblance of order to the chaos inherent with an Ethernet subnet—or any trust boundary where enforcement of bandwidth usage is necessary, such as a Windows 2000 RRAS router—there must be some management of the medium's available bandwidth. Generally, that management includes reserving a certain percentage (20%, maybe) of the LAN segment or router interface for reservations, and the remaining bandwidth is reserved for best-effort usage or unreserved usage. One facet of the ACS is to do just such LAN segment or router interface bandwidth management. In fact, the accepted Subnet Bandwidth Manager (as presented in various IETF documents bearing that name) component of the QOS picture is incorporated in the ACS/SBM QOS component. The ACS/RRAS component implements bandwidth management on Windows 2000 RRAS deployments. The ACS, however, provides more functionality than subnet (LAN segment) or router interface bandwidth management.

There is a more communal position to take when discussing the management of client requests for bandwidth (and therefore network device resource) usage. That communal position is this: if clients that have QOS requests that we "somehow know" will fail could be stopped from sending those requests across the entire network, resources associated with those requests (which are not incidental, by the way) could be preserved. It's the networking version of "an ounce of prevention is worth a pound of cure." ACS performs this function by inserting itself into the front of a Windows 2000 QOS client's QOS reservation path and checking the client's permissions as the first order of business. If the client does not have proper permission to receive its requested service guarantee (QOS request), the ACS ends the reservation request right there and effectively nixes the client's further attempts (In other words, it stops the client from sending the request across the entire network.)

The result of the ACS placing itself at the beginning of the client's QOS request is this: Bandwidth and resources of other LAN segments or network devices in the path beyond the ACS are preserved because the request doesn't go beyond the ACS unless it has sufficient permission to do so. This philosophy works equally well for incoming QOS requests; with ACS on the LAN segment, an incoming QOS request (perhaps initiated by a client located 3,000 miles away) can be monitored by ACS. And if the requesting client doesn't have appropriate permission to use bandwidth on that LAN segment, the process can be terminated before the request gets any further. By monitoring outgoing requests (initiated by clients on the local LAN segment) and incoming requests (initiated by some distant QOS-enabled requestor), the local bandwidth is further secured and preserved. ACS, which controls whether clients' QOS requests are admitted beyond their LAN segment, is aptly named.

ACS is implemented as a service running on a Windows 2000 Server computer.

To provide a concise overview, ACS manages a LAN segment's available bandwidth, and inserts itself into the client's QOS request path in order to conserve network device and bandwidth resources from clients' doomed QOS guarantee requests. ◆

The Policy Element Generator

In order for policy-based admission control services, such as those provided by the ACS, to be effective or even to function at all, policy information must be provided by the client. This provision of policy information (information that identifies the client, so that policies regarding this client can be compared to a given request) on the client's side of things requires that a component prepare requisite policy information and package it into a format that is understandable by the ACS. This policy information is called a *Policy Element (PE)*; on a Windows 2000 client, the software that creates the policy element that comes with Windows 2000 is a MSIDPE.DLL, and it resides on the Windows 2000 QOS client.

The PE provides information that its complementary component on the ACS—called the *Local Policy Module (LPM)*—can intercept and interpret. The relationship between the PE and the LPM is tight, in that they depend on each other speaking the same policy "language" in order to function properly. The PE generator included in Windows 2000 QOS clients contains client information that can be compared against policy information stored in the Windows 2000 Active Directory. The LPM included with the ACS intercepts this information from the client and does the necessary policy lookup. If either the PE generator (MSIDPE.DLL, in this case) or the LPM is replaced with a custom policy enforcement package, the other must also be replaced with a complementary policy-enforcement package.

The PE resides on the Windows 2000 QOS client, and it packages Windows 2000 policy information for submission with QOS guarantee requests for the LPM (on the ACS) to interpret and act upon.

The PE API

The *Policy Element Application Programming Interface (PE API)* enables developers to create custom policy modules that can be used in conjunction with, or in place of, the Microsoft-supplied PE.

The Local Policy Module

In order for the ACS to make decisions regarding client requests for QOS reservations, the ACS must be able to identify a client and compare its request against established permissions. This identification of the client and subsequent comparison against established permissions is done with the help of the *Local Policy Module (LPM)*. Although the PE Generator resides on the Windows 2000 QOS client, its counterpart, the LPM, resides on the ACS computer. The LPM acts as a ferry service between ACS and the Windows 2000 Active Directory for the retrieval of identification information and corresponding client permissions.

The process works like this:

1. The client sends a PE with its QOS request, which is intercepted by the ACS.

2. The ACS hands off the PE to the LPM, which then accesses policy information stored in the Windows 2000 Active Directory, and compares the request against the policy information to determine whether the client has enough permission rights to establish the connection.

3. The LPM passes the verdict back to the ACS.

> #### Note
>
> *It's important to remember that the LPM, which resides on the Windows 2000 Server computer running the ACS for a given LAN segment or router, interacts in a proprietary way with the PE sent by the client, so the two are a functional pair. If the PE Generator on a client is changed, then the corresponding LPM must be added to (or take the place of) the Microsoft-provided LPM. ◆*

The LPM, then, intercepts identity and permission information in a Windows 2000 QOS client's PE, and manages the decision-making process on behalf of the ACS. The decision-making process may entail submitting a request to the Windows 2000 Active Directory to determine whether the client has the appropriate permission to be granted the QOS reservation request.

The LPM API

Much like the PE API, the *Local Policy Module's Application Programming Interface (LPM API)* allows an LPM to communicate with the ACS. Programmers interested in creating customized LPMs (and, of course, in corresponding PE Generators for the client if the information provided in the PE will be in a different format from that expected by the LPM) can use the LPM API to interface with the ACS.

Third Party API (LDAP)

For the LPM to gather information from the Windows 2000 Active Directory, there has to be some sort of preordained process (or at least some sort of agreed-upon protocol) for interacting with the Active Directory. This process, which is really a protocol, is called the *Third Party API* in the context of Windows 2000 QOS. This is actually the Lightweight Directory Access Protocol, or LDAP, and it certainly is not particular or isolated to Windows 2000 QOS. In fact, LDAP is the protocol of choice for accessing the Active Directory or any other directory service information store.

The use of LDAP to gain information from the Active Directory has its roots in gaining policy information, from which a LPM (and therefore, the ACS) can make decisions on whether to grant resource reservations to clients requesting such service. Anyone programming in the Windows 2000 arena will soon be familiar with LDAP, whether they want to or not.

LDAP, then, is the interface to the Windows 2000 Active Directory. In terms of its importance as a Windows 2000 QOS component, LDAP is the protocol used to ferry information back and forth between the LPM and the Active Directory.

> **Note**
>
> *For more information about LDAP, take a look at the book* LDAP: Programming Directory-Enabled Applications with Lightweight Directory Access Protocol, *by Tim Howes and Mark Smith (published by Macmillan Technical Publishing).* ◆

The Role of RSVP

Absent from the discussion thus far has been an answer to the following question: "How does Windows 2000 QOS package these service guarantee (QOS) requests?" The answer comes in the form of an overview explanation of the *Resource Reservation Protocol*, or *RSVP*.

Since its IETF-draft beginnings, RSVP has been designed as a protocol dedicated to carrying QOS-related information to diverse network devices along the path between end devices. Because it has been introduced and submitted as an industry standard, or at least a recommendation, RSVP intends to be the generic but well-defined carrier of QOS information from end node to end node, and to every network device in between.

RSVP allows network devices to reply with an affirmative or negative response to included reservation requests (in non-QOS terms, RSVP means "please reply"), which allows each device in the path to make individual decisions about whether to grant QOS guarantee permissions to requests.

RSVP, therefore, is the protocol of choice for transmitting standardized QOS information to network devices in the path, and Windows 2000 QOS clients are members of that network device party. That is to say, Windows 2000 QOS clients use RSVP to package their QOS requests for transmission across the network.

RSVP Intentions

As you remember from earlier chapters, one of the most difficult challenges looming over the implementation of QOS was the complexity involved in getting all these diverse network devices to be able to communicate with and between one another. With the emergence of RSVP as a de facto standard, a level playing field has been established. Now, if devices can understand, interpret, and act on RSVP messages, devices can be QOS-aware.

The intent of RSVP, at least from the perspective of someone who didn't actually dream up and create RSVP himself (and there are a lot of us out there), is simple but powerful. Create a communication medium that will allow all sorts of vendors to create QOS-aware network devices. By doing this, it becomes more likely that QOS (which is being demanded by these vendors' customers) will become a reality. As more vendors create RSVP-aware devices, QOS will become more entrenched, or at least more available. The services and capabilities that accompany QOS will then create more demand for RSVP and QOS-aware products. With the advent of DSCP, and its more simplistic approach to enabling QOS provisioning, the availability of QOS-aware devices is given an additional method of gaining momentum.

In other words, RSVP standard acceptance creates a self-feeding cycle, kind of like the Windows platform and its wide availability of programs. More available programs meant that more users wanted to use the platform, and more users on the platform drew more programmers (representing potential profits), which created more applications and drew more users. If the intention of RSVP was to create a self-feeding momentum, bringing on its heels more and more products that supported RSVP (or DSCP, and thus QOS), spurring the development of more applications that could take advantage of QOS guarantees, then its intention is taking hold.

RSVP is somewhat complex, and merits longer discussion (see Chapter 6). At this point, it's sufficient to explain that RSVP is the protocol in which QOS guarantees are placed and then transmitted (by using IP) across the network to the next appropriate network device. To switch from a functionality perspective to a "market" perspective, RSVP paves the way—through its standardization of QOS-enabling communications—for QOS to make a stronger foothold in the networking world, and to bring about what the IETF intended for QOS in the first place: network-type convergence. ◆

Part II

Quality of Service in Detail

5 Application-Driven QOS

6 Network-Driven QOS

7 Policy-Driven QOS

8 Uniting Application-, Network-,
and Policy-Driven QOS

With the Quality of Service basics explained in Part I, we now move on to the specifics of the Windows 2000 implementation of Quality of Service. Part I explained what Windows 2000's implementation of Quality of Service is attempting to achieve; Part II goes into detail about how Windows 2000 achieves that implementation.

The Windows 2000 implementation of Quality of Service is necessarily complex—owing largely to its industry-standard, multiplatform interaction with diverse devices that are scattered across the network. In order to properly approach the explanation of the implementation, Part II has been divided and designed specifically to make the explanation of the implementation details as clear as possible. This is done by dividing the explanation of components into three functional categories: application-driven, network-driven, and policy-driven components of Windows 2000.

5

Application-Driven QOS

In Part I of this book, QOS was introduced, and some of the technical challenges that its implementation faces were outlined. This part gets down to the details and presumes that if you've gotten this far, you have a pretty firm grasp on what was discussed in Part I.

Even with a firm grasp on all of the components of QOS, the way that QOS is presented can play a big part in how effectively it is explained. That being the case, there are a number of points to be made about how the explanation of QOS is approached, and how that approach reflects the operation and implementation of QOS in Windows 2000.

Giving Structure to the QOS Beast

Explaining QOS is kind of like eating a large pizza without cutting it into slices: It's big, unwieldy, somewhat difficult to manage, and you're almost guaranteed to have it all over your face before you're done.

To avoid such messy approaches, I've sliced the QOS discussion into three logical parts, enabling us to better digest QOS as a whole. The three QOS discussion parts are as follows:

- Application-driven QOS
- Network-driven QOS
- Policy-driven QOS

It's important to realize that this division is being done for the sake of clarity and to facilitate the proper introduction of QOS-related components that are complicated all by themselves, but they're doubly complicated when interacting with other QOS components. Although it's arguable to state that these components are each initiated (in one way or the other) at the end node, the impact of each component is not necessarily in the client. Instead, its impact is felt in one of these three categories: application, network, or policy.

Although many of the components that make up Windows 2000 QOS technology can function independently to provide limited QOS functionality, QOS is an integrated technology, and it is most effective when the components are working together to provide a comprehensive end-to-end QOS solution.

There is a reason why the division of QOS technology has been made in the places it has. First, there is a logical distinction between application, network, and policy. Second, the influence of each of these three categories (application, network, or policy) has a certain demarcation in the end-to-end solution of QOS that lends itself to such division. So, all of the components have a certain part of the overall solution, in which their influence is the greatest while they work together to create a true end-to-end solution.

Important Departures from the Logical Structure

The structure that's been outlined so far in this chapter works very well from all of the QOS components in Windows 2000, except one: RSVP.

RSVP is kind of its own animal, and RSVP signaling—the transmission of RSVP messages across the end-to-end network connection between end nodes—exerts influence on each of the three outlined areas of influence. Therefore, RSVP will be treated in each of the following three "area-of-influence" chapters, with each entry explaining how RSVP interacts with the components (or end-to-end connection) in each area.

The reason that RSVP is so diverse is that RSVP was invented to be the carrier of all things necessary to either establish or invoke QOS, and its relative complexity (versus other components) reflects its creators' ambitious intentions. So, don't be surprised when you see RSVP in each of the following three chapters, and don't believe that the RSVP protocol is disjointed or broken into three disparate parts; it isn't. It's one protocol (and in this context, one QOS component) that happens to exert influence in every aspect of QOS.

The Complete QOS Technology

Despite this slicing up of Windows 2000 QOS components and grouping such components into logical sections, QOS is a cohesive technology. This dividing of technologies is for convenience (in part). More importantly, however, this division of QOS components lends to an easier, better, more thorough understanding of QOS. And it better explains how QOS interacts with all the devices, protocols, and software it must have in order to function.

So, make no mistake; QOS is a cohesive technology that integrates all of its components to create an end-to-end solution that delivers QOS to Windows 2000 computers... regardless of how far apart they are.

Application-Driven QOS Components

QOS components that are application-driven have their greatest effect in the client. To put this in other terms, these QOS components are largely application-driven. As far as their implementation goes, their greatest influence is in the way that the *client* behaves to QOS (versus how the network reacts to QOS or how policy is implemented for QOS). The following is an all-inclusive list of QOS components categorized as application-driven, each of which is covered in detail in this chapter:

- **RSVP Service Provider (RSVP SP):** Facilitates QOS for Windows clients and applications, and invokes other QOS components.

- **Resource Reservation Protocol (RSVP):** RSVP is the standards-based messaging protocol that's usually invoked by the RSVP SP and carries reserve requests across the network. Note that RSVP can be invoked directly by sophisticated programs or services, and that certain QOS functionality in Windows 2000 (such as Traffic Control) can be achieved without RSVP signaling.

- **Traffic Control Modules:** Facilitators of Traffic Control. These modules include the Generic Packet Classifier and the Packet Scheduler.

- **QOS API:** The application programming interface (API) to the RSVP SP.

- **TC API:** The API to Traffic Control components.

The QOS components that are explained in this chapter have been grouped and branded with *application-driven* as their title because each gets invoked as a direct result of an application or service on a QOS-enabled client calling QOS-invoking function calls (APIs). Also, QOS components belonging in the application-driven group have their greatest influence in the client itself, rather than in the network or in policy-based decision processes.

When you take a look at Figure 5.1, which outlines where each of the three groups of QOS components have their greatest influence, you see that the application-driven group has its greatest effect on the client. You also see that the boundary of their influence largely rests just around the client; although messages that are created or transmitted based on application-driven components (such as RSVP messaging) may extend beyond the client, such messages invoke other components (such as network-driven QOS components).

Because this chapter is interested in getting into the details of application-driven components, it's useful to zoom in to the client and see what's going on in the network stack of a QOS-enabled Windows 2000 computer. In Figure 5.2, which is a conceptual representation of the way QOS components interact and function within the network stack, it becomes clearer how the RSVP SP plays a central role in Windows 2000 QOS.

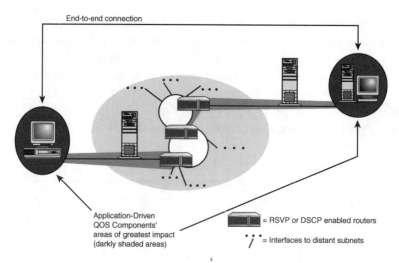

Figure 5.1 *Application-driven components' greatest area of impact—the client.*

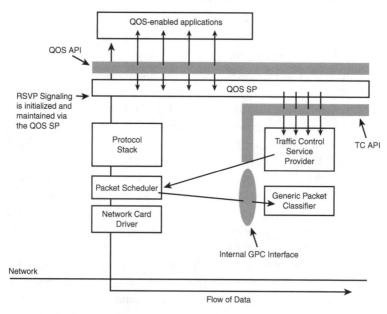

Figure 5.2 *The stack and application-driven components' interaction with one another.*

With the centralized role of the RSVP SP duly illustrated, there is a caveat that should be understood. It is possible to get a certain degree of QOS without ever using the RSVP SP, perhaps by simply invoking Traffic Control without the use of RSVP. You could argue (as many have on both sides of the issue) that QOS has degrees of implementation and degrees of effectiveness. You can get some QOS, you can get comprehensive QOS, or you can simply choose a number of different levels of service—such as levels 0 through 7—and consider differentiation between such data to be a form of QOS.

In Windows 2000 QOS, though, the RSVP SP is central to Windows 2000 QOS, but its participation is not absolutely necessary to get *partial* (or a *lesser degree*) of QOS provisioning for a given flow. Although this may be confusing, it's useful because almost every component of QOS can individually contribute to making better use of the end-to-end network connection. Getting at least some increased efficiency out of such an end-to-end connection is better than not getting any.

The RSVP SP

The detailed discussion starts with the anchor of Windows 2000 Quality of Service implementation: the RSVP SP. If you want an overview of how the RSVP SP theoretically fits within Windows 2000 QOS (rather than its implementation details, which are outlined here), refer to Chapter 4, "Quality of Service Components in Windows 2000."

The RSVP SP is the heart of Windows 2000 QOS. Simply put, the RSVP SP is the hub for just about everything that happens with QOS. It is a service layer that sits between applications and other QOS components, turning applications' QOS requests into directives for other QOS components.

The RSVP SP implements this central role by accepting QOS-specific connection requests, and then by invoking other QOS components on behalf of the application; the RSVP SP manages RSVP signaling for both incoming and outgoing messages, and its API provides the interface by which most application developers QOS-enable their applications. By providing this service layer to applications, the RSVP SP shields application developers from the complexities of directly interfacing with other QOS components, such as RSVP, Traffic Control, and policy identity modules.

As a service layer, the RSVP SP must receive enough information from an application about its service requirements to act or request services on the application's behalf. Because QOS has many different characteristics and because there are many different scenarios in which QOS requirements differ (such as unicast versus multicast), the information that an application must supply to the RSVP SP is significant. However, there is a common ground on which all QOS-enabled transmissions stand: They are all based on creating a "connection" between end nodes, and those connections are established through the use of Windows Sockets, or Winsock. Details of the way that such programming conventions are used, such as the difference between a TCP connection and a connected UDP connection, are explained further in Chapter 11, "QOS for the Programmer."

QOS Connection Characteristics

Before we get too far into implementation details, some basics must be identified. Perhaps one of the most important facts to establish is that QOS-enabled connections have the following traits:

- They are receiver-centric.
- They are largely unidirectional.

Each of these points deserves further explanation because these two points seem to contradict not only conventional wisdom, but what you'll find in the ongoing discussion of QOS components. QOS-enabled connections are generally considered to be *receiver-centric* because the QOS-enabled connection is usually instigated by the end node that is interested in receiving data. Although the sender *can* initiate a QOS-enabled connection through the use of RSVP signaling (by emitting PATH messages), the receiver is the decision maker for the QOS connection because it determines the QOS parameters that go into its RESV message. Only after RESV messages travel back up the path taken by the associated PATH messages is the QOS connection completed. Because the receiver ultimately must make the final decision about QOS provisioning (both parameters and the final step of establishing the QOS connection), QOS connections are generally considered to be receiver-centric.

QOS-enabled connections are *unidirectional* because QOS provisions for a given flow apply to only one direction (usually, data going *to* the receiver). Either direction of a bidirectional connection may have QOS-enabled transmission characteristics, but the receiver is generally the one most interested in receiving QOS-enabled data. RSVP is based on that premise.

Let's say that you want to get some information over the telephone (perhaps because you want to buy something from a telephone-based retailer), so you place a telephone call. You just created the two-way connection and the connection is complete, but there is no service quality established yet. Once connected, data/information begins flowing your way and you can modify the service you get by making decisions about certain parameters of the conversation ("Hello, welcome to Telemarketers International. Press 1 for more options"). During the course of this telephone connection, you are the receiver of most of the information—after you begin making choices from the list of options, you're directing the service you want. This is similar to instigating service quality on an already-established connection—you're required to send certain control information ("Press 2 now for game software sales") at certain prompts, which is essentially a decision that you make based on a "path" being offered to you by the service. In this example, you initiated the call because you wanted the bulk of the information (how to order your Quake III). Yet, there was another direction in which information could travel (you received, but you also sent by pressing 2), largely for control information.

This example is similar to the way that QOS is receiver-centric (you initiated the call because you wanted information) and largely unidirectional (most of the data/information was coming your way). Yet the connection required interaction from the sender (it had to answer your call and respond to your requests), and it could transmit data in two directions (at certain points, you directed the conversation by choosing to modify the data by pressing 2).

Notice that the connection was established without need for immediate service quality parameters; there may be a direct line to game software sales, though, in which case you could (in comparison) be specifying the type of service you wanted *upon establishment* of the initial connection.

Similar to this telephone call example, each QOS connection has transmission characteristics for both directions. This works well for unidirectional data, such as video feeds or online radio transmissions, but what about real-time teleconferencing? What about situations in which each side is interested in receiving QOS-enabled data? Simple: Use two QOS-enabled connections (sockets), so that each receiver instigates a QOS-enabled connection. Not one socket with QOS for each direction of the socket, but two sockets, where each client is primarily sending on one and receiving on the other.

QOS-Enabled Applications

Applications that are *QOS-enabled*—that is, they have been written (or retrofitted) with the capability to take advantage of a QOS-enabled Windows 2000 client—are capable of the following:

- They set up a network connection that can be QOS-enabled by invoking the RSVP SP.
- They request QOS provisioning on the connection (this can be done during the connection setup or at a later time).
- They receive and/or send QOS-enabled data, perhaps modifying QOS transmission characteristics over the life of the socket.
- They cancel QOS provisioning the QOS-enabled connection (socket).
- They close the QOS-enabled connection (socket).

Note

It's possible to combine setting up the network connection and enabling QOS provisioning (the first and second bullets) into one step. It's also possible to combine the last two bullets, canceling QOS on the connection and closing the network connection, into one step. ◆

From these steps, all things QOS come to life, data is sent from end node to end node with service quality guarantees based on QOS-specific parameters and, upon closing of a socket, things come to an end. Once the QOS-enabled socket is connected (actually, even when it's listening), the RSVP SP is interpreting QOS parameters that the application has provided; and, based on those parameters, invoking other QOS components, as appropriate.

Getting the RSVP SP Its Parameters

How does the RSVP SP know the particulars of which QOS parameters the application requires? What is entailed in providing the RSVP SP with QOS parameters? Good questions—and the answers really help to explain the basis on which the rest of the QOS components operate.

As previously explained, Windows 2000 QOS is implemented through the use of Winsock functions. Primarily, applications use the following Winsock functions to begin the process of creating a QOS-enabled connection between two end nodes, which inherently invokes the RSVP SP:

- WSAConnect
- WSAJoinLeaf
- WSAAccept
- WSAIoctl (SIO_SET_QOS)

Don't worry if you aren't a programmer; this information is just for reference right now, and I won't get bogged down in programmatic detail. The reason I'm making you endure this programming slant for the moment is because it is through one particular parameter, which each of these functions use, that all QOS parameters are derived: the FLOWSPEC. Even for the non-programmer, the FLOWSPEC is interesting and necessary to understand. And if you are a programmer and are hungry for more details on particular programmatic call sequences for QOS-enabling applications, don't worry: programming details are provided in Chapter 11. But the following information is good—and necessary—to understanding how QOS works.

Through the use of the FLOWSPEC structure (a *structure* is a programming element with multiple categories, into which programmers can place data), the QOS-enabled application provides the RSVP SP with the information it needs to establish a connection with service quality tailored to the application's needs. The parameters of the FLOWSPEC structure are based on the Token Bucket model (explained in Chapter 2), and each direction of a QOS-enabled connection is called a *flow* (thus the FLOWSPEC, or a given flow's specifications). The FLOWSPEC has the following members:

- TokenRate: The TokenRate (Token Rate) member specifies the rate at which data is allowed to be transmitted for the given flow. If the "transmission tokens" are not used immediately, they accrue to allow data transmission up to a certain periodic limit—which is the value of the PeakBandwidth member for the FLOWSPEC structure. Accrual of credits is limited, however, to a specified amount (the value of the TokenBucketSize member). This limiting of total transmission tokens avoids situations in which flows that are inactive for a while end up flooding available bandwidth with large amount of accrued tokens. Because flows may accrue transmission credits over time (at TokenRate) only up to a certain maximum number of tokens (the TokenBucketSize), and because flows are limited in "burst transmissions" to their PeakBandwidth, Traffic Control and network-device resource integrity are maintained. Traffic control (discussed later in this chapter) is maintained because flows cannot send too much data at once, and network-device resource integrity (such as routers or switches) is maintained because network devices are spared from large traffic bursts. TokenRate is represented in bytes per second.

- TokenBucketSize: The TokenBucketSize member places a limit on the amount of "transmission tokens" that a given flow can accrue, regardless of time. By placing a limit on the number of transmission tokens that a flow can accrue, flows are kept from hogging available network bandwidth by accruing unlimited transmission tokens (from being idle for a long period), and then transmitting sustained streams of large amounts of data. TokenBucketSize is expressed in bytes.

- PeakBandwidth: The PeakBandwidth member places upper limits on how much data a given flow can transmit over a given period of time, essentially placing a throttle on a flow's transmission privileges, regardless of how many transmission tokens the flow has accrued. In quick terms, PeakBandwidth is a burst limit. PeakBandwidth keeps flows from overburdening network resources with one-time or cyclical data transmission bursts. PeakBandwidth is expressed in bytes per second.

- Latency: The Latency member of the FLOWSPEC structure indicates the maximum amount of acceptable delay between transmission (by the sender) and reception (by the receiver or receivers) of a given packet (actually of any given bit). This particular member of the FLOWSPEC structure is useful for time-sensitive transmissions such as real-time audio or video; if too much latency is experienced while transmitting the given data, then the picture/audio on the other end will not have an acceptable level of quality. Latency is expressed in microseconds.

- DelayVariation: The DelayVariation member is a little less intuitive than other members of the FLOWSPEC structure; in essence, DelayVariation provides a range (of time) that a given packet will be delayed between transmission and receipt. By providing such bounds, you can make certain arrangements. Applications also make certain arrangements based on this value, such as how much buffer space they'll need, and so on. DelayVariation is expressed in microseconds.

- ServiceType: The ServiceType member of the FLOWSPEC structure is actually a structure itself (that's right, this is a structure within a structure; we'll see more of this soon). ServiceType determines how QOS provisions (that is, the parameters provided in the FLOWSPEC structure) are handled by everything involved in QOS provisioning—the client, network devices, transmission mediums, WAN interfaces...everything. There are a number of predefined service types available in Windows 2000 QOS (such as best effort, controlled load, and guaranteed), any of which can be specified by name in this ServiceType member to have the RSVP SP provide the appropriate type of service to the specified flow. Service Types details are explained in the "QOS Service Types" section, found later in this chapter.

- MaxSduSize: The MaxSduSize (Maximum Serviced Data Unit Size) specifies the maximum packet size permitted or used for the given flow. The MaxSduSize member is expressed in bytes.

- MinimumPolicedSize: The MinimumPolicedSize member specifies a minimum size for a packet's specified flow and still receive the quality of service requested for the flow. The MinimumPolicedSize member is expressed in bytes.

These parameters and the service quality provisions they represent are the building blocks upon which QOS provisioning is built. Quality of Service—for each client, access medium, and network device in the path between end nodes—is derived from the values provided in these parameters.

As you may have noticed, all these members of the FLOWSPEC structure are particular to a flow. Earlier, I mentioned that each connection has two flows (although the flow going toward the receiver that initiated the connection is generally the flow of interest). So, what about the other direction? The FLOWSPEC contains all of this information, but it is actually part of the all-encompassing QUALITYOFSERVICE structure that specifies QOS parameters for the entire socket. There is a very clear relationship between the QUALITYOF-SERVICE structure (governing the entire socket's QOS characteristics) and the FLOWSPEC structure (specifying the QOS parameters for a given flow). The QUALITYOFSERVICE members are as follows:

- SendingFlowspec: As you may have guessed, this member is a FLOWSPEC structure (another structure within a structure) that specifies QOS parameters for the sending direction of the given flow.

- ReceivingFlowspec: Surprise, surprise...this member is a FLOWSPEC structure (yet another structure within a structure) that specifies QOS parameters for the receiving direction of the given flow.

- ProviderSpecific: There are certain times when a programmer wants to be able to fine-tune particular parameters or values of a QOS-enabled connection that would otherwise be unreachable. This member of the QUALITYOFSERVICE, which is in the form of a WSABUF structure (WSABUF is a well-known Winsock structure type), enables programmers to do just that. Its presence in the QUALITYOFSERVICE structure is good to know about, but we won't get into its programmatic specifics here. Just know (as a programmer, IT professional, or CIO considering QOS for your organization) that Windows 2000 QOS has the capability to fine-tune QOS parameters to meet very specific needs.

QOS Templates

With so many parameters, there are countless ways to direct the QOS SP to prepare and invoke QOS capabilities for a given application's needs. However, many applications fall into one category or another, and their needs for QOS provisioning are similar. For example, QOS parameters for the FLOWSPEC structure could be similar for all IP telephones, video transmission applications, or mission-critical SQL queries. In such cases, it's conceivable that a certain set of QOS parameters could be preordained as appropriate for such application types. In a word, applications could make use of FLOWSPEC *templates*. The QOS SP provides for such rubber-stamping of FLOWSPEC parameters.

> **Note**
>
> *Using a QOS template is much like popping a TV dinner into the microwave. There's no need to break out all sorts of pots and pans to cook up the veggies, potatoes, meat-substitutes, or desserts; and no messy cleanup afterwards. Simply choose the TV dinner that most closely resembles what you can stomach, open the TV dinner's box, peel off the protective wrap, and apply a little heat. Voila! You have dinner.* ◆

With QOS templates, the process (and avoided messes) is similar. You can leverage well-known QOS settings (for the QUALITYOFSERVICE structure) simply by choosing the available QOS template that most closely resembles your required transmission characteristics and applying the template to the appropriate socket. Using QOS templates can greatly reduce the complexity associated with QOS-enabling an application. Even if your application has specific needs, you can create a QOS template with settings for SendingFlowspec and ReceivingFlowspec (members of the QUALITYOFSERVICE structure) that are appropriate, and (programmatically) install it on the system, after which it's available for use whenever needed.

Of course, without available templates, the idea of using templates is just that (an idea), and it's not terribly useful. The RSVP SP automatically supplies a fair number of QOS templates. The following lists the templates included in Windows 2000 as a matter of course:

Template G711
Services packets sized at 340 bytes; suited up to 27 packets/second; provides Guaranteed Service.

Sending FLOWSPEC Values

ServiceType	3
TokenRate	9250
PeakBandwidth	13875
TokenBucketSize	680
MaxSduSize	340
MinimumPlicedSize	340
DelayVariation	-1
Latency	-1

Receiving FLOWSPEC Values

ServiceType	3
TokenRate	9250
PeakBandwidth	13875
TokenBucketSize	680
MaxSduSize	340
MinimumPlicedSize	340
DelayVariation	-1
Latency	-1

Template G723.1
Service packets sized at 68 bytes; suited for approximately 32 packets/second; provides Guaranteed Service.

Sending FLOWSPEC Values

ServiceType	3
TokenRate	2200
PeakBandwidth	3300
TokenBucketSize	136

MaxSduSize	68
MinimumPlicedSize	68
DelayVariation	-1
Latency	-1

Receiving FLOWSPEC Values

ServiceType	3
TokenRate	2200
PeakBandwidth	3300
TokenBucketSize	136
MaxSduSize	68
MinimumPlicedSize	68
DelayVariation	-1
Latency	-1

Template G729

Service packets sized at 40 bytes; suited for up to 50 packets/second; provides Guaranteed Service.

Sending FLOWSPEC Values

ServiceType	3
TokenRate	2000
PeakBandwidth	4000
TokenBucketSize	80
MaxSduSize	40
MinimumPlicedSize	40
DelayVariation	-1
Latency	-1

Receiving FLOWSPEC Values

ServiceType	3
TokenRate	2000
PeakBandwidth	4000
TokenBucketSize	80
MaxSduSize	40
MinimumPlicedSize	40
DelayVariation	-1
Latency	-1

Template H263QCIF

Service packets sized between 80 and 2500 bytes; accrues transmission tokens at 12,000 bytes/second; provides Controlled Load Service.

Sending FLOWSPEC Values

ServiceType	2
TokenRate	12000
PeakBandwidth	-1
TokenBucketSize	6000
MaxSduSize	2500
MinimumPlicedSize	80
DelayVariation	-1
Latency	-1

Receiving FLOWSPEC Values

ServiceType	2
TokenRate	12000
PeakBandwidth	-1
TokenBucketSize	6000
MaxSduSize	2500
MinimumPlicedSize	80
DelayVariation	-1
Latency	-1

Template H261QCIF

Service packets sized between 80 and 2500 bytes; accrues transmission tokens at 12,000 bytes/second; PeakBandwidth (burst rate) is not specified; provides Controlled Load Service.

Sending FLOWSPEC Values

ServiceType	2
TokenRate	12000
PeakBandwidth	-1
TokenBucketSize	6000
MaxSduSize	2500
MinimumPlicedSize	80
DelayVariation	-1
Latency	-1

Receiving FLOWSPEC Values

ServiceType	2
TokenRate	12000
PeakBandwidth	-1
TokenBucketSize	6000
MaxSduSize	2500
MinimumPlicedSize	80
DelayVariation	-1
Latency	-1

Template H261CIF

Service packets sized between 80 and 8192 bytes; accrues transmission tokens at 16,000 bytes/second; PeakBandwidth (burst rate) is not specified; provides Controlled Load Service.

Sending FLOWSPEC Values

ServiceType	2
TokenRate	16000
PeakBandwidth	-1
TokenBucketSize	8192
MaxSduSize	8192
MinimumPlicedSize	80
DelayVariation	-1
Latency	-1

Receiving FLOWSPEC Values

ServiceType	2
TokenRate	16000
PeakBandwidth	-1
TokenBucketSize	8192
MaxSduSize	8192
MinimumPlicedSize	80
DelayVariation	-1
Latency	-1

Template GSM6.10

Service packets sized at 86; suited for approximately 25 packets/second; accrues transmission tokens at 2,150 bytes/second; provides Guaranteed Service.

Sending FLOWSPEC Values

ServiceType	3
TokenRate	2150
PeakBandwidth	4300
TokenBucketSize	172
MaxSduSize	86
MinimumPlicedSize	86
DelayVariation	-1
Latency	-1

Receiving FLOWSPEC Values

ServiceType	3
TokenRate	2150
PeakBandwidth	4300
TokenBucketSize	172
MaxSduSize	86
MinimumPlicedSize	86
DelayVariation	-1
Latency	-1

QOS Service Types

Service types are used to specify service quality requirements for a given QOS-enabled connection, and can loosely be equated to the rigidity with which an application needs QOS parameters (provided in the FLOWSPECs in the QUALITYOFSERVICE structure) to be followed. The service type specified by the application or service invoking QOS enables the QOS SP to decide the type of requests that it should pass on (or invoke) to other QOS components.

Imagine that you need to have a package delivered to you. Although the package may have certain characteristics—such as size, weight, fragility, need to stay dry, and so on—there may be a number of different delivery requirements that you need—such as ground delivery (as soon as reasonably possible), two-day delivery, or next-day delivery. Now, imagine that you need many packages sent to you, that you're paying for shipping, and that you must stick to a budget. If you have fifty packages sent to you, your budget may only be able to send a few packages next-day, some second-day, but most may have to go ground because you don't have the *resources* (budget) to send them all with the highest degree of priority (next-day delivery).

QOS service types are similar; one provides the best effort of transmission as reasonably possible, one provides fairly prioritized transmission, and one provides the highest degree of priority as possible. By applying service types to QOS-enabled connections, the QOS SP can categorize submission characteristics and make other appropriate choices on the requesting application's behalf.

Just as in the package-sending example, there are three primary service types available to the QOS SP, each of which is based on work done by the IETF IntServ Working Group. These three primary service types are the following:

- Best Effort
- Controlled Load
- Guaranteed

Applications that initiate QOS connections choose which service type is most appropriate for them, based on traffic characteristics, performance requirements, user preferences, or anything else that influences how the application's data should be transmitted. Service types can also be used by senders to respond to QOS-enabled requests, such as identifying (to the receiver) which service types are being offered to the receiver.

The Best Effort Service Type

Selecting Best Effort as a service type instructs the QOS SP to make a reasonable effort to transmit the application's data with the QOS parameters as guidelines. However, the important point is that the QOS SP makes no guarantees; the application can ask the QOS SP as nicely as it wants, but when Best Effort is the specified service type, the QOS SP makes a reasonable effort, and that's all.

There's another important point to glean from this explanation: QOS provisioning isn't really necessary for Best Effort because all networks (that don't specifically suppress certain types of data) provide Best Effort service, regardless of whether they're QOS-enabled.

That gleaning is true to the Windows 2000 implementation of QOS: Only QUALITYOFSERVICE structures that have the other two service types (Controlled Load or Guaranteed) specified in the ServiceType member of the FLOWSPEC invoke QOS SP service for that corresponding direction (SendingFlowspec or ReceivingFlowspec).

The Controlled Load Service Type

With the Controlled Load service type, the RSVP SP provides end-to-end service quality that approximates the behavior achieved from the Best Effort service type *under unloaded (lightly loaded) conditions*. From this definition of Controlled Load, the following can be assumed to be true about a transmission that specifies Controlled Load:

- Delivery of a very high percentage of packets will occur (packet loss approximates basic packet-error rates for the transmission medium).

- Transit delay by a very high percentage of transmitted packets will not greatly exceed the minimum transit delay experienced by any successfully delivered packet.

These two defining characteristics are obviously technical definitions of the Controlled Load service type; they're both based on definitions provided by the IETF.

The Guaranteed Service Type

The Guaranteed service type is the most rigid service type of all, and, as its name implies, the approximation of service levels isn't its intention. With the Guaranteed service type, the QOS SP (as well as other invoked QOS components) attempts to guarantee the service quality specified in the transmission's QOS parameters. More specifically, when the Guaranteed service type is specified, queuing algorithms isolate the application's flow in order to provide the following service characteristics:

- As much as possible, the application's flow is isolated from other flows.

- Transmission of data at TokenRate is guaranteed for the duration of the connection.

- If TokenRate is not exceeded over time, latency is also guaranteed.

Administrative Service Types

There are also a number of administrative service types that enable applications to monitor or modify service provisioning for a flow over the life of the connection. Administrative service types also enable end nodes to communicate (and negotiate) the QOS parameters and provisions that are requested (by receiver), accepted or rejected (by sender), or negotiated (offered by sender, accepted, or dropped by receiver). Note that these are more for administrative use than for the application of a particular type of service quality; however, their availability exemplifies the versatility that service types can bring to an application.

- NOTRAFFIC: Specifying NOTRAFFIC (for the programmers, it's actually SER-VICETYPE_NOTRAFFIC) specifies that no QOS services are required in the associated direction, so that if SendingFlowspec NOTRAFFIC, then traffic *sent* on the specified connection would not receive QOS provisioning.

- NO_CHANGE: Specifying NO_CHANGE as the service type is useful when making changes to QOS parameters for the *opposite* transmission direction of a given flow. Using NO_CHANGE (for programmers, it's actually SERVICETYPE_NO_CHANGE) enables an application to indicate changes in one (the opposite) direction of a flow, without having to respecify unchanged QOS parameters for the other direction of the flow.

- GENERAL_INFORMATION: The GENERAL_INFORMATION service type is used in the SendingFlowspec parameter of a QUALITYOFSERVICE structure to indicate that all service types are available for the requested flow. Because Best Effort is almost always available, GENERAL_INFORMATION is really advertising that Controlled Load and Guaranteed service types are available for the flow. Note that routers in the path between end nodes may indicate that they do not support one or both Controlled Load or Guaranteed service types.

- NETWORK_UNAVAILABLE: The NETWORK_UNAVAILABLE service type is used when network service has been lost in the specified direction.

RSVP: Getting the Request Out

In order for QOS parameters, such as those in the QUALITYOFSERVICE structure discussed in the previous section, to get from one end node to another end node in the end-to-end QOS solution, there must be some way for such end nodes to communicate their requests. That mechanism is RSVP.

RSVP is an industry-standard protocol, and it has to be; the information that RSVP messages transmit between end nodes must be (at least partially) readable by all devices in the path between end nodes. Why? Because RSVP messages are the primary mechanism used by the RSVP SP to create end-to-end QOS-enabled connections, and are the building blocks on which QOS is enabled in each network device (or medium) across the network.

Invoking RSVP

RSVP is invoked in one of two ways:

- Automatically, when the RSVP SP determines RSVP signaling is required.

- Directly, through a programmatic interface specifically exposed to enable fine-tuning of RSVP signaling (such as with the RSVP_RESERVE_INFO object).

Most applications depend on the RSVP SP to invoke RSVP (this is the easiest way to QOS-enable an application or service), thereby removing the need to write programs that directly manipulate RSVP signaling. However, there are certain circumstances in which the capability to directly specify RSVP messages is warranted; for those circumstances, the RSVP_RESERVE_INFO object and its bundled capabilities are made available in Windows 2000.

> **Note**
>
> *Because the focus of this chapter is to understand application-driven QOS components, and not on programming, this section foregoes the programming details for RSVP. For more information on programming RSVP, check out Chapter 11, "QOS for the Programmer."* ◆

RSVP Filter Styles

RSVP uses *filter styles* (similar to service types in the QOS SP) to define how an RSVP-compatible network device treats QOS-enabled data, and sends filter style and other information across the network in RSVP messages.

When the QOS SP invokes RSVP, it uses information that the application (on whose behalf it is acting) provides to determine the most appropriate RSVP filter style, and then instructs RSVP to apply that style to the message it sends out (again, on behalf of the application). The QOS SP can decide which filter style is most appropriate, based on information in the FLOWSPEC. However, a particular RSVP filter style can be specified (even if it contradicts the style that the QOS SP would otherwise choose).

The RSVP protocol has three filter styles (sometimes called *reservation styles*) that dictate the way RSVP-enabled network devices treat packets QOS-enabled packets:

- Fixed Filter (FF)
- Wildcard Filter (WF)
- Shared Explicit (SE)

When an application specifies the connection type (unicast or multicast) or service type that it wants for a given flow, the RSVP SP automatically translates that connection type or service type into the appropriate RSVP filter style. The following sections define each of these three RSVP filter styles.

Fixed Filter

The Fixed Filter (FF) reservation style implies a couple of facts about the reservation in question:

- It has a distinct reservation.
- The reservation has an explicit sender.

These implied facts about the reservation are in contrast with other RSVP filter styles, mainly because packets associated with a FF reservation style are *not* shared among multiple receivers (both WF and SE reservation styles can share packets among multiple receivers). Figure 5.3 clarifies the FF reservation style.

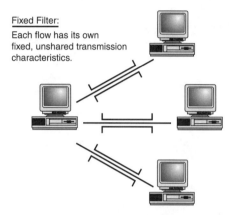

Figure 5.3   *FF, when applied with real end nodes and senders.*

FF reservations require a one-to-one relationship between sender and receiver. FF is used for unicast sessions, such as those (logically required) using TCP (versus UDP). In fact, the QOS SP uses FF for all reservations that use TCP.

Wildcard Filter

Use of the Wildcard Filter (WF) reservation style implies the following about the reservation:

- The receiver is participating in a shared transmission.

WF enables upstream senders (such as routers) to make more efficient use of network bandwidth availability by taking advantage of multicast techniques. In a multicast scenario, many downstream senders (or recipients) may require the same packet, but rather than sending multiple identical packets that use bandwidth unnecessarily, a single packet is sent and propagated to all down-stream senders (or recipients). Figure 5.4 clarifies the WF reservation style.

WF is appropriate (and its definition implied) for use with multicast sessions.

Shared Explicit

The Shared Explicit (SE) reservation style is a hybrid of FF and WF reservation styles. The SE style enables the receiving application to share a single reservation with (explicitly) selected senders. Figure 5.5 clarifies the way the SE reservation style operates.

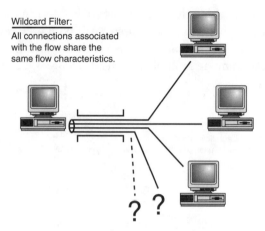

Figure 5.4   *WF, when applied with real end nodes and senders.*

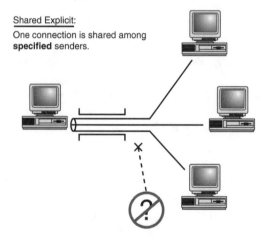

Figure 5.5   *SE reservation style, when applied with real end nodes and senders.*

The SE reservation style is somewhat specialized because it's only appropriate for applications that can explicitly benefit from its transmission capabilities. In fact, it's so unusual that the QOS SP doesn't use SE by default; use of the SE reservation style requires that applications specify SE through direct programming of RSVP through the use of the RSVP_RESERVE_INFO object. For example, TAPI 3.0 uses SE reservations for video streaming during conferencing, enabling it to select and optimize the network traffic that the video uses.

RSVP *PATH* and *RESV* Messages

Just setting RSVP reservation styles (FF, WF, or SE) that correspond to the QOS service types isn't enough to establish a QOS-enabled connection, based on all the information that the application provides the QOS SP.

To revert to the earlier package-sending example, reservation styles simply determine transmission characteristics, such as next-day, second-day, and ground transportation. In order for all QOS parameters to be achieved, RSVP—as the carrier or all such QOS information—must also provide specifics that characterize the actual data being transmitted, such as TokenRate, TokenBucketSize, Latency, and so on. The mechanisms that facilitate the conveyance of such information are RSVP PATH and RESV messages.

PATH and RESV messages have very specific headers, but they then base the information that can be carried in each message on a set of available RSVP objects. Although there are many objects from which PATH and RESV messages choose to include in their messages (different circumstances may merit different objects), PATH and RESV messages have mandatory objects that must be included in each of their messages; these mandatory objects are essentially QOS parameters. So, in essence, the QOS SP *maps* its QOS parameters to equivalent RSVP message objects. This mapping enables a particular implementation of QOS (such as the Windows 2000 implementation) to communicate with industry-standard protocols (RSVP), and thereby communicate with heterogeneous network devices (routers, switches, and WAN equipment made by all sorts of vendors) that understand the format of RSVP objects.

Establishing a Connection

The establishment of an RSVP session is a little bit counterintuitive and somewhat complex, so be prepared.

To enable the connection of QOS-enabled end nodes, RSVP uses PATH and RESV messages, as mentioned earlier. Under such circumstances, the sender and receiver(s) play specific roles to establish the RSVP session:

- The sender emits PATH messages toward the receiver (or receivers).
- The receiver waits until the PATH message corresponding to the flow arrives, and then issues a RESV message.

QOS provisioning can be initiated on an existing socket or when a socket is opened. Also, the sender or receiver can initiate QOS provisioning. Information in the PATH and RESV messages is derived from the SendingFlowspec and ReceivingFlowspec members of the QUALITYOFSERVICE structure.

PATH Messages

PATH messages get their QOS parameters from the SendingFlowspec and apply those parameters to objects that are required to be included in every PATH message. The use of industry-standard objects enables different implementations of RSVP to communicate QOS requests and guarantees among one another. Note that QOS-enabled connections are initiated by the receiver, but PATH messages are created on (and transmitted by) the sender. The reason that PATH messages are being discussed first is because PATH messages are the first RSVP of the two messages (PATH and RESV) to be transmitted.

There's a certain amount of information that the RSVP SP must pass to RSVP in order to generate a PATH message. Table 5.1 outlines that information and explains how QOS parameters provided by the application in the FLOWSPEC structure correspond to parameters in a PATH statement.

Table 5.1   Mapping FLOWSPEC *parameters to* PATH *messages.*

RSVP PATH object/parameter	Equivalent Receiver-based parameters
Sender Tspec	SendingFlowspec member of the QUALITYOFSERVICE structure
SenderTemplate	Source IP address/port to which sending socket is bound
Session	Destination IP address/port and protocol ID to which the socket is sending (sockaddr_in)

Note the following:

- The Sender Tspec contains QOS parameters for sent traffic.
- SenderTemplate contains the sender's address.
- Session contains the destination of the sent traffic.

Details about how FLOWSPEC parameters map to the Sender Tspec are explained in the following section.

RESV Messages

RESV messages get their QOS parameters from the ReceivingFlowspec, and, as with PATH messages, they apply those parameters to objects required to be included in every RESV message. The use of industry-standard objects enables different implementations of RSVP to communicate QOS requests and guarantees among one another. Similar to a PATH message, a RESV message is created from information that the RSVP SP gets from the application, and then maps into a RESV message. Table 5.2 outlines that information and explains how QOS parameters provided by the application in the FLOWSPEC structure correspond to parameters in an RESV statement.

Table 5.2   Mapping FLOWSPEC *parameters to* RESV *messages.*

RSVP RESV object/Parameter	Derived from the following Winsock parameter
flowspec	ReceivingFlowspec member of the QUALITYOFSERVICE structure
filterspec (source(s) from which QOS traffic will be received)	Address(es) of peer(s) from which the socket is receiving
Session (destination of sent traffic)	Local IP address and port to which the receiving socket is bound (unicast), or multicast session address on which the socket is a leaf (multicast)

Note the following:

- The RSVP *Flowspec* object contains desired QOS parameters for traffic to be received.

- The RSVP *Filterspec* object contains the source or sources from which QOS-enabled traffic will be received.

- The RSVP *session* object contains the destination of the sent traffic.

Also, the *filterspec* parameter in an RESV message can be generated without knowledge of the sender's address. Such RSVP RESV messages are considered to be WF style, such that they apply to all senders in the session.

RSVP *Tspec, Rspec,* and *Adspec*

As you've seen, PATH and RESV messages use parameters derived from FLOWSPEC structures to specify transmission and service quality characteristics for a given QOS-enabled connection. Since the QUALITYOFSERVICE structure was created (with its SendingFlowspec, ReceivingFlowspec, and ProviderSpecific buffer), subsets of its information are used at certain steps in the RSVP messaging process to fill certain parameters or create certain RSVP objects. This process of going from parameters in the QUALITYOFSERVICE structure (a specific implementation of QOS) to RSVP objects enables cross-platform QOS parameter communication.

The RSVP Tspec and Rspec are also derivatives of these Windows 2000 QOS parameters. Tspec and Rspec are derived from certain information in the FLOWSPEC, and used by RSVP and other components (such as packet schedulers or classifiers in Windows 2000 clients, or on network devices such as routers) to characterize and qualify data for a given flow. In essence, these boiled-down pieces of information can be thought of as RSVP primitives.

So, within PATH and RESV messages, certain values (within their requisite RSVP objects) are used to represent the traffic and to specify requested QOS parameters. These parameters enable a sender and receiver to establish service quality parameters for a given flow, per the following:

- The Tspec (T represents traffic) specifies the parameters available for the flow. Both senders and receivers use Tspec (SenderTspec and ReceiverTspec, respectively).

- The Rspec (R represents reserve) specifies the requested QOS parameters, and is used by the receiver in RESV messages to transmit requested reservation parameters.

- The Adspec (ad for advertisement) enables QOS-enabled network devices in the path between sender and receiver to advertise their resource availability and transmission characteristics.

Tspec

Tspec is used by both senders (the SenderTspec) and receivers (the ReceiverTspec). The Tspec derives its parameters from the SendingFlowspec, as Table 5-3 outlines.

Table 5.3   *Mapping* SendingFlowspec *Parameters to* Tspec *Parameters.*

SendingFlowspec Parameter	Tspec
TokenRate	TokenBucketRate
TokenBucketSize	TokenBucketSize
PeakBandwidth	PeakRate
MinimumPolicedSize	MinimumPolicedUnit
MaxSduSize	MaximumPacketSize
DelayVariation	
Latency	

Adspec

Each RSVP PATH message may also include an Adspec, which provides a place within the PATH message for QOS-enabled network devices (that are in the path between sender and receiver) to advertise their resource availability, transmission characteristics, and available services.

Traffic Control

All the work that the RSVP SP does in enabling applications to specify QOS parameters, and all the work that RSVP does in ferrying traffic between end nodes would amount to nothing if there weren't a traffic cop sitting somewhere, keeping all those flows and connections honest. As mentioned in Chapter 4, this whistle-bearing mechanism—the one that makes sure packets conform to the flows that their applications have set up—is aptly called *Traffic Control*.

Some form of Traffic Control can be found in various strategically placed QOS-enabled network devices, including clients, routers, WAN devices, or even LAN segment switches. The presence of Traffic Control in certain places, such as the end node or certain boundary routers, is a must. As I've said, without proper Traffic Control, QOS provisioning becomes little more than a good intention, and good intentions get as far with networking as they do with bill collectors. Traffic control in the Windows 2000 implementation is application-driven, it is kernel-driven (meaning that it's a part of the core operating system and not a user-mode add-on), and it has a number of capabilities and responsibilities:

- Traffic Control classifies packets, based on source, destination address, port, and protocol. Such classification patterns are used by other QOS components in the Windows 2000 client, as well as certain other parts of the operating system.
- Traffic Control marks packet priorities, based on QOS parameters.
- Traffic Control schedules the transmission of packets onto the network, based on specified QOS parameters.
- Traffic Control manages the placements of packets onto the network medium.

Fittingly, Traffic Control is implemented in Windows 2000 through the use of three distinct modules:

- Generic Packet Classifier
- Packet Scheduler
- Packet Shaper
- The TCP/IP stack, which handles DSCP marking

First, however, there are some things to know about Traffic Control in order to get a firm grasp on how and why the components do what they do.

Invoking Traffic Control

Traffic Control is invoked at the same time that RSVP is invoked—when QOS SP functionality is initiated by an application that wants to transmit QOS-enabled data. As with RSVP, Traffic Control may also be invoked or modified through the use of the Traffic Control API, which enables fine-grained control over the behavior of the three Traffic Control modules.

Dealing with Nonconforming Packets

Traffic Control is tightly integrated with the QOS SP and RSVP, and its behavior is largely based on the parameters provided to the QOS SP through the FLOWSPEC structures. However, because of the focused responsibilities of Traffic Control modules, and because controlling traffic presents options that aren't necessarily answered by the parameters provided in FLOWSPEC structures, the packets that pass through Traffic Control modules have an additional set of rules applied to them. These rules dictate the way Traffic Control modules treat nonconforming packets, supplementing the QOS parameters provided in the FLOWSPEC.

Note

When we get a driver's license, we implicitly agree to abide by the posted rules and regulations that govern the way people transmit themselves (drive) over our roads. And on our streets and highways, we (the people) have posted the specifics of those transmission characteristics (driving regulations) through the use of speed limits, stop signs, traffic laws, and so on. But if you've ever driven a vehicle, you may have noticed that not everyone abides by those laws. What's the answer to such a dilemma? Traffic cops. And what do traffic cops do? They decide—based on regulations that have been given to them by some governing body—how to deal with nonconforming motorists. That's exactly what Traffic Control in Windows 2000 QOS must do, as well. ◆

There is a specific set of options that Traffic Control provides for handling nonconforming packets, and which option is chosen determines the fate of nonconforming packets. That fate ranges from sending the packet when the device is less busy to discarding the packet entirely. The following is a list of available SD (Shape/Discard) modes, by which Traffic Control handles nonconforming packets, and what effect each mode has on nonconforming packets:

- **Borrow Mode:** Borrow mode (known programmatically as TC_NONCONF_BORROW) directs Traffic Control (specifically, the Packet Shaper) to "borrow" remaining available transmission resources after all flows that have a higher priority have been serviced. In other words, nonconforming packets that are associated with flows that are set to Borrow Mode will have such nonconforming packets relegated to a priority that is below best effort. Only after everything else has been serviced—including non-QOS-enabled transmissions—will such nonconforming packets be serviced.

- **Shape Mode:** Shape mode (TC_NONCONF_SHAPE to the programming interfaces for Traffic Control) directs Traffic Control (again, specifically, the Packet Shaper) to hold onto nonconforming packets until sufficient "transmission credits" have accrued to get the packet into conformance. So, if a given flow is attempting to transmit a 1200-byte packet and there are only 1000 bytes accrued (in the Token Bucket) by the flow, then Traffic Control must hold onto the packet until such time that the flow has accrued 1200-bytes-worth of transmission "credits."

- **Discard Mode:** Discard mode (known as TC_NONCONF_DISCARD to the programming types) is the nastiest, least forgiving, and most unsavory of the Traffic Control modes; as such, it should be used with care. When Discard mode is used, Traffic Control (specifically, the Packet Shaper) discards all nonconforming packets, no questions asked. There's no waiting for enough credits and no queuing; just a quick, remorseless discarding of data.

When these traffic-cop modes are in place, coupled with the QOS parameters provided to the QOS SP by the application (through the QUALITYOFSERVICE structure) and complementary RSVP signaling, QOS traffic is ready to roll out of the client and across the network in very controlled, systematic, and largely deterministic pieces.

The Generic Packet Classifier

In order to determine the characteristics of any given packet, there must be some mechanism by which information pertinent to that packet (such as whether it belongs to a given flow or matches an established flow's pattern) is provided or exposed. This information characterizes, or classifies, the packet, enabling network components (such as QOS components) to use such packet classification to determine the way the packet should be treated. The *Generic Packet Classifier*, or *GPC*, is the component that services classification requests.

Network components (QOS-related and otherwise) within a given Windows 2000 client use the GPC to classify packets into a number of classification families. By allowing network components to register as clients of the GPC, the sharing of traffic-control related information is streamlined for the entire client (not just one given network component), centralizing classification operations and enabling any network component that needs such facilities to use one component's (the GPC's) well-known interface. The GPC's well-known interface is called the *Generic Packet Classifier Interface (GPC Interface)*.

The process of packet classification works something like this:

1. A packet is sent to the GPC for classification (such as determining whether it matches an established flow) by some QOS component (usually the Packet Scheduler).

2. The GPC looks at the packet, compares certain elements of the packet to lookup tables that the GPC maintains, and provides the requesting component with certain classifying information, thereby enabling the QOS component to treat the packet according to established flows (or RSVP sessions, or a given socket's QOS parameters).

Packet classification, therefore, provides a way for packets to be prioritized by other QOS components or by the OS itself. Such classification and prioritization can affect the packet's CPU processing attention or the timeliness of its transmission onto the network.

The importance of the GPC is based on its capability to provide lookup tables and classification services within the network stack (and, therefore, to multiple network components). Because of its classification faculties, the GPC is the first step in an overall prioritization scheme for QOS packets.

The Packet Scheduler

At the center of Traffic Control functionality in Windows 2000 QOS is the Packet Scheduler. The *Packet Scheduler* is the QOS-enforcement traffic cop; it regulates how much data a given flow is allowed, when those packets are put onto the network, and in which order such packets that are ready for transmission are sent. In essence, the Packet Scheduler enforces QOS settings and mitigates transmission of data onto the network.

The Packet Scheduler uses three mechanisms to carry out its packet scheduling:

- **The Conformer:** The Conformer is responsible for ensuring that packets conform to the QOS parameters established for their flow. The Conformer's treatment of nonconforming packets is based on the associated SD (Shape/Discard) mode associated with the flow (Borrow Mode, Shape Mode, and Discard Mode).

- **The Packet Shaper:** The Packet Shaper takes the naturally bursty nature of computer network transmissions and smoothes things out, alleviating one of the major causes of network congestion. The advantage of doing so has to do with getting more effective use out of the network; bursty transmissions tend to use lots of network bandwidth in a short spurt, thereby clogging the network for a short period during the transmission burst. A better approach is to smooth out such bursts of data into a still acceptable, but slightly longer period of time. Figure 5.6 shows the advantage of this approach in terms of network resources.

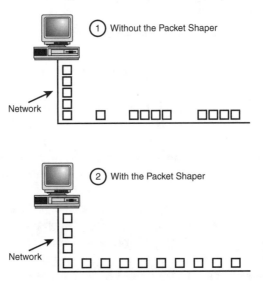

Figure 5.6   *The Packet Shaper smoothes bursty transmissions, leaving more network resources available for other network nodes.*

The advantages of this approach can be felt on the network—the smoothed use of the network medium and resources along the path. It can also be felt in the client—it enables a round-robin approach to transmitting packets, similar to a CPU timeslice, which aids the continued transmission for all flows.

- **The Sequencer:** The Sequencer is responsible for managing the transmission of packets onto the network. It must take packet and flow characteristics, such as service type (Best Effort, Controlled Load, Guaranteed) and priority (explained in the next paragraph) into consideration when making transmission decisions.

To differentiate between flows *on the same client*, Windows 2000 QOS has the capability to set numerous relative priorities for a given flow's packets, regardless of service type. These priority settings, including those done for DSCP, for 802.1p, and for other QOS components, enable the Sequencer to establish transmission priority within the same service type. Thus, a flow with a Controlled Load service type with a higher priority setting gets better network transmission priority than a flow with a lower setting.

Under congested conditions, however, the Sequencer initiates a round-robin approach to the transmission of packets onto the wire, rather than servicing all flows with a Guaranteed service type, then all flows with a Controlled Load service type, and so on. The Sequencer also initiates this within a service type, so that all flows of the Controlled Load service type are serviced in a round-robin fashion as well. An internal priority mechanism also helps to avoid *starvation*, in which a flow of relatively low priority is unable to transmit any packets, as long as flows with higher priority are waiting for transmission.

The QOS API

Windows 2000 QOS functionality must provide applications with some way to QOS-enable their applications, so that QOS capabilities can be leveraged from everything from die-hard gamers to mission-critical SQL queries. QOS capabilities in Windows 2000 are accessed through the use of application programming interfaces, or APIs.

Note

The QOS API comes with a number of QOS-specific function calls, structures, and objects. This section gives a quick rundown of each of these. For more detailed information, check out the Windows SDK, available with an MSDN subscription or online at msdn.microsoft.com. ◆

QOS Functions

The WPUGetQOSTemplate retrieves a named QOS template for a particular service provider, which contains an associated QUALITYOFSERVICE structure. WSAGetQOSByName initializes a QUALITYOFSERVICE structure based on a named template. This function can also be used to retrieve an enumeration of all available template names.

WSCInstallQOSTemplate installs a QOS template (which includes a QUALITYOFSERVICE structure with its values filled in), based on a QOS name. The QUALITYOFSERVICE structure and its settings can subsequently be retrieved by calling WSPGetQOSByName with the associated QOS template's name. One caveat worth noting: this function's caller must have administrative privileges.

WSCRemoveQOSTemplate removes a named QOS template. Again, this function requires administrative privileges.

WSPGetQOSByName initializes a QUALITYOFSERVICE structure based on a named template. This can also be use to retrieve an enumeration of available template names, and has one more parameter (for retrieving an error message) than WSAGetQOSByName.

QOS Structures

FLOWSPEC is the carrier of all things QOS. More technically and in a little more detail, the FLOWSPEC structure provides QOS parameters to the QOS SP, thereby enabling QOS-aware applications to invoke, modify, or remove QOS settings for a given flow. The parameters of the FLOWSPEC structure and their explanations were provided earlier in this chapter, in the section called "Getting the QOS SP its Parameters."

QUALITYOFSERVICE is the carrier of the FLOWSPEC; it enables applications to do fine-grained tuning to the RSVP SP, RSVP, and Traffic Control. The QUALITYOFSERVICE structure has the following members:

- SendingFlowspec: Specifies QOS parameters for the sending direction of a particular flow and has the form of a FLOWSPEC structure.

- ReceivingFlowspec: Specifies QOS parameters for the receiving direction of a particular flow and also has the form of a FLOWSPEC structure.

- ProviderSpecific: Pointer to a WSABUF structure (used often in Winsock programming), the customizable contents of which enable application programmers to provide additional, very specific QOS parameters for a given flow through the use of QOS objects.

QOS Objects

If you read the previous sentence, you already know that QOS objects enable application programmers to provide the QOS SP with customized settings for QOS signaling, including RSVP and Traffic Control parameters. In essence, QOS objects are knobs with which the tuning of Windows 2000 QOS can be done.

QOS objects follow a stringent structure; they always include an information header (specifying the type and length of the attached QOS object), and then include the object itself.

QOS_OBJECT_HDR specifies the format of the QOS header itself.

QOS_OBJECT_PRIORITY specifies the absolute priority of a given flow; it is used by Traffic Control's Packet Scheduler (in its Sequencer mechanism) to determine the priority of a flow with respect to other flows of the same service type.

QOS_OBJECT_SD_MODE is the object that enables an application programmer to specify the Shape/Discard mode that Traffic Control—through the Conformer mechanism in the Packet Scheduler—provides for (or inflicts on) nonconforming packets for a given flow. The specifics of the three modes— Borrow, Shape, and Discard—were discussed previously in this chapter, in the section titled "Dealing with Nonconforming Packets."

RSVP_ADSPEC enables application or service programmers to read the information provided in the RSVP Adspec object. The Adspec is sent in some, but not all, RSVP PATH messages.

RSVP_RESERVE_INFO is the QOS object that enables application or service programmers to fine-tune RSVP signaling and characteristics for a given flow by overriding, modifying, or resetting default RSVP settings. The RSVP_RESERVE_INFO is actually a structure, but it belongs here. The following is a list of RSVP_RESERVE_INFO structure members:

- ObjectHdr: The QOS object header (see QOS_OBJECT_HDR).

- Style: The RSVP reservation style to be applied to the flow (FF, WF, or SE). Because only FF or WF reservation styles are applied through the QOS SP, the only mechanism available to apply the SE reservation style to a flow is through the use of this structure. RSVP reservation styles (also called *filter styles*) were explained previously in this chapter; see the section "RSVP Filter Styles" for more information.

- ConfirmRequest: Used to get the QOS SP to issue a reservation request confirmation (notification of when a RESV CONFIRMATION message arrives) for an RSVP session.

- NumPolicyElement: Specifies the number of policy elements included in the next member.

- PolicyElementList: Pointer to the set of policy elements. Policy information for RSVP is explained in Chapter 7, "Policy-Driven QOS."

- NumFlowDesc: Specifies the number of FLOWDESCRIPTOR structures included in the next member.

- FlowDescList: Pointer to the list of FLOWDESCRIPTOR structures.

RSVP_STATUS_INFO provides information about an existing flow, such as error information, and is useful for retrieving RSVP-specific status and error information.

The Traffic Control API

The Traffic Control component of Windows 2000 QOS also has built-in capabilities that enable application programmers to fine-tune its characteristics. Because Traffic Control APIs aren't quite as central to understanding how QOS operates, I've included a list of the available functions to give you an idea of the kind of things that are possible with Traffic Control, but have omitted explanations for each:

TcAddFilter	TcGetFlowName
TcAddFlow	TcModifyFlow
TcCloseInterface	TcOpenInterface
TcDeleteFilter	TcQueryFlow
TcDeleteFlow	TcQueryInterface
TcDeregisterClient	TcRegisterClient
TcEnumerateFlows	TcSetInterface
TcEnumerateInterfaces	

As you can gather from the number of programmable elements in the Traffic Control API (their names are intuitive, as well), there's a lot that can be done to fine-tune Traffic Control behavior, and to get information about what's going on or available in the various Traffic Control components.

Previously in this chapter, I mentioned that various network components can register as a client of the GPC (see the section titled "The Generic Packet Classifier"). When a network component registers as a client of the GPC (as the QOS SP does behind the scenes), it must expose the following callback functions to enable the GPC to interface with it (Cl stands for Callback):

ClAddFlowComplete

ClDeleteFlowComplete

ClModifyFlowComplete

ClNotifyHandler

Summary

This chapter set the groundwork for all others. It explained the bulk of the specifics that make QOS in Windows 2000 work, and set the groundwork for the rest of the chapters. This chapter started with the QOS SP, discussed how QOS SP parameters are put into RSVP and its messages, and then discussed how QOS SP parameters affect and invoke certain Traffic Control components. And finally, a quick look was taken at the APIs that enable application programmers to take advantage of all of this QOS functionality. Once the QOS-enabled packets leave the client, they must traverse a network that has the capabilities to carry out the parameters set forth in RSVP messages. Such network device interaction means that there must be QOS components, or at least elements of QOS components, that enable network media and devices in the path between end nodes to fulfill QOS requirements. Such QOS components have their greatest effect in the network, and therefore are considered to be network-driven QOS components.

6

Network-Driven QOS

The next step in explaining the details of the Windows 2000 QOS implementation is to address those technologies that are considered to be network-driven. As a reminder, *network-driven QOS components* are so named in this discussion of Windows 2000 QOS because they have their greatest impact on the way that the network (the collection of transmission mediums and network devices that sit between the end nodes in any given QOS-enabled connection) reacts to QOS provisioning.

The following is an all-inclusive list of QOS components that are categorized as network-driven:

- **802.1p**: A mechanism by which packets traversing an 802 LAN segment, such as an Ethernet segment or Token Ring segment, can be differentiated based on aggregated queues that contain packets with the same priority.

- **Subnet Bandwidth Manager (SBM)**: Manages shared-media network bandwidth. In the Windows 2000 QOS, SBM functionality (which has been outlined in various IETF documents) is incorporated in the QOS Admission Control Service (QOS ACS) through its QOS ACS/SBM capabilities. As such, every SBM capability in Windows 2000 QOS is explained in the context of QOS ACS, and this is the last time you'll see it with its own section.

- **DiffServ Codepoint (DSCP)**: Enables priority marking for IP packets as they pass through a DiffServ-capable network, establishing priority for packets as they are handled in Layer 3 switches (routers). The DSCP has taken the place (literally) of TOS (Type of Service). The DSCP uses six of the eight bits in the IP header TOS section that were planned to specify IP Precedence values.

- **L2 Signaling**: The mapping of RSVP objects to Layer 2 signaling, such as Frame Relay network devices or ATM switches.

- **Resource Reservation Protocol (RSVP):** Yes, RSVP also gets its spot in network-driven components. The network-driven aspect of RSVP includes the way RSVP carries and disseminates QOS information to QOS-aware network devices (such as routers) along the path between end nodes.

The Boundary of Network-Driven QOS Components

The Windows 2000 components that are detailed in this chapter have their largest effect on the network. Despite the fact that these components are initiated by clients that initiate (or respond to) QOS-enabled connection requests, and therefore have the roots of their existence in actions or responses that occur within the client, these components affect how the network handles the existence of QOS-enabled connections.

Remember that the network-driven distinction that's being applied to these components helps with the clarity of this discussion of Windows 2000 QOS, but it does not isolate these QOS components from other Windows 2000 QOS components. QOS is an end-to-end solution; these components simply happen to be doing their part to enable networks to implement QOS functionality.

With the soft network-driven distinction thereby explained, the boundary of network-driven QOS components is best reflected in Figure 6.1:

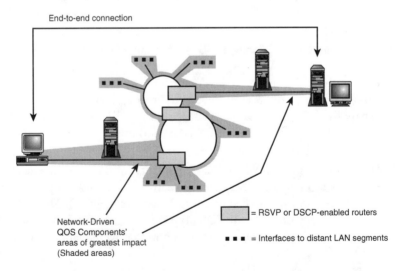

Figure 6.1 *The boundary of network-driven QOS components.*

As mentioned in Chapter 5, "Application-Driven QOS," the exception to the boundary of these components is RSVP. Because RSVP is the messenger of QOS requests, status, and other requisite communications between QOS-enabled connections, RSVP crosses the boundaries of each of these QOS-component groupings.

> **Note**
>
> *In order to continue providing a thorough explanation of the way that these components work together, RSVP is again explained in this chapter. However, the emphasis of the discussion of RSVP in this chapter is the way RSVP facilitates communication to and among the various network-driven QOS components that are also covered in this chapter.* ◆

Network-Driven QOS Component Details

One issue to keep in mind is the following:

> Windows 2000 isn't running on all of the network devices that participate in end-to-end QOS.

This means that the implementation of QOS in Windows 2000 is intended to interact with network devices that can interpret agreed-upon QOS information. The distinction is as follows: Windows 2000 may not be running on the network device that implements the network-driven QOS solution (perhaps an Ethernet switch). However, Windows 2000 must provide the information necessary for that particular network device (such as the Ethernet switch) to understand the QOS provisions that the Windows 2000 client is requesting, and to handle such requests accordingly.

This chapter, then, explains how Windows 2000 QOS ensures and enables the communication of Windows 2000 clients' QOS requests to the various network devices that provide QOS-enabled network transmissions. Often, such communication between a Windows 2000 client and the network device is achieved through the Windows 2000 client's setting of a bit or bits on headers that are subsequently sent off across the network. The anticipation, of course, is that the network device in question will interpret these set bits (for example, bits that are set to indicate 802.1p priority) and act accordingly. Wherever possible, I anticipate where confusion about this interaction between bit-setting (in the client) and bit-reading (in the network device) is likely to raise its ugly head, and then take extra steps to ensure that such confusion is minimized—perhaps with further explanation of the QOS bits/network device interaction.

802.1p

The great majority of clients that are connected to a network in any organization—whether a small company, worldwide enterprise, or campus network—are connected by some sort of 802 network. These 802 networks, such as Ethernets or Token Rings, are therefore the first leg of a QOS-enabled packet's journey onto or across the network. It is vitally important that any part of the network, including this first step, is capable of providing differentiated or even deterministic transmission of QOS packets.

The capabilities of 802.1p are what enable QOS provisioning over 802 networks. However, to get a grasp on how 802.1p operates, it's necessary to first understand the constraints under which it has to operate, the physical conditions under which 802.1p is effective, and (by process of elimination) conditions under which it is not effective.

Hubs versus Switches

First, it's necessary to understand the difference between a hub and a switch. A *hub* is an Ethernet device that shares one 10Mbps or 100Mbps wire among all attached devices, which is why hubs are sometimes referred to as *shared Ethernet*. When an Ethernet LAN segment is being serviced by Ethernet hubs, the access for any given device attached to the hub is determined by CSMA/CD, which is essentially a "first come, first served" means of regulating access to the Ethernet transmission medium (the "wire"). As you can imagine, such random, non-prioritized, and non-differentiated means of regulating access to the wire doesn't lend itself well to implementing the deterministic or differentiated services that QOS provisioning must, by definition, provide. In fact, it is impossible to determine what the possible delay of a given Ethernet datagram may be when heavy congestion on the hub is being experienced.

To put it another way, the possible delay of any given Ethernet datagram serviced by shared Ethernet (a hub) is unbounded. What are the implications of such unbounded potential delay and the corresponding logical conclusion? Ethernet LAN segments that are being serviced by a hub (rather than a switch) are essentially out of luck when it comes to QOS provisioning, for a couple of reasons:

- First, switches are the devices of choice, especially if QOS is a priority for a given network and the switches' deployment (versus hubs) is on the rise.

- Second, it's much more complex to attempt to implement priority in shared Ethernet segments (not necessarily impossible, but difficult and likely to require changes to existing MAC protocols). Simply deploying a switch is probably an easier and less painful solution.

The bottom line is that QOS provisioning isn't probable, in practical terms, for LAN segments serviced by hubs.

With Token Ring, access to the wire is governed by an access token, and it is therefore not subject to the chaos associated with the less deterministic CSMA/CD method. This makes Token Ring an immediate candidate for providing QOS provisioning capabilities in its LAN segments. One issue to be concerned about with Token Ring, however, is the fact that its large packet size introduces the potential for increased jitter when many nodes reside on the same ring. Administrators and IT Managers should consider this fact when dealing with their Token Ring segments and take appropriate action (such as reducing the MTU for segments on which QOS is being implemented).

A *switch* is a different animal altogether. In direct contrast to hubs (or Token Ring MSAUs), which share the available bandwidth among all connected nodes, a switch provides the specified bandwidth to *each* connected node. This approach is somewhat akin to a telephone (a circuit-switched network). Any time you pick up a telephone and dial a telephone number, you are provided with a dedicated circuit. (Granted, it is a virtual circuit or VC, but as far as you're concerned—virtual or not—the line is dedicated to your conversation.) The net effect of this circuit-switching technology is that the chaotic, non-deterministic approach of regulating access to the wire with CSMA/CD is nullified with the use of a switch.

With a switch, there is the capability to quantitatively know the delay bounds that may be introduced to any given Ethernet (or Token Ring, in the case of Switched Token Ring) datagram. Because delay is bounded when using a switch (or, more accurately, because delay is not unbounded when using a switch), the capability to provide QOS provisioning in switched LAN segments becomes viable. In other words, it's possible to control a datagram's delay with an Ethernet switch; with an Ethernet hub, it is not possible.

I've mentioned that each node in a switched LAN environment is provided with a *dedicated* connection at the switch rated transmission speed (such as 10Mbps or 100Mbps), which means that the wire is always available to the end node, resulting in no contention for access to the wire. Well, that "no contention for access to the wire" is almost true; it depends on the type of connection that the end node has to the switch.

Half-Duplex versus Full-Duplex

There are two kinds of connections that a node might have to a switch: half-duplex or full-duplex. The type of connection may have significant impact on QOS provisioning capabilities within your LAN segment.

Half-duplex connections mean that the wire is shared among two nodes, the end node and the switch itself. Remember that a connection to a switch enables the sending *and receiving* of data from the network. Such bi-directional transmission means that from the end node perspective, data is both going out and coming in from the network over the connection to the switch; with a half-duplex connection, only one or the other can occur at any given instance. If the switch is sending data across the connection to the end node, the half-duplex connection is in use and is unavailable for transmission of data in the opposite direction. This constraint is similar to that of a pair of traditional walkie-talkies; you can speak or you can listen, but you can't do both at the same time.

Full-duplex connections to a switch provide individual sending and receiving circuits, enabling a connection between a switch and an end node to send and receive at any given instant at the same time. This capability is similar to the observed behavior of a telephone connection between you and your brother across the country; you can speak and receive sounds from the other end of the connection at any given instant.

The importance of the distinction between half-duplex and full-duplex connections to a switch is most prevalent when Guaranteed Service QOS provisioning is at issue. Controlled Load and best-effort are less stringent, and are, therefore, less contingent upon the absolute immediate access to the wire that a full-duplex switch connection provides.

Where does 802.1p fit into all of this? To be precise, it fits into the potentially crowded connection that a switch has to the rest of the network. Even if 16 or maybe 1,000 clients on your Ethernet switch have full-duplex connections to the switch, the connection (or connections) to the rest of the network are finite. On a 16-port 100Mbps switch, for example, you have 16 end nodes with a 100Mbps connection to the switch, but that switch may have only one 100Mbps connection to the nearest router. The result is that those 16 end nodes have to share the switch's connection to the router, which gets back to the switch's capability to provide differentiation between and among the datagrams transmitted by its 16 nodes. To get a better view of this situation, let's take a tour of the inside of a QOS-enabled 802.1p-enabled switch, as discussed in the next section.

Inside the QOS-Enabled Switch

With multiple end nodes contending for the finite bandwidth that connects the switch to the rest of the network, some sort of mechanism must be in place to determine which packet goes through the switch to the rest of the network first, and then which packet is next. This is the heart of QOS provisioning in the switch. The specific framework in which datagrams are classified (in the end node) and subsequently queued and chosen for transmission (in the switch) is the embodiment of 802.1p.

In order to provide differentiation between different priority classes, a switch must provide two or more different transmission queues. How these queues are managed, how many queues exist (there must at least be two queues by definition of differentiation), and how transmission choices are made within the switch really aren't our concern, as long as such requirements (as set forth in the corresponding standards documents) are met. The reason we can say that transmission choices aren't our concern is because the standards documents dictate the behavior that must be available and/or implemented in a switch before it can claim to be 802.1p-capable. Such standards documents almost never say how the required implementation must be achieved, just that it must meet certain requirements.

For Controlled Load transmissions, the maintenance of individual queues for each priority class goes a long way to provide the necessary QOS provisioning. This is because Controlled Load transmissions are largely qualitative; they have transmission requirements that aren't extremely stringent, so they can be serviced by network devices that have relative transmission quality or relative transmission priority capabilities. For Guaranteed Service transmissions, however, the requirements are much more stringent, and can be considered to be quantitative requirements ("provide 15ms or less latency").

The quantitative requirements of Guaranteed Service require a certain type of transmission quality to exist within an 802.1p switch. Guaranteed Service requires that the 802.1p-compliant switch transmit such packets within the specified service constraints. This probably means that a switch reserves a certain portion of its available bandwidth for a nearly zero-delay transmission queue for packets requiring Guaranteed Service, and to ensure that this high-priority queue isn't oversubscribed. To provide an example, suppose that a switch had the capability to transmit 100 packets per second (PPS) and reserved 10% of that bandwidth for this nearly zero-delay queue. The switch should constrain that queue to 10 PPS because that is the maximum rate at which the bandwidth reserved for high-priority can transmit without queuing (delaying) such packets. Note that this example doesn't consider statistical multiplexing or the grabbing of other available bandwidth; such considerations are implementation details, and thus the concern of switch manufacturers. We just want to ensure that properly marked packets are provided with the treatment we expect.

Within the switch, an 802.1p-compliant switch must maintain multiple queues to properly service packets of different priorities. Although the switch doesn't necessarily have to maintain individual queues for each of the eight available 802.1p priority classes, it must at least provide two (or hopefully more). Providing multiple queues, inspecting the priority class of each packet and placing it in the appropriate queue, and then providing some logic mechanism to determine the order of transmission among the different queues provides differentiated service quality. Those requirements and their implementation inside the switch enable 802.1p to provide QOS-enabled transmission in theLAN segment.

802.1p Priority Classes

802.1p expresses priority class by setting three bits in a Layer 2 MAC header, whose binary values 0 through 7 represent eight distinct priority classes. When the switch receives a datagram from one of its connected end nodes, it reads the value of these three bits, and maps the value (0 through 7) to the appropriate transmission queue. The IETF Integrated Services over Specific Link Layers (ISSLL) Working Group has a draft version of recommended default values for these seven values:

0	Default (assumed to be best effort)
1	Reserved
2	Reserved
3	Reserved
4	Delay sensitive, no bound
5	Delay sensitive, 100ms bound
6	Delay sensitive, 10ms bound
7	Network control

The default setting of 0 represents standard best-effort service. The values of 1 through 3 are reserved, but a value of 1 (in some implementations, 2 as well) denotes a service quality that's *worse* than best effort. The reasoning behind this is to provide a way to penalize flows that are transmitting outside of their specified or allowed bounds. The use of the value of 7 for network control traffic is necessary to avoid a situation in which a heavy congestion of high-priority packets disables the network's capability to communicate functionally critical network control information.

> **Note**
>
> *There are a couple of things to keep in mind about IETF Internet Drafts and recommendations: They're drafts and they're only recommendations. To elaborate on those points, drafts generally go through a number of changes before they are either relegated negation, supersession, or golden status as an RFC, and they are guidelines within which (or outside of which) individual implementations can be deployed. By the time you read this, these seven priority classes may have been completely reordered. Check out the ISSLL Working Group's section in the IETF Web site (www.ietf.org) for the most recent version of "Integrated Service Mappings on IEEE 802 Networks" for the most up-to-date information on these recommendations.* ◆

Note, too, that these recommendations are being presented as default values, which means that they are subject to customization or configuration by network administrators who have special or specific needs for 802.1p tagging in their network. As you'll find out in the following section, such reconfiguration of 802.1p tagging is not recommended in a Windows 2000 deployment environment. ◆

How Windows 2000 Uses 802.1p

You may have noticed that 802.1p has a linear classification model, while RSVP and the QOS API provide the capability to specify multifaceted transmission specifications, such as all of those parameters of the FLOWSPEC structure. This seemingly wide gap in implementation priorities may seem like a problem, but for the programmer and the implementer, it isn't. Windows 2000 maps QOS parameters to appropriate 802.1p priority classes under the hood.

In fact, it's not a good idea to take 802.1p tagging into your own hands, for a number of reasons. Admittedly, it would be very difficult for programmers to actually do this (you could, but it's not as easy as setting a registry entry or anything like that; the tagging is done in the NIC driver). The reasoning for letting the operating system handle this tagging is worth laying down, however.

Primarily, Windows 2000 QOS implements admission control (through the QOS ACS) that enables QOS-enabled clients to request a certain set of transmission parameters. If such a request fails, it could be a permission-based rejection or a resource-based rejection. Either way, the QOS-enabled client shouldn't be transmitting for that particular flow. If the client has taken 802.1p tagging into its own hands, then the effectiveness of the QOS ACS and the overall efficiency of permission-based, QOS-enabled transmissions are degraded.

Also, the Windows 2000 QOS ACS may have information about the state of the network or the switch to which the QOS-enabled client is attached that could merit a different 802.1p priority class than might otherwise (or generally) be applied. The conditions under which such a change might occur could be complex...too complex and perhaps too dynamic to enable static 802.1p to be as effective as if Windows 2000 specified the appropriate priority class. Part of this "state of the network" information might also entail dynamic modification of queues or priority classes, based on information that Windows 2000 or the QOS ACS has gained as a result of QOS-enabled clients' RSVP transmission requests. If such requests aren't being made (in the case of a client that's doing its own 802.1p tagging), the information may not be complete, and the efficiency of the network configuration may not be optimal.

Subnet Bandwidth Manager

An Internet Draft created by the ISSLL Working Group of the IETF has outlined the proposed specification and standards for SBMs. The Windows 2000 implementation of SBM closely (if not precisely) follows those guidelines.

SBM is designed to enable the policing and provisioning of available bandwidth for a given subnet or LAN segment *in a logical manner*. The premise behind the operation of the SBM is that a given amount of bandwidth, such as 10Mbps, can and should be logically reserved for traffic that is requesting better than best-effort transmission. The specification of a logical reservation (as opposed to a physical reservation) means that requests for transmission and their possible rejections are not regulated on the wire; rather, they are admitted or denied with the expectation that the client complies with the results of such requests.

In Windows 2000, the SBM is part of the overall functionality of the QOS ACS. You may have gathered that implementing management of subnet bandwidth implies the capability to include some identifying criteria for a given request (such as user, application, requester's address, or the user's group membership). Without such criteria, reservations could be approved or denied only on a first-come, first-served basis. This isn't the spirit of QOS, and the mechanism for implementing policy-based decisions in Windows 2000 is part of the QOS ACS. Therefore, it makes sense to couple the policy-enforcing component and the bandwidth management component, which is what the QOS ACS is.

Because SBM is part of the QOS ACS, the details of SBM are provided within the context of the QOS ACS, which is detailed in Chapter 7, "Policy-Driven QOS."

DiffServ Codepoint

If we consider the path that a given packet or flow takes from one end node to another end node (presumably across a network), the next step in the process of transmitting a packet across a QOS-capable network is to traverse the mesh of routers in the path between QOS-enabled end points. In order for the mesh of routers to provide QOS provisioning, some sort of deterministic or differentiated service must be provided. One such approach is the implementation of the *DiffServ codepoint framework*, or *DSCP*.

The DSCP is the result of the IETF DiffServ Working Group's labors. One of the guiding facets of DiffServ's charter, as described on the IETF Web site (www.ietf.org), is to provide "relatively simple and coarse methods of providing differentiated classes of service for Internet traffic." In response to that charter, DiffServ created a framework in DSCP that uses an existing field in the IP header (the TOS field) to create 64 values, or *codepoints*.

Some of these are reserved for standardized use and others are reserved for local configuration, but all of them are intended to be used as building blocks for creating differentiated services across an IP network or networks.

Perhaps most important, with DSCP, DiffServ has created a scalable framework for QOS provisioning—a framework that doesn't need to maintain resource-intensive, per-flow information; yet can still provide the varied and sometimes specific requirements that end nodes require with a given QOS connection. This scalable and effective framework is a much-needed improvement in terms of the probability of its deployment, and has the capability to address the diverse and growing industry-wide need for a QOS-capable network. The nature of the improvement is that DSCP removes the need to implement RSVP at every network node and provides more prioritization queues than IP Precedence. The details of this improvement, however, are best explained when DSCP is compared to its predecessors: IP Precedence and RSVP signaling.

Where DSCP Is Marked

The DSCP codepoint can be marked in the Windows 2000 client or, if appropriate, at various network devices across the network. The existing IP field that DSCP uses to mark its codepoint for IP packets is the TOS field for IPv4 and the Traffic Class field in IPv6. The TOS field consists of eight bits; the DSCP uses the first six of those bits to set its range of 64 values (0–63), and leaves the remaining two bits of the TOS field unused. Figure 6.2 shows where the TOS field is in the IP header, and shows which of those bits are used for DSCP.

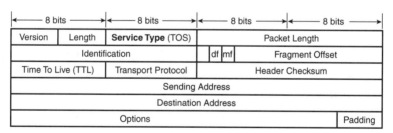

df = Don't Fragment Flag
mf = More Fragments Flag

Figure 6.2   *The TOS field in an IP header, and the bits being used for DSCP.*

Other IETF standardizations have used the TOS field to specify certain service provisioning classes, so, as you can imagine, using the TOS field for DSCP excludes it from being used for other information. Although a slight exception to this exists with DSCP backward-compatibility measures (as discussed in the "DSCP Value Mappings" section), in general, the use of DSCP "takes over" the TOS field. Therefore, two previous IETF RFCs have been made obsolete with the publication of the DSCP RFC. Those two obselete RFCs are RFC 1455, "Physical Link Security Type of Service," and RFC 1349, "Type of Service in the Internet Protocol Suite."

DSCP is defined in RFC 2474 and functions within the framework of RFC 2475. Both RFCs can be found on IETF's Website, www.ietf.org.

DSCP versus IP Precedence

Before the advent of DSCP as an official IETF RFC, the TOS field of an IPv4 header was divided differently. As Figure 6.3 illustrates, the first three bits of the TOS field were used to designate IP Precedence, which generates the capability to designate eight different values. The remaining bits weren't used by IP Precedence; they had been planned for use in *TOS routing* (an identification of different paths through the network, based on variables such as delay, cost, and path reliability). The approach didn't scale well in implementation attempts, however, so the bits were freed for use in DiffServ.

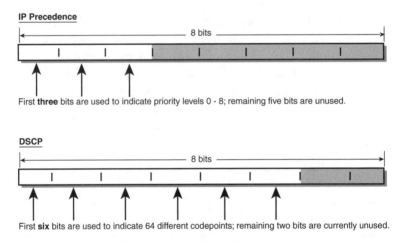

Figure 6.3   *The TOS field of an IPv4 header and how it's used in IP Precedence versus its use by DSCP.*

DSCP has absorbed IP Precedence functionality. The good news about DSCP, especially because IP Precedence is already in fairly wide use in IP networks around the world, is that DSCP is backward-compatible with IP Precedence. This backward compatibility is achieved through the use of DSCP's Class Selector Codepoints. This compatibility is by design, and it is done to enable existing IP Precedence-compatible routers to interact seamlessly with DSCP-enabled networks. DSCP is a superior design over IP Precedence because IP Precedence, although it provides some class-based priority capabilities, is not as flexible nor as specific as DSCP, and it is probably not specific enough to enable networks to provide predictable QOS provisioning.

The specific codepoints that enable DSCP to be backward-compatible with IP Precedence are explained in more detail in the upcoming section called "DSCP Value Mappings."

DSCP versus RSVP

You may have been thinking that there's a bit of overlap in QOS components or QOS technologies as you compared the capabilities and intentions of DSCP and the use of RSVP by RSVP-enabled routers. If so, you are correct—there is overlap in their capabilities. However, their approach to solving the problem of providing QOS provisioning over the Internet (or any IP network) is so significant that the complexity of one (RSVP) begot the other (DSCP).

The reasoning and background on how DSCP has come into existence due to RSVP's complexity merits explanation. So, at this point, a little bit of background on DiffServ is needed.

The DiffServ working group was created out of an industry need to address problems with existing QOS-enabling technologies. Specifically, the existing means of providing QOS provisioning across a network, RSVP, was complex and had problems with scalability. The industry was in need of a QOS-provisioning framework that provided a less complex, less resource-intensive (in the router) means of providing QOS provisioning across a network. RSVP is resource-intensive, buffer-intensive, and CPU-intensive because of its requirement to maintain information and separate queues for individual flows (also referred to as *microflows*) that are associated with each active QOS session. With the potential for individual end nodes to initiate and maintain several flows at any given time, and the potential for many end nodes (perhaps even thousands of them) to be routed through a single router at certain edges of a given network, the overhead associated with maintaining information about what could be tens of thousands of simultaneous flows is enormous... prohibitively so.

The premise behind RSVP's hefty resource consumption is its implicit requirement that very granular, detailed service specifications be met at each hop along its packets' journeys across the network. In other words, RSVP requirements dictate qualitative service provisions, such as 10ms delay and bandwidth of 150K/sec; versus quantitative service provisions, such as "this packet has a higher priority that packets in these other priority classes."

These qualitative, deterministic requirements make RSVP scale poorly because there is not economy of scale and no aggregation of packets for a given queue. In fact, quite the opposite of "economy of scale" occurs with RSVP. Because each flow's queue must be isolated from other flows and information about each flow must be maintained in each router along the path between QOS end points, the resources required to service RSVP in routers grow by leaps and bounds as it attempts to scale to larger networks.

DiffServ's DSCP attempts to address such scalability with a two-pronged approach. First, aggregating traffic into priority-based queues (rather than tracking individual flows) lightens the resource load on routers and enables it to scale better than RSVP. Also, offering a large number of service code-points (64 in all) enables sufficiently differentiated service provisioning to be mapped to individual codepoints. This enables granular, specific service capabilities (rather than TOS' sparse eight values) within the DSCP-enabled network. Adding to the attractiveness of DSCP is the fact that it is backward-compatible with the existing priority-routing technology, IP Precedence.

Despite DSCP's advantages in scalability and complexity over RSVP, there is still a very useful and necessary place for RSVP in clients and near the edge of the network. The need and appropriate place for RSVP is discussed more in Chapter 9, "Uniting Application-, Network-, and Policy-Driven QOS."

DSCP Value Mappings

As previously mentioned, DSCP uses the first six bits of the TOS field in an IP header to represent its 64 available values. Within this range of 64 values, three pools of DSCP values have been created by RFC 2474 to promote the appropriate use of the finite number of codepoints available within the six-bit DSCP range. Incorporated into these policies and pools that regulate the use of available DiffServ codepoints is the reservation of values that correspond to existing IP Precedence values. This reservation of IP Precedence values is possible because IP Precedence uses the first three bits of the DSCP's six bits, as illustrated in Figure 6.3.

Table 6.1 specifies the pools of DSCP values and their intended usage. Pool 1 is reserved for standardization by appropriate standardization organizations. Pool 2 is intended for local use (including experimental use). Pool 3 is also intended for local use, but that allotment is an initial ruling. If the need for standardized codepoints exhausts the 32 codepoints available in Pool 1, then Pool 3 may be grabbed and used for further standardized codepoints. The use of x indicates that the value can be 0 or 1.

Table 6.1   *The pool of DSCP bitwise values and their intended uses.*

Grouping	Codepoint Space	Assignment Policy
Pool 1	xxxxx0	Standardization
Pool 2	xxxx11	Local Use
Pool 3	xxxx01	Local Use (may be used later for standardized codepoints)
Best Effort	000000	Always reserved for Best Effort service
Class Selector Codepoints	xxx000	Reserved for backward-compatibility with IP Precedence

The term used to associate the codepoints in Table 6.1 that are reserved to provide backward-compatibility are called *Class Selector Codepoints* (as in Class of Service). Note that the RFC actually requires that routers claiming to be DSCP-compatible must provide compatibility with the existing installed base of IP Precedence-compatible routers.

Despite the fact that these compatibilities with previous IP Precedence values and the RFC's requirement that DSCP-compliant network devices implement such Class Selector Codepoints for backward-compatibility, network administrators shouldn't depend on the implementation of such backward-compatibility.

Although all this pooling and grouping of available DSCP values are good for the industry, there must be some mapping of values to associated or expected behavior, or else the pooling is for naught. Fortunately, two IETF drafts have been written that address the creation of what are called per-hop behaviors, or PHBs. These enable the setting of a given codepoint to an associated treatment with which packets of these given codepoints can be expected to be handled. Remember that IETF drafts are just that—drafts—but it's pretty likely that these drafts will eventually become RFCs. For more disclaimers on drafts, check out the section "802.1p Priority Classes" earlier in this chapter.

Understanding PHBs

In order for the idea of differentiated treatment of IP packets traversing a network to have a meaningful implementation for QOS provisioning, there must be at least two levels of service—one presumably receiving better treatment than the other. For the sake of explanation, we'll call these levels priority A and priority B, with priority A receiving preferential treatment. Such differentiation between the treatment of packets marked with priority A and priority B requires that a network device's forwarding behavior adhere to certain transmission requirements. Presumably, that behavior at the very least provides a differentiation between the transmission priority of A and B packets.

To put this another way, all these DiffServ codepoints have to map to some sort of anticipated behavior at the network device. That "anticipated behavior" must somehow be specified, explained, and should probably be standardized so that certain different QOS requirements expect certain standardized behavior out of a network device, as long as the packet is tagged with the corresponding codepoint. Here's a simple example. If all we want from a network are two types of service (immediate service and best effort service), we could map priority A to immediate service and map priority B to immediate service. We could then assign a PHB so that all priority A traffic is transmitted before any priority B packets are transmitted. (As an aside, we can also state that only 10% of the bandwidth be available for priority A packets and use some sort of mechanism to communicate availability of that 10% to a policy enforcer. This would presumably then not allow any more clients to transmit priority A packets until some of that 10% bandwidth becomes available).

Thus, within the framework of available codepoints, there must be a mapping of anticipated service for a given codepoint to the per-hop behavior that network devices will provide for that same given codepoint. The first step, even before such mapping can occur, is that such PHBs must be defined. Fortunately, the IETF has already done much of this work.

The Assured Forwarding PHB Group
The *Assured Forwarding (AF) PHB group* is the primary group of PHBs (in conjunction with the EF PHB) that Windows 2000 uses to enable QOS provisioning across an IP network. The AF PHB group provides four classes of service, and within each of those four classes of service, drop precedence can be assigned from among three drop-precedence choices.

This PHB group takes DiffServ codepoints—simple binary values within a constrained range of available values—and provides structure within those twelve values (four classes × three drop-precedence levels per class) by assigning required behaviors for any given packet with a value that maps to any PHB in this group. In other words, an otherwise linear set of codepoints is provided multi-faceted behavior characteristics by defining classes, and then by adding stratification within each class. This structured use of available DiffServ codepoints enables service quality to be provisioned from building blocks of service differentiation, and as you'll see, the DiffServ codepoint structure provides even further customization. With so many codepoints available (64 in all) and the capability to provide so many different and customized PHBs, DSCP appears to have all the ingredients to create simplified, yet highly differentiated services across any given IP network.

The AF PHB is much easier to understand when its values are put into table format. For the technical explanation of the AF PHB, right from the IETF Working Group's site, you can read the AF PHB Group paper in the DiffServ area of the IETF Web site, www.ietf.org. Table 6.2 helps to visualize the structure of the AF PHB codepoints.

Table 6.2   The AF PHB codepoints.

	Class 1	Class 2	Class 3	Class 4
Low Drop Precedence	001010	010010	011010	100010
Medium Drop Precedence	001100	010100	011100	100100
High Drop Precedence	001110	010110	011110	100110

The naming conventions that are being assigned to these classes make sense, but are a little bit counterintuitive, so you have to pay close attention to these conventions when discussing the AF PHBs to ensure that you don't get things screwed up. That brings us to the next question and its corresponding explanation. How do these classes compare to each other with regard to relative service transmission quality? And furthermore, how do the AF PHBs compare to the types of QOS provisioning that we've grown to know and love?

First, an explanation of what the AF PHBs codepoint values and classes mean in terms of relative service transmission quality. The higher the class number, the better the transmission service; to put it differently, the higher the class number, the higher transmission priority provided to the packet. As a result of the AF PHB class ordering, and because speaking in binary is just not intuitive or particularly effective, the AF PHBs have a naming convention that is explained in Figure 6.4.

The higher the drop precedence, the more likely it is that the packet will be dropped when congestion occurs, based on the requisite behavior that a given network device must exhibit in relative treatment of these packets. The reason that this is somewhat counterintuitive is that a packet with the highest AF number (which would be AF43) is not the "most important" packet in the AF PHB. I know, this isn't a requirement, but when the treatment of the packet (based on its class) gets better as the class number increases, one is led to believe that the drop precedence would be "better" as that number (the drop precedence) increases. That isn't the case. The best treatment that a packet receives when marked with a DSCP from the AF PHB group is when that packet is marked AF41. This doesn't make the AF PHB numbering scheme wrong nor does it make my sense of intuitiveness right—there's probably an argument to be made that the strict sense of "drop precedence" implies that a higher number means a higher likelihood of being dropped. That's fine, but most administrators will look at the AF PHB number as a whole, draw conclusions about the numbering scheme from the first half of its explanation (the class-numbering scheme), and believe that the higher the number, the better is the overall service. This is not the case.

	Class 1	Class 2	Class 3	Class 4	
Low Drop Precedence	AF11	AF21	AF31	AF41*	Better Service
Medium Drop Precedence	AF12	AF22	AF32	AF42	
High Drop Precedence	AF13*	AF23	AF33	AF43	Worse Service

Worse Service ← ←   Better Service → →

* AF13 provides the worst service; AP41 provides the best service.

Figure 6.4   *The AF PHB corresponding names.*

It's important to understand that all packets of the same class are serviced in the same queue in a given network device, regardless of drop precedence. That means that all Class 1 packets are serviced in the same queue, including AF11, AF12, and AF13 packets. When congestion occurs, however, packets with a higher drop precedence will be more likely to get dropped than packets with a lower drop precedence, so AF13 packets will get dropped more than AF11 packets.

Another important point to remember about the AF PHB's differentiated service scheme is that delay parameters or other service quality measurements are not quantitative. That means that there's relative priority, there's drop precedence, but none of the service classes provide any quantification of the probable delay that a packet will endure as it passes through the device. This is by design (and in direct contrast with RSVP), and it enables DSCP to be lightweight in a device's implementation of its transmission algorithms, and essentially makes the capability to implement DSCP-enabled network devices less resource- and CPU-intensive. Which, in realistic terms, translates into a much higher probability of industry acceptance and deployment.

Also, although it's not a hard-and-fast rule, the AF PHB group is certain to be equated with the QOS provisioning scheme known better as Controlled Load. To generalize the intentions and requirements behind marking packets for Controlled Load service, transmission characteristics such as delay variation, latency, and other quantitative transmission measurements aren't as important (or at least not intended to be provided) as providing service comparable to unloaded conditions. More important than quantitative provisioning is the qualitative approach, which is to say that Controlled Load packets get better transmission service than best effort traffic, for example.

The Expedited Forwarding PHB Group

The *Expedited Forwarding (EF) PHB group* is a bit of a special case because its behavior defines the mapping to a single DiffServ codepoint. The reason that the EF PHB group can be so narrow in its singular codepoint is because it has a very specific intentions: to provide assured bandwidth, low delay variation, and low latency transmission of packets through any given DSCP-enabled network. To read between such lines of required behavior, the EF PHB intends to provide the closest approximation of traditionally defined Guaranteed Service to DSCP network devices.

The EF PHB specification requires that a network device claiming EF PHB capability has some characteristics that enable that device to introduce as little delay as possible, and essentially introduce no queuing delay.

The recommended EF PHB codepoint is 101110, although other codepoints can be used. Network devices that implement EF PHB must isolate the EF PHB queue from other PHB groups.

There are a few salient requirements of the EF PHB implementation on any given network device. The first of these requirements pertains to the amount of bandwidth allocated to EF PHB packets and the device's capability to transmit at that specified rate.

During the course of any given period of time, a certain amount of bandwidth is reserved for packets marked with the EF PHB codepoint. To provide example numbers, perhaps 1MB/sec is the configured minimum (the amount must be configurable, per the EF PHB specification) bandwidth reserved for EF PHB packets; the network device must have the capability to transmit packets at or above that given rate. In other words, if the reservation is 1MB/sec, the device must be able to transmit packets at a rate of 1MB/sec or greater. The implication is that as long as packets marked with EF PHB are given higher priority than all other packets arriving at the network node, there will be no queuing (or very short queuing as packets are inspected) delay introduced to the packets. The network node can forward them as fast as the configured EF PHB incoming rate. The only delay introduced to the packet, therefore, is the time necessary to inspect the packet and then send it on its way.

Another salient requirement is that EF packets are still aggregated; they don't receive individual queues, such as what happens with RSVP implementations. However, because the configured rate cannot exceed the network device's transmission capability, the implied result is that the packets get through the device as fast as possible—nullifying any potential gains from more sophisticated (complex and difficult-to-implement and sustain) approaches.

There are other details about the EF PHB that can be found on the IETF Web site, including the required behavior of border routers (those on the edge of a network connection between two independent networks). A couple of ways to implement the EF PHB is to use *Weighted Fair Queuing (WFQ)*, or to map it to ATM's CBR or rtVBR. More information on border routers is provided in Chapter 8, "Uniting Application-, Network- and Policy-Driven QOS."

Class Selector PHB Requirements

In consideration of DSCP's forefather (IP Precedence) and because IP Precedence is in use today, the adoption and viability of DSCP suggests that packets with their TOS field marked in the ways of IP Precedence receive treatment that approximates the treatment expected by the corresponding IP Precedence behavior. Such required per-hop behavior of IP Precedence-marked packets has been assured by Class Selector PHB Requirements. Class Selector PHB Requirements are requirements placed on the PHB treatment of packets that map to Class Selector Codepoints. As you recall from Table 6.1, Class Selector Codepoints are codepoints that are reserved for backward-compatibility with IP Precedence. Within the six-bit DSCP codepoint, they map to those bits used in IP Precedence.

In addition, the Class Selector Codepoints must honor the default value of best effort traffic, which is all zeros (000000).

DSCP in Windows 2000

With the wide range of values available to the DSCP, and the fairly large number of codepoint-to-PHB mappings associated with the AF PHB, you may think that the complexity associated with applying the appropriate DSCP with a given QOS flow specification will be daunting and complex. Perhaps it is, but, fortunately, it isn't complicated for us. Essentially, we users, implementers, or programmers don't have to do a thing.

Why? Because Windows 2000 makes DSCP mapping decisions under the hood.

The reason that Windows 2000 is making such decisions has a lot to do with ensuring that traffic traversing the network goes through the appropriate policy check before transmitting. In fact, much of the DSCP architecture, at least in probable implementation scenarios, depends on such policy checks being made by the client prior to transmission. More details on such interaction between DSCP and the overall deployment of Windows 2000 QOS are provided in Chapter 8, "Uniting Application-, Network- and Policy-Driven QOS," and Chapter 10, "QOS for the Integrator and Administrator."

L2 Signaling

The issues surrounding L2 signaling can be embodied in the following question: How do RSVP parameters or DSCP PHBs get mapped to L2 technologies, such as ATM or Frame Relay? The answer is that the IETF provides guidance, recommendations, and standards for such mapping issues, which enable WAN technologies such as ATM and Frame Relay to interoperate with the standards-based Windows 2000 implementation of QOS.

The interoperation of RSVP (or other QOS-enabling service request media) with WAN technologies is made possible by the fact that WAN technologies already have QOS-enabling mechanisms built into them. Examples include committed information rates, drop precedence bits, traffic management, delay variation, latency-specification capabilities, and others. These built-in capabilities mean that the building blocks for enabling Windows 2000 QOS to interoperate with such L2 technologies are already there. All that needs to be done is to map Windows 2000 QOS requests/requirements—which are communicated through the use of RSVP—to the QOS building blocks present in the various L2 signaling technologies. Such work is easier pointed out than completed.

Most of the work that the IETF's ISSLL working group has done on L2 signaling has been focused on mapping the IntServ model's use of RSVP signaling to request, reserve, and provision QOS guarantees to ATM. Naturally, the two types of service quality provisioning that have been targeted by ISSLL for ATM implementation are Controlled Load and Guaranteed Service. The third non-service quality service type, Best Effort, is also included.

QOS and ATM L2 Signaling

The much-boiled-down version of ISSLL's work on IntServ interoperation with ATM is that Controlled Load service and Guaranteed service map best to certain ATM services, as outlined in Table 6.3. There are other possible mappings, but those outlined in Table 6.3 represent the best choices. Earlier versions of the ATM Forum's UNI specification (versions 3.0 and 3.1) have ATM services that map to particular UNI 4.0 services, and are included in parentheses after the UNI 4.0 ATM services.

Table 6.3   *Mapping Controlled Load service and Guaranteed service to UNI ATM services.*

IntServ Service Type	Best-Choice ATM Service Mapping
Guaranteed service	CBR or rtVBR (BCOB-A)
Controlled Load service	NrtVBR (BCOB-C) or ABR with a minimum cell rate
Best Effort service	UBR or ABR (BCOB-C or BCOB-X with the Best Effort indication set)

In Table 6.3, the ATM service mappings equate to the following:

CBR = Constant Bit Rate

rtVBR = Real-time Variable Bit Rate

nrtVBR = Non–real-time Variable Bit Rate

UBR = Unspecified Bit Rate

ABR = Available Bit Rate

Table 6.3 includes the following ATM UNI versions 3.0/3.1 services in parentheses:

BCOB-A = Constant rate, timing required, unicast/multipoint

BCOB-C = Variable rate, timing not required, unicast/multipoint

BCOB-X = Can substitute either of the above parameters, as long as its dependent parameters, such as traffic type and timing requirements, are appropriately set

Again, this is a simplified version of the actual issues that go into determining and even provisioning the mapping of RSVP requests to ATM service type. Other important, but ATM-specific issues are addressed, including SVC (switched virtual circuit) setup and teardown based on reservation request, whether to aggregate like-reservations over a single VC, and whether to use the data VC for RSVP signaling. (The current recommendation is to use the best effort VC rather than the data VC for RSVP signaling). These important issues are specific to ATM implementations, and their detailed discussions are outside the scope of this book. For those eager to get their hands on such information, however, the RFC that outlines this information (RFC 2381) is a clearly written and easily understood document, so go there for further information.

Note, however, that there's a group of RFCs that largely depend on each other for supportive information or implementation recommendations, so you may need to read three or four RFCs to round out the recommendations found in RFC 2381. Those "grouped" RFCs are RFC 2382, 2379,

2380, and 2381. Reading them in that order may yield the best results because there is a sort of information-building and detail-drilling that occurs through that progression of documents.

QOS and Frame Relay L2 Signaling
Not much work has transpired on the mapping of the IntServ model to Frame Relay. Indeed, as mentioned earlier in this section, Frame Relay has built-in QOS-enabling parameters such as FECN (Forward Explicit Congestion Notification Bit, which notifies upstream nodes of congestion problems), BECN (Backward Explicit Congestion Notification Bit, which is used to notify downstream nodes of congestion problems), and DE (Discard Eligibility) bits that make it a ready-made candidate for QOS mechanisms in the end-to-end solution. Despite these QOS-enabling features, work must be done to create a mapping scheme from IntServ's RSVP signaling to Frame Relay QOS provisioning.

Though it hasn't happened as of this printing, it's almost certainly in the works. If you want to keep a close finger on the pulse of Frame Relay QOS parameters and the IntServ (or perhaps DSCP) model, you can check the IETF's ISSLL working group's Web site regularly.

RSVP: the Communications Medium
As you may have gathered from other sections in this chapter, RSVP plays a central role in the process of communicating Windows 2000 QOS reservation parameters across the network.

RSVP-enabled routers also play a part in the network-driven QOS component arena. Although RSVP is more complex than DSCP, it may prove the best approach for some smaller networks, in which scalability isn't as large an issue. If DSCP may be the solution of choice for large networks or the Internet's interior, RSVP may be implemented in smaller satellite networks or intranets. The general belief, too, is that an RSVP-enabled network node makes more efficient use of network resources than does DSCP (despite RSVP's increased overhead). Also, RSVP is useful when the size of the resource request equates to a significant portion of available bandwidth. Therefore, there are certain situations in which RSVP can be a more efficient solution than DSCP.

Despite RSVP's relative complexity and overhead, its capability to carry QOS requests across a network provide it with a firm place in the overall scheme of network-driven QOS. (It enables those requests to be parsed by whichever network devices require such information to properly reserve or provision appropriate transmission characteristics for associated packets.)

As the section "L2 Signaling" explained, many WAN technologies use RSVP to determine the appropriate L2 signaling for a given reservation. Another place where RSVP has an important and even central role is in carrying user information to admission control

7

Policy-Driven QOS

In order for QOS to be meaningful in any deployment, there must be a means of implementing and enforcing policy on resource reservations and priority requests. The final step of explaining how Windows 2000 provides a complete end-to-end QOS solution is to provide the functional details of how policy is implemented and enforced in Windows 2000 QOS.

From an overall perspective, the policy-enforcing capabilities of a QOS solution must be capable of providing identification of which user (or group, or even which application) is requesting the QOS provisioning for a given flow or session. The next step in providing policy-based QOS mechanisms is to determine whether the identified entity (user, group, or application) has the appropriate permissions to reserve the bandwidth that such a reservation would require. After that, it must then determine whether there are enough resources on the transmission medium—LAN segment, WAN link, router, or other network device—to service the request.

These QOS requirements are implemented by the cooperation and interaction of the following, all-inclusive list of Windows 2000 QOS components:

- **QOS Admission Control Service (QOS ACS):** The QOS ACS manages the admission of QOS-enabled (RSVP-signaled) flows and sessions through LAN segments or across router interfaces. The QOS ACS has the capability to manage LAN segments through its QOS ACS/SBM implementation, and it manages router interfaces connected to Windows 2000 RRAS routers through the implementation of QOS ACS/RRAS. The QOS ACS makes no differentiation between its SBM and RRAS implementations; the interface and the treatment of both are identical.

- **Local Policy Module (LPM):** The LPM is a Microsoft-provided service that makes network resource–access decisions for the ACS. The LPM interacts over the network with the client-based Policy Element.

- **Local Policy Module API (LPM API):** The LPM API is the application programming interface for the LPM.
- **Policy Element (PE):** The PE is a policy component that provides authentication information on the client, enabling the creation of resource-reservation requests.
- **RSVP:** In its policy-driven aspect, RSVP carries policy objects between end nodes and all RSVP-enabled network devices in the path between the end-to-end QOS connection, including the QOS ACS. RSVP also carries rejections of admission requests back to the requesting or sending node, providing information about the nature of the error or reservation rejection.
- **Third Party API (LDAP):** This application programming interface exposes policy information stored in the Windows 2000 Active Directory. This Third Party API uses the Lightweight Directory Access Protocol (LDAP), enabling a standardized way of acquiring policy information from the Active Directory.

The Boundary of Policy-Driven QOS Components

The most interesting aspect of policy-driven QOS is that there really are no boundaries. This is necessary because at any network node, network cloud, or network device along the path between each end of the end-to-end QOS connection, there must be the capability to reject a given QOS connection, based on certain criteria. If this aspect of QOS were not as pervasive as it is, then there would be no means of differentiation between those requesting the QOS-enabled reservation, and therefore the idea of reserving resources would be mute. For whom would they then be reserved, and moreover, on what basis would such reservations be approved?

The mechanism of choice for ferrying all this policy information from one end node, across the network, through network devices and WAN links, and then perhaps back through other networks and to the other end-device, is RSVP.

Policy-Driven QOS Component Details

One of the primary challenges that network-driven QOS faces, as mentioned in the previous chapter, is that not all network devices are necessarily going to be running Windows 2000. The communication between Windows 2000 or other Windows 2000 QOS components and such non-Windows devices, therefore, is achieved through some agreed-upon medium such as RSVP or DSCP (see Chapter 6, "Network-Driven QOS").

This communication challenge is equally evident for policy-driven QOS components, but the solution is a bit different than the solution for network-driven QOS. For policy-driven QOS components, there is already an agreed-upon medium for passing policy information for a given QOS-enabled request: RSVP. The challenge faced by policy-based QOS components is largely subverted to that of translating RSVP-based requests (and its included policy elements) into something usable by policy-driven QOS components. Better yet, they can simply interpret (or directly access) the policy information that RSVP carries. In this chapter's discussion of RSVP, the way that such policy information is included in RSVP messages is explained in detail.

In each of the components explained in this chapter, the issue of the way such policy information is handled, parsed, or otherwise used is included as part of the explanation—sometimes, it's the central issue; sometimes it's peripheral. Regardless, knowing how such policy information is created, disseminated, or interpreted is a large part of the policy-driven QOS component picture. Often, the defining feature of a policy-driven QOS component is how it works with such policy information.

QOS ACS

Windows 2000 QOS ACS enables Windows 2000 end nodes and RSVP-enabled routers to reserve resources on local 802-based LAN segments or on WAN interface connections using industry-standard RSVP signaling. By doing this, QOS ACS enables more effective, manageable, and differentiated use of the network media that it manages. QOS ACS achieves such management, differentiation, and increased efficiency by managing network bandwidth and by admitting only RSVP-enabled QOS requests that traverse its managed segment if resources are available and if policy allows.

QOS ACS has two implementations:

- QOS ACS/SBM
- QOS ACS/RRAS

The QOS ACS/SBM provides admission control and bandwidth reservation functionality for LAN segments, whereas the QOS ACS/RRAS provides admission control functionality for Windows 2000 RRAS routers (RRAS stands for *Routing and Remote Access Service*). Despite this duality of capabilities, the management of either QOS ACS/SBM or QOS ACS/RRAS is the same: Windows 2000 QOS does not differentiate between them from a management or setup standpoint.

Note

When a Windows 2000 server running the QOS ACS service is doing its duty on a given LAN segment or WAN interface connections (that is, when QOS ACS is providing admission control services) that LAN segment or WAN interface is considered to be managed. For the sake of clarity, I'll refer to a LAN segment or a WAN interface being managed by QOS ACS as a managed segment. A managed segment can be a shared LAN segment, an ATM Virtual Circuit (VC), an ISDN connection, or any other connection that can be managed by QOS ACS. ◆

Both routers and end nodes make use of QOS ACS functionality. The reasoning and usage by both become clearer as more details about how QOS ACS works are provided, but the short version is as follows. QOS ACS intercepts both RSVP PATH and RESV messages to exert its management on a managed segment; both routers and end nodes make use of the admission control functionality built into QOS ACS because both are involved in PATH and RESV message transmissions. Therefore, throughout this discussion of QOS ACS I'll refer to end nodes (such as Windows 2000 clients) and RSVP-enabled routers as *RSVP-enabled devices* or *nodes*. When you see such terms, remember that the context of either can mean Windows 2000 clients or routers.

There are two important points to keep in mind about QOS ACS and its capabilities. If you keep the following two points about QOS ACS in mind while going through its explanation, the explanation of how QOS ACS works, its role in the overall scheme, and even explanations in the next chapter (which ties how all these QOS components work together in a given deployment) are much easier to understand.

First, QOS ACS only works with RSVP-enabled requests. Fortunately, all Windows 2000 clients are RSVP-enabled, as are RSVP-capable routers. Another way of putting this is to say that QOS ACS is an RSVP-based service that resides on a Windows 2000 computer. Either way you look at it, the fact that QOS ACS only interoperates with RSVP messages implies, correctly, that the transmission of traffic over a managed segment that doesn't use RSVP to reserve resources is not regulated by QOS ACS.

Second, QOS ACS only provides *logical* management of bandwidth resources, and therefore can't enforce its policies. This fact requires that RSVP-enabled devices be well-behaved when it comes to abiding by potential rejections from QOS ACS for bandwidth/service reservations. Contrary to sometimes-observed behavior, computers don't have a mind of their own, so the requirement of RSVP-enabled devices doesn't present as much of a breach of security as one might think. More explanation on QOS ACS security is provided later in this chapter.

How QOS ACS Gets Involved

QOS-enabled nodes, including Windows 2000 clients and RSVP-compatible routers, learn about the presence of the QOS ACS by listening on a specific multicast IP address. The QOS ACS/SBM then jumps into the path of PATH and RESV messages by becoming a hop in the network node path between either end of the end-to-end QOS solution.

In order to fully explain how this process works, there are a couple of explanations that have to occur in parallel; that is, both are required to fully explain how it is that QOS ACS/SBM goes about inserting itself into the RSVP message path. Those two parallel explanations are as follows:

- How QOS ACS/SBMs Operate
- Getting QOS ACS/SBM In the Path

The explanations follow that order; by the end of the second explanation, it will be clear how QOS ACS/SBM gets itself involved in clients' requests, and thereby provides the necessary QOS capabilities that it was created to solve.

How QOS ACS/SBMs Operate

The IETF's ISSLL working group has created an SBM standard, in which the design and implementation specifics of the way SBMs should operate, communicate, and behave are described. As mentioned earlier, QOS ACS incorporates SBM functionality into its services. Therefore, it is an SBM, and it follows the SBM standards recommendations. Part of that SBM specification instructs SBMs to broadcast their presence to SBM-aware devices (which includes Windows 2000 clients, RSVP-aware routers, SBM-aware switches, and any other network device that's interested in SBM service) at certain intervals. Windows 2000 clients, RSVP-aware routers, and other devices (such as other ISSLL SBMs, QOS ACS/SBMs, or otherwise) listen to the address that the SBM specification has indicated is appropriate for advertising SBM service, They thus know how to reach the SBM. However, there may be multiple SBMs on a given managed segment. In fact, there actually should be multiple SBMs, whether they are QOS ACS/SBMs or other SBMs, on a given managed segment to ensure that the failure of one machine doesn't bring down the SBM design's QOS-enabling functionality.

The question that comes to mind is this: How does a Windows 2000 client or a router know to which SBM they should send its reservation request? The answer is that it must send its RSVP reservation request messages only to the *Designated SBM*, or *DSBM*.

SBMs and SBM-aware nodes (such as Windows 2000 clients, routers, and switches) use two reserved multicast IP addresses for communication; one is called the *AllSBMAddress* (224.0.0.17), the other is called the

DSBMLogicalAddress (224.0.0.16). The choice of these IP multicast addresses, which were selected from the range of local multicast addresses, were chosen based on the following:

- They aren't passed through routers—no need to do so with SBM capability, so the fact that routers don't forward such messages makes the addresses functionally plausible.
- They do pass through non-SBM aware switches or hubs.
- They can be made permanent members of a switch's database so that messages directed to the AllSBMAddress or DSBMLogicalAddress can be sent directly to the SBM management entities in the switch device itself (if any such management entities exist).

SBMs monitor the AllSBMAddress multicast IP address for the presence of a DSBM. In the event that a DSBM is not detected or the status of DSBM comes up for grabs, a DSBM election occurs to determine which SBM on the managed segment becomes the DSBM.

The DSBM Election Process

The DSBM election process merits further explanation. When an SBM comes online, it listens on the designated IP multicast address (AllSBMAddress) for messages sent out by the current DSBM, which indicate the existence of an active DSBM. Such messages are called I_AM_DSBM, and they have a specified format in which they provide information about the DSBMs, including IP address, Layer 2 address, and SBM priority value in individual fields. The order of these fields is strictly defined, as is each field's length, so the interpretation and handling of I_AM_DSBM is an industry standard, and therefore easier to manage in terms of implementation and interoperability between devices from different manufacturers.

When the SBM receives the I_AM_DSBM message, it records the information contained in the message, and then remains idle until such a time that status as DSBM becomes available. DSBM status becomes available either through timing out of the I_AM_DSBM messages or from a specific message sent by the DSBM, stating that it's no longer going to be DSBM (such as the case when it does a graceful shutdown). Because I_AM_DSBM messages must be sent to the appropriate IP multicast address on a periodic basis, an SBM can listen for a certain interval (a timeout interval) for I_AM_DSBM messages; if that interval times out, the status of DSBM becomes subject to an election.

The election process occurs on the same IP multicast address as the I_AM_DSBM messages (AllSBMAddress), and is accomplished and decided through the exchange and comparison of DSBM_WILLING messages. DSBM_WILLING messages have a specific format, in which they provide the SBM's addresses (IP address and Layer 2 address) and its SBM priority. The process is simple;

whichever SBM has the highest SBM priority wins the election, becomes the DSBM, and begins transmitting its I_AM_DSBM messages on the specified periodic basis. SBM priority values range from zero (meaning it isn't eligible to be DSBM, as is the case with an I_AM_DSBM message prior to the DSBM's graceful shutdown) to 255. Higher numbers indicate higher DSBM priority.

SBM-aware clients forward only PATH *or* RESV *messages to the DSBM, and only the presence of a DSBM constitutes (and functionally results in) a managed segment. How do SBM-aware clients, such as a Windows 2000 client or SBM-aware router, know about the DSBM? Easy. They monitor the AllSBMAddress for I_AM_DSBM messages, just like an SBM does. Because the I_AM_DSBM message contains the IP and L2 address of the DSBM, SBM-aware clients know where to forward their* PATH *and/or* RESV *messages in order to get QOS ACS/SBM service (that is, to have their QOS reservation requests considered, and either admitted or rejected)* ◆

Note that there are a number of configuration parameters, such as the listening interval time, after which the DSBM is presumed dead (the SBMDeadInterval *value) and the time an SBM has to wait in response to* DSBM_WILLING *messages before it deems itself DSBM (the* ElectionInterval*). These values can be stored in the Active Directory on an enterprise-wide basis, enabling QOS ACS/SBM servers to pull such information from the Windows 2000 directory store (the Active Directory), and thereby be centrally and easily managed on an enterprise-wide basis. Otherwise, such values are likely entered statically in the device.* ◆

Getting QOS ACS/SBM In the Path

Now that you know how SBMs (including QOS ACS/SBM) determine which of them is the DSBM, the question of how the DSBM gets inserted into the end-to-end network path of a QOS-enabled connection needs to be answered. Fortunately, it isn't as complex or long as how SBMs interoperate. After all, if the DSBM is just another node on a LAN segment, getting from the router to the next appropriate hop on the way to the other end of the QOS connection doesn't require going through the DSBM. Indeed, going through the DSBM introduces an *extra* hop along the way.

Keep in mind, too, that the end node to which the RSVP message is traveling may not reside on the managed segment in question. Depending on topologies, a given RSVP message (such as a PATH message) may have to traverse numerous LAN segments just to get to a network backbone (which itself may have an additional DSBM). There may be six different DSBMs from which a PATH or RESV message require admission before the QOS reservation can be put in place.

Because SBM-aware nodes (routers and end nodes, and even switches) monitor the AllSBMAddress and therefore receive (and read) I_AM_DSBM messages, they have knowledge of the DSBM's IP and L2 address. That being the case, SBM-aware nodes simply treat the DSBM as the next logical hop on the way toward their QOS-enabled destination. Conversely, each DSBM in the network path between end nodes acts on such RSVP messages accordingly, setting up state and maintaining RSVP information for all such reservations, just as any other RSVP-enabled network node must do.

By getting into the path of all RSVP messages, the QOS ACS/SBM can interpret the QOS-provisioning requests of SBM-aware nodes on the network. Remember, that includes Windows 2000 clients and routers, and thereby regulates admission of RSVP-enabled flows onto the shared 802-based LAN segment medium, at least logically (rather than physically).

What About QOS ACS/RRAS?
Unlike QOS ACS/SBM, QOS ACS/RRAS doesn't have to contend with SBM elections or other work that needs to be inserted into the RSVP message path. However, the device on the other side of the QOS ACS/RRAS point-to-point link, over which the flow's packets are transmitted, may also be managed by QOS ACS/RRAS and its resources appropriately managed by the QOS ACS/RRAS management and admission control functionality. This is necessary because either RRAS router may be in a different domain or Organizational Unit (OU), may have different policies based on user or application, and may therefore reject a given QOS-provisioning request where the other RRAS router has approved it, or vice versa.

Such placement for admission control—in routers or other network devices, rather than on a PC server running Windows—brings up a probable trend worth mentioning. It's likely, and actually anticipated, that the responsibility for admission control functionality, such as that incorporated in QOS ACS, will shift from PC server-based operation to being incorporated into routers and/or switches as the implementation of QOS broadens and QOS-enabled devices become more commonplace.

Let's get back to the issue of why QOS ACS/RRAS is exempt from the complexities associated with managing DSBMs on LAN segments. It gets away with not requiring "designation" complexity because it is already a network device in the path between end nodes in a given QOS flow. Otherwise, why are the packets going to cross the RRAS interface? By definition, QOS ACS/RRAS is already and undeniably in the path between end nodes, allowing it to concentrate on the job of reserving bandwidth and administering policy.

Reserving Bandwidth and Administering Policy

With the functionality explanations out of the way, discussion of just what QOS ACS does can finally be tackled. As the *admission control* part of Admission Control Service suggests, QOS ACS manages the admission of RSVP QOS reservation on LAN segments and RRAS routers. This admission management performs two functional checks to determine whether a reservation is granted: a policy check and a resource (bandwidth) availability check. The process that the QOS ACS goes through is the same for either a QOS ACS/SBM or a QOS ACS/RRAS.

QOS ACS makes its admission requests in the following order: policy check first, and then bandwidth availability check. In the spirit of providing a good reading flow, though, the reservation of bandwidth is addressed first (the policy check logically takes us to the next QOS component discussion). However, keep in mind that the failure of either check results in the failure of the QOS reservation request, so the order in which the admission control activities is done isn't functionally necessary...just comprehensively pertinent.

Reserving Bandwidth

The comparison of a given QOS reservation request and the LAN segment resources available for reservations implies that the QOS ACS somehow knows how much bandwidth is available for reservations. The QOS ACS knows the amount of bandwidth available for reservation by configuration. Any given QOS ACS is configured from the QOS ACS MMC administrative snap-in, and part of that configuration includes creating reservation policies that, by their collective definitions, constitute the amount of bandwidth available to a given QOS reservation.

For example, a QOS ACS may have 1.8Mbps reserved for sending Guaranteed Service reservations, with a maximum peak data rate of 500kbps for any given reservation and a maximum of 100 flows. That same QOS ACS may also have a reservation policy that makes 2.5Mbps available for receiving applications requesting Controlled Load reservations, with a maximum data rate of 100kbps. In addition, it may also have a bandwidth policy for JoeCEO that enables a reservation of 1.0Mpbs with a peak data rate of 1.0Mpbs. These collective reservation policies constitute the overall reservation parameters for the configured QOS ACS. There may be default configurations for all QOS ACSs in the enterprise, which provide default configuration information, from which individual QOS ACSs can base and customize their reservation policies to accommodate local LAN segment needs. There are a number of other configuration parameters that are available to QOS ACSs, all of which are discussed in detail in Chapter 10, "QOS for the Integrator and Administrator."

Remember, though, that these reservations are logically enforced, not physically enforced, requiring applications and end nodes that request such reservations to honor the reservation guidelines. However, because Windows 2000 QOS components in the Windows 2000 clients such as Traffic Control interoperate with RSVP, such guidelines are (once the reservation is in place) enforced locally—within the Windows 2000 client.

Therefore, when an RSVP-enabled QOS reservation request is passed to the QOS ACS/SBM, one of the checks that QOS ACS/SBM does to determine whether the reservation should be admitted is to see available resources. Because the policy that has been configured for the given QOS ACS/SBM defines available bandwidth and because QOS ACS/SBM maintains state for each QOS reservation that it admits, QOS ACS/SBM has the capability to determine how much reservable LAN segment bandwidth is available for the type of QOS reservation being requested. If there aren't enough resources available, the reservation request fails.

An important point to remember about QOS ACS/SBM is that it does not have knowledge about how resources within a switch are used or allocated. Even if a given switch has the capability to provide line-level bandwidth to *each* attached link (for example, 100Mbps to each line in a 100Mbps switch, not 100Mbps shared between all of them), QOS ACS still subtracts a reservation of resources from a single total (a shared total, so to speak). It essentially presumes that the bandwidth is shared between all switches. This assumption is necessary because QOS ACS doesn't know the internal bandwidth capabilities of a given switch. This is an argument for putting QOS ACS on a given switch; if QOS ACS were implemented on a switch, QOS ACS *could* manage each link more appropriately, therefore being more accurate (and more efficient or effective).

Administering Policy

In order to determine whether the user or application has appropriate permission to reserve bandwidth with a given RSVP-based QOS request, the QOS ACS must have some means of identifying the user and/or the application requesting the reservation. The requirement that the QOS ACS be able to determine the user making the request is fairly straightforward; usage policies have long since been basing admission to resources based on a given user's identity or group membership. This same principle can be extended to applications.

There are all sorts of applications that use network resources, such as Quake III and SAP, just as there are all sorts of users who make use of network resources. To be blunt, some applications are more important or more mission-critical to the ongoing functions of a business than others, just as some users are more business-important or more mission-critical. Often, users with such mission-critical importance have preferential access to resources (such as salary and parking places); in a differentiated-service-quality network environment, mission-critical applications should also have preferential access to such resources. After all, without the ongoing functionality of such mission-critical applications, the business can suffer. For this reason, the capability to provide preferential treatment on a managed segment for certain applications makes sense. That's why the capability for QOS ACS to base policy decisions on user identity and/or application is important.

The QOS ACS solution to administering policy is implemented in a modular fashion. Strictly speaking, the QOS ACS doesn't actually interpret user identities or application identities included in the RSVP QOS reservation request. Such user or application identification, and any subsequent decision-making on whether the reservation should be admitted (based on the policy check) is done by the Local Policy Module, or LPM.

In a broad sense, the LPM can be considered part of QOS ACS, but this discussion isn't geared toward the broad sense; it's geared toward details, and these details shouldn't be overlooked. When QOS ACS receives an RSVP message that includes a reservation request, it parses the RSVP message and forwards the request (in a specific internal format) to the appropriate LPM for policy check. If any report of failure is returned by the LPM, the reservation request fails.

QOS ACS and Security

In order to avoid the theft of QOS or denial-of-service attacks (reserving QOS-enabled bandwidth for the express intent of denying such service to others), reservation requests must implement some form of security. The Windows 2000 QOS ACS security model is a reflection of and is married to the implementation of the pervasive security found in Windows 2000.

Security is a big subject. There could be tomes and volumes of even only reference material dedicated to the subject, so any section in a given chapter that attempts to provide a full account of such measures is doomed to fall short. Therefore, I'll provide information on what QOS ACS uses to implement security, and leave the dedicated tomes and reference volumes to do the rest.

Windows 2000 QOS ACS servers utilize the Kerberos approach to securing and identifying the authenticity of users and QOS requests. The approach uses the concept of public key/private key technology, along with digital signatures, to assure that the users who make the request are who they say they are. This approach effectively thwarts nefarious attempts by users to "listen to the wire" and steal a ticket or key, and thereby attempt to steal QOS service or generate denial-of-service attacks. Note that Kerberos only authenticates users; it does not provide secure application identity. You should at least partly trust the user identity before trusting the application's identity.

Local Policy Module

Local Policy Module (LPM) is a generic term used to refer to a piece of software, usually implemented in the form of a .dll, that provides policy-based decision-making for QOS ACS servers. LPMs generally provide such policy decisions by accessing the information contained in some (perhaps centralized) policy store and comparing user/application or other identity and the reservation information provided in the request. They then make appropriate decisions and pass them back toward the QOS ACS.

Multiple LPMs can reside on a single QOS ACS server at any given time. In order to manage the presence of multiple LPMs, and furthermore to manage the fact that multiple responses for a single reservation request may be returned (due to multiple LPMs or multiple policy data being involved), another component is responsible for managing the interaction between the QOS ACS and its potentially multiple resident LPMs. The component responsible for handling the interaction between QOS ACS and its LPMs is called the *Policy Control Module (PCM)*. The PCM's primary responsibility is to send policy information to each LPM installed on the QOS ACS server, to gather the responses provided from each LPM, and then to aggregate the responses and hand the single response back to QOS ACS.

By implementing policy enforcement as a modular component that interacts with QOS ACS, Windows 2000 makes the creation and implementation of additional LPMs possible—even easy.

The LPM that ships with Windows 2000 creates a decision-making link between QOS ACS and the policy information stored in the Windows 2000 Active Directory. The LPM retrieves and returns policy information from the Active Directory. Based on that policy information and resource policy information configured for the QOS ACS administering the reservation request, it makes policy-based admission control decisions and returns such decisions to the PCM. The PCM, in turn, passes an aggregated decision back to QOS ACS. By using the Active Directory, user, group, or application information can be stored on an enterprise-wide basis, and the policies enforced on QOS ACS servers throughout the enterprise can be set as defaults or locally customized.

The LPM included in Windows 2000 is implemented through a DLL called msidpe.dll.

As previously mentioned, QOS ACS sends the policy information that is provided in the RSVP reservation request message (in the form of one or more RSVP POLICY_DATA objects) on to PCM. It then passes that information on to each LPM installed on the QOS ACS server for policy-based decision making. Just as there may be more than one LPM installed on a given QOS ACS server, any given RSVP reservation request message may—and quite likely does—contain more than one policy object. For example, the RSVP message may contain user information in one of its policy objects, and then may contain application information in another policy object. Because of the structure of RSVP messages, multiple RSVP objects, including policy objects, may be carried in a single RSVP message.

The carrying of multiple policy information enables any given LPM to consider multiple policy information when determining whether a given reservation should be admitted. For example, user MackDaddy might not have appropriate permissions, based on his user identity, to reserve Guaranteed Service for a QOS reservation traversing a given LAN segment. However, the application that he is using may be a mission-critical database lookup program, which *does* have overriding permission to make Guaranteed Service reservations. Because the RSVP message carried information about both the user and the application (in multiple policy data objects), and because the LPM could process these requests individually (and hand them back to the PCM for aggregation before handing the verdict back to QOS ACS), the mission-critical reservation succeeds based on the importance of the application, not the importance of the user.

In order for the LPM to be able to interpret the data contained in the policy objects being provided by RSVP messages, however, there must be an understood format for passing such data. More precisely, the format in which policy information is expressed must be synchronized between the creator of such information (the PE) and the reader of such information (the LPM). This requires that the LPM and PE work together to enable policy-based admission control. In other words, it's a functional pair; if you have one without the other, your policy-based admission control won't work. Fortunately, the LPM and PE that ship with Windows 2000 work together nicely, and they both work in conjunction with policy information stored in the Active Directory.

At the time of this writing, third-party development efforts outside of Microsoft are already underway to take advantage of the extensibility of LPM...and big companies are getting behind it. Intel is working on an LPM that interferes with its COPS policy servers (servers that implement the IETF Common Open Policy Service recommendation), for use with Windows 2000 QOS. For more information, check www.ietf.org/html.charters/rapcharter.html.

LPM API

The modular approach of the LPM enables software developers or security organizations that want to develop customized policy-enforcement modules to do so, and simply replace the LPM (and the corresponding Policy Element on any clients wishing to make use of the customized LPM) and, thereby, implement the new policy-enforcement module.

As mentioned previously, LPMs communicate with QOS ACS through a go-between called the Policy Control Module (PCM). The PCM takes the multiple responses that LPMs can generate from various policy objects passed to them for a given (single) reservation request, and aggregates the information so that QOS ACS can get a "yes or no" answer. Because LPMs must communicate through the PCM in order to provide their policy-based decision making, the interface between LPMs and Windows 2000 QOS must be defined; that is exactly what the LPM API does.

The LPM API provides the following seven functions for interfacing with the PCM:

- LPM_Initialize
- LPM_Deinitialize
- LPM_AdmitRsvpMessage
- LPM_GetPolicyData
- LPM_CommitResv
- LPM_DeleteState
- Lpm_IpAddressTable

The LPM API also defines the following callback functions:

- cbpAdmitRsvpMsg
- cbpGetPolicyData

To round things out, the LPM API also implements the following three structures:

- LPMIPTABLE
- PALLOCMEM
- PFREEMEM

The details of these programmatic interfaces are available through Microsoft's subscription service, MSDN.

Because the reasoning behind creating a customized LPM might not be too clear, consider this example. If the WeAreCrypto company wants to create an LPM that enforces its high-security measures for the LAN segment, it can develop an LPM and a PE. It can put the LPM on any involved QOS ACS servers, put the PE on all Windows 2000 clients, and the new policy mechanism will be in place.

Why is such a theoretical replacement (or supplement) to the LPM so easy? Because of its modularity: If the LPM were intricately included in QOS ACS, the WeAreCrypto company would have to develop an entirely new admission control package to replace QOS ACS, an undertaking that would likely be effort-prohibitive. With the modularity of the LPM and its corresponding PE, dropping in new policy-enforcement LPM/PE pairs is much easier.

Why might this be necessary? Perhaps the WeAreCrypto company wants identity information to be more stringently protected, and therefore introduces some cryptography scheme that puts its user-identity information in a format that is scrambled by the PE and can only be unscrambled by their corresponding LPM. There are all sorts of reasons, each of which is probably very important to the company or organization that wants to implement it.

Policy Element

The PE is the client-side half of the LPM-PE functional pair. The PE provided in Windows 2000 clients places identity information into RSVP policy objects, which are then placed in RSVP reservation requests that are forwarded to QOS ACS servers. After QOS ACS intercepts the RSVP reservation request, it parses the RSVP message and forwards the PE-generated policy data to the PCM, which then manages the submission of the policy data to each LPM installed on the given QOS ACS. The LPM that corresponds to the PE that generated the policy data is able to interpret the included policy information because the policy information is in a format that the LPM/PE pair specifically understands.

The LPM that functions with the PE provided in Windows 2000 clients then compares the provided policy data with information provided in the Windows 2000 Active Directory, and returns the appropriate policy decision to the PCM. It then aggregates the (potentially) multiple responses from each LPM, as well as the (potentially multiple) policy information from multiple LPMs. Once aggregated, the PCM hands the decision back to QOS ACS.

The PE represents a modular component that can be replaced or supplemented on Windows 2000 components. Microsoft plans to provide the API that will enable the development of additional PEs. At the time of this writing, the API hasn't been released. Because the PE and LPM are a functional pair, the creation of additional or replacement policy-information generating (PE) and policy-decision making (LPM) pairs will have to wait until the PE API is made available.

RSVP

If you read the other sections in this chapter, it's probably evident that RSVP plays a central role in the Windows 2000 implementation of policy-driven QOS. Because its place in the ferrying of policy objects, reservation requests, QOS reservation parameters, and the enabling of QOS ACS functionality have already been discussed throughout this chapter, I won't rehash its importance here.

To help complete the discussion of how RSVP messages can effectively communicate and articulate QOS requests and QOS flow maintenance, it's useful to have a list of the message types and the objects that those messages may (or must) carry. The reason for introducing this list toward the end of the detailed discussion of QOS components is one of pain management. Rather than having this information at the beginning and being distracted with the way each message carried corresponding data to the various component in the Windows 2000 QOS picture, it seemed a better approach to first explain the components, and then provide detailed RSVP messages to chew on.

RSVP messages carry their information in what are called *RSVP objects*. The following is a list of RSVP message types and RSVP objects that an RSVP implementation must recognize. Between the message types and their available RSVP objects, these collections enable RSVP to communicate information. Note that additional object types might be available for specific RSVP-enabled technologies, such as is the case with SBM.

RSVP Message Types

The following is a quick list of the seven different RSVP message types defined in the RSVP specification (RFC 2205). Each of these messages can (or must, in some cases) carry particular RSVP objects:

- PATH
- RESV
- PathErr
- ResvErr
- PathTear
- ResvTear
- ResvConf

Each RSVP message must also contain what's called the *Common Header*. The Common Header includes in its specified format the protocol number, flags, the message type (), a checksum, the TTL, and the length of the entire message (including the header and all objects).

RSVP Objects

The following list provides the RSVP objects defined in the RSVP specification, and quick explanations of each of their functions:

ADSPEC: Used to carry "One Path With Advertising" (OPWA) information in PATH messages. This information can be used by the receiver to determine certain transmission-quality information. RSVP-enabled nodes in the path (should) update information in this RSVP object when it passes through the node.

ERROR_SPEC: Used to specify errors in ResvErr, PathErr, or a confirmation in ResvConf messages.

FLOWSPEC: Defines QOS parameters.

FILTER_SPEC: Defines the attributes used to uniquely identify packets that should be identified with the flow being requested.

INTEGRITY: Carries cryptographic data that's used to authenticate that the sending node is who it says it is.

NULL: Used to include four bits of nothing, which is good for rounding out messages. Ignored by RSVP-enabled devices.

POLICY_DATA: This has been the object of our discussion for much of this chapter. It carries the information that enables the LPM to determine whether a given reservation request should be admitted. This object can appear in PATH, RESV, PathErr, or ResvErr messages.

RESV_CONFIRM: Carries the IP address of a receiver requesting reservation confirmation. The RESV_CONFIRM object can appear in RESV or ResvConf messages.

RSVP_HOP: Used to manage next- and previous-hop information.

SCOPE: Used to create a list of specific network nodes that are involved in the end-to-end connection. The SCOPE object can appear in RESV, ResvErr, or ResvTear messages.

Session: Provides unique identifier of the session with which the message is associated. Every RSVP message must have a session object.

SENDER_TEMPLATE: Contains the sender IP address and other optional information.

SENDER_TSPEC: Defines the traffic characteristics associated with a sender's flow. Every PATH message must have a SENDER_TSPEC object.

STYLE: Provides the reservation style, and includes style-specific information not included in FLOWSPEC or FILTER_SPEC objects. Every RESV message must have a session object.

TIME_VALUES: Contains refresh period information used by the message's creator. Every PATH and RESV message must have a TIME_VALUES object.

For a more in-depth and complete treatment of these messages and RSVP in general, check out RFC 2205 on the IETF's Web page, www.ietf.org.

8

Uniting Application-, Network- and Policy-Driven QOS

It's one thing to have detailed information about all the individual Windows 2000 QOS components, but in order to understand how Windows 2000 QOS intends to make networks function more efficiently, it's necessary to show you how these components work together. This chapter does just that.

Because most networks don't deploy new technologies immediately, in every corner of the network, and at the same time, knowing what happens when certain components may not be working (or aren't QOS-enabled) is equally important. This chapter covers that issue as well, at every step of the networking way.

Removing Application, Network and Policy Boundaries

Because QOS is an end-to-end solution, the grand scheme of QOS functionality in a network has no boundaries. Although it may serve a good and necessary purpose to divide the discussion into logical groups (such as application, network, and policy) when QOS goes from end-to-end, these logical groups behave as one unit. This is evident when you take a few steps back from the desk, launch a QOS-enabled audio/video demonstration, and watch it work its magic. The solution occurs as one seamless event, not as three different QOS areas trying to work together. In other words, when put to practical use, QOS has no boundaries.

To best explain how this unified end-to-end cooperation functions, it's best to go through the connection process, the reservation process, and the actual transmission of QOS-enabled data, just as such things would happen in a given QOS-enabled connection. This approach helps dust out fuzzy corners of a full understanding of QOS, and should clean up any remaining functional questions of the Windows 2000 QOS solution.

Initiating and Establishing the QOS-Enabled Connection

The initiation of a QOS-enabled connection can be the cause of a lot of uncertainty for someone trying to understand how QOS actually works. Although part of that confusion may stem from the flexibility that is built into QOS, the process must be explained thoroughly for a discussion of QOS to be complete. Certainly, there is a programmatic foundation to the initiation of QOS connections, but understanding how QOS provisioning is initiated (and thereafter established) is a requirement for understanding the overall QOS picture.

QOS-enabled reservations can be compared to transaction-based operations. By that, I mean that there are events that must occur, as pieces of the overall "QOS-enabling" sequence of events, in order for QOS provisioning to occur. The easiest transaction-based event example is that of a funds transfer between bank accounts (transferring "from" one account "to" another). The process includes a withdrawal from one account (the "from" account), with the corresponding reduction in its balance; and a deposit into another account (the "to" account), with the corresponding increase in its balance. The transaction must occur as a whole or not at all; you can't withdraw from one account (the "from" account) and reduce that account's balance, and then not increase the value of the account into which that transfer is going (the "to" account). It must occur as one complete event or not at all.

QOS reservations are similar to the transaction model because there must be a socket opened between receiver and sender, the sender must transmit PATH message(s), and the receiver must respond with RESV message(s) before QOS provisioning is set up for a given flow. Another way of looking at these requirements is this: Both sender and receiver must invoke QOS on their respective ends to enable provisioning for any given flow; senders transmit a PATH message, and receivers transmit a RESV message once a corresponding PATH message is received.

Each of these events must occur for a given QOS-enabled connection to be valid. However, within the framework of those events, there is flexibility, which contributes to the complexity of QOS. That flexibility includes which end initiates QOS first (sender or receiver—either can), how such initiation is handled in the context of the socket, and what finally constitutes a "completed" QOS-enabled connection. The following paragraphs clarify these points:

- **Sockets:** QOS can be enabled on an existing socket, or it can be requested at the same time a socket is opened. One socket can support bidirectional data transmission, but QOS provisioning is unidirectional. A unidirectional QOS-enabled transmission provision is considered a *flow*, and a flow has unique QOS characteristics. QOS

provisioning is unidirectional and unique, given its identifying characteristics (based on sender/port, receiver/port, and other information
that is collectively considered a *filter*). Because sockets can be bidirectional, one socket connection can have independent QOS-provisioning
for each transmission direction. For example, a unicast bidirectional
socket can have certain QOS provisioning specified for one direction
and different specified QOS provisioning in the other direction.
Multicast sockets (also referred to as a *session*) may have more QOS
specifications associated or aggregated at certain multicast points yet,
which means that a given socket may have many different QOS specifications (filters) associated with it. More information about multicast is
provided toward the end of this chapter.

- **Initiation:** Either the sender or the receiver may initiate QOS provisioning. If the receiver requests the QOS provisioning, the sender may
respond with a PATH message if it is QOS-enabled. If the sender initiates
QOS-enabling, it does so by sending out PATH messages (it doesn't have
to wait for the receiver to request QOS provisioning). Note that it is
the application's responsibility to request QOS provisioning; RSVP is
not automatically initiated for applications.

- **Connection Establishment:** Regardless of whether the sender or
receiver initiates QOS-enabling on the socket, there must be a RESV that
is specifically associated with the corresponding PATH message in order
for the QOS provisioning to occur. Whether sender or receiver initiates
the QOS-enabled connection, local state is established on either end
node to await the arrival of the message that indicates QOS connection
establishment. On receivers, the system establishes local RESV state and
waits for an incoming PATH message that matches the RESV state. On
senders, the system establishes local PATH state and starts sending out
PATH messages, waiting for the arrival of the corresponding RESV message to establish the QOS-enabled connection.

Until the QOS-enabled connection is established, end-to-end QOS provisioning is in place. However, note that senders can begin transmitting data
right away, regardless of whether the QOS-enabled connection has been
established. Such transmissions are provided with best-effort service until
the RESV message is received by the sender (and therewith, the QOS-enabled
connection is established).

It's important to realize that all RSVP-enabled network nodes in the path
between end nodes intercept these PATH and RESV messages, and that the
passing through of these messages sets up flow state for each flow. Therefore,
the setting up of a QOS-enabled connection also primes all RSVP-enabled network nodes in the transmission path between end nodes for the impending
transmission of the associated QOS-enabled data between these end nodes.

You'll often hear that QOS connections and the establishment of QOS provisioning is *receiver-centric*. This perspective is due largely to the fact that the receiver is the decision maker in regard to the level of QOS (the QOS provisioning) that it requires for a given flow. This is a twist on the perspective provided in RSVP signaling, in which QOS is sometimes considered to be *sender-centric* because the sender begins the RSVP process of provisioning QOS between end points with the transmission of a PATH message. It is the receiver, however, which ultimately decides on the transmission characteristics of the flow. Again, this is a matter of perspective; the technical details remain unchanged.

In essence, the PATH is extending an RSVP offer, whereas the RESV is taking the sender up on the RSVP offer, often based on how much data it can (or needs to) process. To do a little personification, the sender sends out a PATH message that states "I can do this level/specific type of QOS provisioning." The receiver is the decision maker and it says: "Hmm, based on that PATH statement, I want this level of service." Of course, the receiver can't request "better" or "more" service than what the sender is offering because the sender can't or won't support "better" or "more" service. But the receiver may choose to request less resource-intensive (or lower "quality") service than what the sender is offering, for whatever reasons the receiver may have (perhaps it doesn't want to pay for the sender's offering of 1.5Mbps transmission rate because it only needs 200kbps). The receiver then sends back a RESV message, which states: "I'll take this level/specific type of QOS provisioning, based on your PATH statement offer."

Non-QOS Applications

It is presumed that QOS-enabled applications handle the initiation of QOS provisioning through the use of QOS-enabled Windows Sockets calls. However, because the implementation of full-featured QOS capability is new to Windows 2000, there are a number of applications out there that are not inherently QOS-aware.

For these applications, there is a component available in Windows 98 (but alas, not in Windows 2000) called *TPQOS (Third-Party QOS)* that invokes QOS provisioning for non-QOS-aware applications, per the individual client's configuration.

Enforcing QOS in the Client

First and foremost, RSVP signaling in Windows 2000 carries user and/or application identity with it when PATH or RESV messages traverse the network path between end nodes. At every hop, LAN segment, or network device along the way, the enforcement of admission policies can be implemented, which means than any given hop, LAN segment, or network device can reject a connection request and stop the reservation request in its tracks. Therefore, RSVP signaling is an important part of the enforcement of QOS in the client. The presumption throughout much of the rest of this discussion is that the RSVP signaling between end nodes successfully established a QOS-enabled connection, leaving the following discussion's focus on how the parameters of that reservation are enforced as data gets transmitted between end nodes.

The sender is presumably going to begin transmitting QOS-enabled data once the QOS-enabled connection is established. Within the Windows 2000 client itself, classification, shaping, and policing is done to its own transmissions to ensure that the application conforms to the provisions set forth in the QOS reservation.

Because a flow's packets are sent down through the network stack from the application, its packets are classified by the Generic Packet Classifier (GPC) to associate them with a given flow. As that packet continues down the stack toward the network transmission point (the wire), a few things happen:

1. Packets are tagged with their DiffServ Codepoint (DSCP): The TCP/IP part of the network stack tags packets with their appropriate DSCP, enabling the proper routing of the packet through DSCP-aware network regions. The TCP/IP stack knows how to tag packets with the appropriate DSCP because the packet has been classified by the GPC.

2. Packets are policed by the Conformer: Packets are checked to ensure that they adhere to QOS parameters, such as `TokenRate`, `PeakBandwidth`, and `TokenBucketRate`. The Scheduler (through its subcomponent, called the *Conformer*) ensures that the packets being sent through the client (down the stack) for transmission adhere to their QOS flow parameters. If any given packet does not conform, the Conformer may either demote the packet or completely discard the packet, depending on the shape/discard mode applied to the QOS connection. Demotion may be to best-effort, or even to less-than best-effort, for the nonconforming packet.

3. Packets are shaped. Packets that get past the Conformer, which can be conforming packets or nonconforming packets that were demoted, are shaped by the *Packet Shaper* (another Scheduler subcomponent). The Packet Shaper smoothes out bursty data transmissions by spreading their transmissions out onto the wire. Note that packet shaping must be requested by the application in the course of establishing QOS provisioning.

4. Packets are sequenced. While the Packet Shaper smoothes out bursty transmissions, the *Sequencer* manages the transmission of packets onto the network. This ensures that the packets' transmission is within required delay variation or latency transmission guidelines, which avoids clumped packet transmissions that otherwise might clog the wire without sacrificing (or undermining) transmission requirements.

Note

One point worth directing attention to is the timing of certain QOS enforcement within the client. As soon as an application requests QOS provisioning, the associated classification, shaping, and policing is begun within the client. DSCP and 802.1p tagging, on the other hand, is only done once the reservation request is granted. In this respect, clients are well-behaved even before a reservation is granted (because their data is being shaped and policed), furthering the goal of making better use of the network. The previous numbered list, as mentioned in that list's introduction, presumes that the QOS-enabled reservation is already established. Classification, shaping, and policing occurs as soon as the application requests QOS provisioning, and therefore is being done before the reservation is established. ✦

Client QOS without RSVP

If there is no RSVP connection made, as would be the case if the receiver were not RSVP-aware, there is still QOS provisioning that can occur. Because Windows 2000 exposes traffic control capabilities through the Traffic Control API (TC API), a certain degree of in-client QOS can be achieved without RSVP.

Because the submission of packets that go through classification, shaping, and sequencing (and perhaps even the setting of their 802.1p value or their DSCP) can contribute to better quality of service across the LAN segment or DSCP-enabled network nodes, certain elements of QOS can be achieved. In such cases, the QOS elements that can be enabled help with the transmission service quality, but the end-to-end quality is not as pervasive or complete as when RSVP signaling is involved.

Non-QOS Clients

Because Windows 2000 QOS is quite dependent on RSVP for its end-to-end solution, clients that are not QOS-enabled (all Windows 2000 products are QOS-enabled) have a hard time participating unless the TC API is used directly. Windows 98 supports RSVP, but is not capable of traffic control.

Admission Control on the LAN Segment

Because the QOS Admission Control Service (ACS) inserts itself in any RSVP PATH or RESV message traversing its managed segment, it catches reservation requests initiated by Windows 2000 clients (or other RSVP-enabled end nodes). The LPM (Local Policy Module) component of the QOS ACS checks user identity against its Windows 2000 Active Directory policy store (some of which may be cached locally for performance's sake) and hands an admission decision back to QOS ACS. If the request should be admitted according to the LPM, QOS ACS submits the reservation request (PATH or RESV message) to the next hop.

If the reservation request is not permitted, QOS ACS returns an error to the sender of the RSVP message with an error code that indicates the reason for rejection (it can be policy-based rejection, bandwidth-based rejection, or something else).

If QOS ACS rejects the reservation, remember that the receiver can still receive the data by using best-effort.

Non-QOS Clients

Because QOS ACS uses RSVP signaling to enforce its admission control, clients that are not RSVP-enabled are unable to take advantage of its LAN segment management and admission control capabilities.

Non-QOS Traffic on the LAN Segment

Remember that QOS ACS is only logically managing the segment, and that it isn't managing best-effort traffic. That means that although you may have reserved 2Mbps of your Ethernet LAN segment for non-best-effort traffic, if best-effort traffic is flooding your LAN segment, there's really nothing you can do to stop it. Your logically reserved 2Mbps of bandwidth will be relegated to enduring the same congestion-induced transmission quality degradation that all other (best-effort) traffic on the LAN segment is suffering. That is, unless your LAN segment has an 802.1p-aware switch, described in the next section.

QOS ACS/SBM and 802.1p

If all your LAN segment switches are 802.1p-aware, the need for the admission control capabilities of QOS ACS/SBM is reduced, but not removed.

With 802.1p, there is an overlapping of LAN segment management responsibility. Because 802.1p physically manages bandwidth on a LAN switch, an 802.1p-enabled switch can ensure that best-effort traffic will not interfere with higher-priority traffic. And because Windows 2000 QOS sets 802.1p bits in the stack based on QOS reservation provisioning, which can't happen without a successful QOS-enabled reservation, an 802.1p LAN switch with Windows 2000 does much of the work that QOS ACS/SBM intends to provide on a given LAN segment.

So, why does QOS ACS/SBM exist? Because it will likely be some time before all LAN segments are serviced by switches (802.1p doesn't work on shared segments, as you remember), and it will likely be some time before all switches have 802.1p capabilities. But perhaps more importantly, QOS ACS/SBM manages the amount of high-priority traffic that is admitted onto the LAN segment. Without QOS ACS/SBM, it would be possible to flood an 802.1p switch by tagging all traffic as high priority; QOS ACS/SBM can keep that from happening.

As 802.1p takes hold, and as switch technology replaces shared LAN segment hardware, a couple of things will likely take place. 802.1p functionality will become commonplace, and SBM functionality will be built right into the switch, obsolescing the need for the SBM functionality of QOS ACS/SBM (though perhaps not the overall admission control features of QOS ACS).

Until then, however, QOS ACS/SBM and 802.1p play important roles in end-to-end QOS for Windows 2000.

No QOS ACS/SBM

Without QOS ACS, there is no logical management of a LAN segment or RRAS router interface, and RSVP-enabled connections can reserve as much of the available bandwidth as there is available (or more than that, in fact). This can cause QOS guarantees that should be functioning under certain delivery constraints to report that the reservation is available. However, the delivery characteristics may be much degraded (due to congestion on the LAN segment or RRAS router interface). Because there's no way of determining, based on the LAN segment, how much bandwidth is reserved by RSVP-enabled QOS connections without QOS ACS, it is impossible to determine whether the service quality being reserved is anywhere near what should be available to the LAN segment or router interface. It's also impossible to determine whether too many RSVP-enabled connections are using more than their fair share of the available bandwidth and perhaps starving (because of upstream RSVP-enabled and enforceable network-node hops) best-effort traffic.

No 802.1p

Without the use of an 802.1p-aware switch, there is no means of regulating best-effort traffic on a LAN segment. Although QOS ACS will logically regulate RSVP-enabled traffic, there is no physical guarantee that any prioritized data transmissions will receive better service than best-effort transmissions receive. Furthermore, there is no way to differentiate between higher-priority QOS-enabled traffic and lower-priority QOS-enabled traffic. For example, a Controlled Load QOS reservation that simply wants to reserve 50kbps on an ongoing basis (perhaps with an 802.1p-equivalent priority value of 2) has the same chance of transmitting its data in a timely manner as a 500kbps mission-critical application (with perhaps an 802.1p-equivalent priority value of 6) .

Enforcing QOS across the Network

As mentioned earlier, as PATH and subsequent RESV messages are transmitted between end nodes establishing a QOS-enabled connection, RSVP-aware network nodes set up state for these connections in anticipation of data corresponding to the established flow. This state can include policy control of data associated with a given flow, enabling an RSVP-aware node to become a policing point for QOS-enabled data traversing the network. In this RSVP-enabled situation, Windows 2000 end nodes' data transmissions interact with RSVP-aware network nodes through RSVP signaling, creating a tightly knit communication and network-transmission enforcement medium. This tightly knit medium, of course, has one major drawback: overhead. The DSCP approach to regulating (and QOS-enabling) the transmission of QOS-enabled data has much less overhead. Note, however, that if a network node has both RSVP and DSCP capabilities enabled, RSVP will take precedence.

With Windows 2000 QOS-enabled connections, then, as the packets cross through the LAN segment or segments cross onto the "core network" with either their DSCP value, RSVP value, or both, the network nodes through which they pass undergo the following handling mechanisms:

- **RSVP-enabled network nodes:** By virtue of the RSVP standard, RSVP-enabled nodes keep state information about each active flow passing through it. Therefore, packets that are associated with an established flow are provided transmission treatment according to the RSVP connection established and maintained in the node.

- **DSCP-aware network nodes:** Because DSCP functions on an aggregated queuing logic rather than a per-flow state, packets are put *in order* into the queue that corresponds with their marked DSCP, and are then transmitted through the node according to the DSCP's prescribed per-hop behavior. The importance of the packets being in order is that DSCP requires that there be no reordering of packets (packet #3 of a given flow must be transmitted after packet #2, even though DSCP doesn't keep flow state) for a given transmission. Although some queues are serviced with more priority than others (and, therefore, perhaps a given queue has a disproportionate amount of packet transmissions compared to another queue), no reordering of packets within a given flow occurs. This is because all packets of a given flow are transmitted with the same DSCP value, and packets within a given queue are transmitted in order.

When packets pass through WAN links, if the WAN link is connected to an RSVP-aware or DSCP-aware router, then the WAN link will likely have a VC (or create a VC) that corresponds to the service level indicated by the flow/DSCP value. Any disassembly/reassembly of the packet is managed as part of the QOS-enabled VC, and such chopping up and reassembling of the packet should fall within the transmission constraints of the service quality guarantee.

DSCP versus RSVP

RSVP doesn't scale well; DSCP does. Although RSVP plays an important part in provisioning and communicating an end-to-end QOS reservation, its per-flow queue isolation overhead doesn't bode well for implementation in backbone network nodes. DSCP does scale well, so there will likely be a combination of the two, with DSCP in the core network and RSVP in smaller networks and in the end nodes.

Note

Note that RSVP messages do not affect scalability when they pass through network nodes that do not have RSVP capabilities. In other words, a Windows 2000 client's use of RSVP signaling to establish end-to-end QOS provisioning won't penalize the scalability of a non-RSVP network node infrastructure. Those RSVP messages pass through non-RSVP network nodes without RSVP processing, so they don't introduce any more overhead on such network nodes than a standard data packet. ◆

Non-RSVP Network Nodes

When RSVP-enabled packets pass through a non-RSVP network node, the use of the Time To Live (TTL) field and its comparison to fields within the RSVP message (which gets transmitted transparently through non-RSVP nodes) indicates that a non-RSVP network node is in the path between end nodes. Presumably, all network traffic passing through non-RSVP network nodes is given best-effort traffic, so any QOS provisioning guarantees are impossible to predict, let alone guarantee. However, with the use of the RSVP object Adspec, some information about the likely transmission quality from end-to-end can be discovered. Regardless, non-RSVP network nodes essentially break the end-to-end QOS service chain, and can't be trusted to provide any quantitative (or even qualitative) service packets quality.

Non-DSCP Network Nodes

When DSCP-enabled packets packets pass through non-DSCP network nodes, the same premise that applies to non-RSVP network-node transmission quality applies.

Multicast QOS

Multicast is a complex and inherently difficult subject for implementation or explanation, but its basis is the following:

> *Don't transmit duplicate packets if you don't have to.*

To extend this premise to QOS, we can add the following:

> *Preserve network resources by aggregating service quality at every opportunity.*

Of course, this QOS addition requires further explanation, but first, an explanation of multicast is in order.

The premise of multicast is similar to that of broadcast. With multicast, however, the receivers of the data are specified. To preserve bandwidth, a given multicast can transmit only one packet down a network path toward a group of receivers, until that path diverges. At that point, the packet must be copied and sent down each path on which its receivers reside. This creates a tree, with the branches continuing to diverge until the end nodes are reached. In the tree analogy, these end nodes are like leaves. Figure 8.1 illustrates the concept.

When we start the transmission path from the end node (the leaves), the explanation of multicast becomes a bit easier. Each leaf may have a different QOS transmission requirement. For the sake of simplicity, let's say that these QOS requirements are identified as levels 1 through 10, with level 10 being extremely high (resource-intensive) QOS requirements. As Leaf A sends its transmission requirement for a given multicast session up its branch (it requires level 3), it eventually merges with another leaf's branch—we'll call this Leaf B, which requires level 5 service. Because Leaf B requires higher service than Leaf A, the node at the merge-point between Leaf A and Leaf B's branches (a router) only forwards Leaf B's request. Because it remembers Leaf A's requirements, when it receives a multicast packet for the given session, it can copy it and transmit it to Leaf A under the QOS constraints (level 3 service) required by Leaf A. This process of service level aggregation continues up the branches until only one path from the sender remains. At that point, the service level requested is good enough to service all leaf nodes scattered out among the multiplied merged branches.

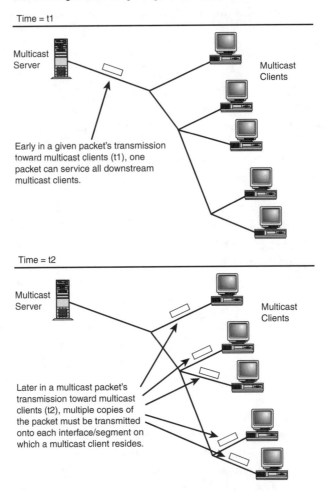

Multicast packet must be copied onto each interface whenever multicast clients no longer reside along a single downstream path.

Time = t1

Multicast Server

Multicast Clients

Early in a given packet's transmission toward multicast clients (t1), one packet can service all downstream multicast clients.

Time = t2

Multicast Server

Multicast Clients

Later in a multicast packet's transmission toward multicast clients (t2), multiple copies of the packet must be transmitted onto each interface/segment on which a multicast client resides.

Figure 8.1 *The multicast structure.*

This process of aggregating QOS requests to provide only the level of QOS provisioning required to meet the necessary QOS constraints is called *Lowest Upper Bound*, or *LUB*. At each step along the way, permission-checking (such as that done by RSVP signaling) is done for each leaf's QOS request, and the rules that apply to a standard end-node-to-end-node, QOS-enabled connection (that is, a point-to-point or unicast connection) still apply. This aggregation of requests includes the aggregation of policy—routers merge multicast requests and, therefore, the RESV message grows. To abate this expansion of the multicast RESV message, QOS ACS replaces individual identities (on which policy decisions are based) with a group identity. Logically, this replacement of individual identities with group identities for the explicit intent of reducing the size of these (router-merged) multicast RESV messages requires that the QOS ACS reside between the clients and routers—that is, in the LAN segments.

Part III

Quality of Service in the Real World

9 QOS in Windows 2000

10 QOS for the Integrator and Administrator

11 QOS for the Programmer

After the explanations and implementation discussions are complete, the task of actually deploying Quality of Service remains. For anyone in the networking field—whether an administrator, network integrator, applications programmer, or IT manager—the importance and details of deploying a technology is as important as understanding it in the first place. Decisions can be complex, issues diverse, and planning requirements daunting. These decisions, of course, must be made in addition to an already-full schedule of responsibilities.

Part III has been written to address these challenges, and aims to help you—the decision and deployment professional—get guidance and ideas on how to make QOS work for your application, within your departmental network, or across your enterprise.

9

QOS in Windows 2000

After the explanation of the way Quality of Service functions and how the collection of QOS components in Windows 2000 interoperate and enable QOS across the network, the task of explaining how Windows 2000 QOS components are actually installed on Windows 2000 computers remains.

Although the installation of QOS on Windows 2000 is not terribly difficult, it is not automatic, and the process doesn't necessarily jump out at integrators or administrators who must complete such tasks. Understanding where such installations take place, what steps must be taken to ensure that these components get properly installed, and how these processes look is important for providing a complete view of Windows 2000 QOS.

How Is Windows 2000 QOS Installed?

As you know, the Windows 2000 implementation of QOS is centered around reservation requests that are transmitted on behalf of a client (in the form of RSVP messages). It is examined by QOS-enabled nodes across the network (such as 802.1p-aware switches, QOS ACS servers, RSVP- or DSCP-aware routers, and QOS-aware WAN connections). It is then received by the other end of the QOS connection (such as a Windows 2000 server). As this progression of events suggests, there are three primary points at which Windows 2000 is likely to be active in the QOS-provisioning connection:

- In the receiver
- At the QOS ACS
- At the Windows 2000 sender

Of course, the use of client and server in this example is subjective. Any Windows 2000 client can be either sender or receiver, providing that Windows 2000 is running on that end node, and providing that QOS capability has been installed on that Windows 2000 computer.

Therefore, the questions are "How is QOS capability installed in Windows 2000 computers?" and "How does the QOS ACS get installed on a Windows 2000 Server?" These questions are answered independently for the Windows 2000 client and the Windows 2000 QOS ACS Server.

Installing QOS On the Client

There are two primary requirements for QOS to function properly on a Windows 2000 client:

- TCP/IP must be installed and must be functioning properly
- Packet Scheduler must be installed

There are other requirements, such as having a functional network card in the computer, but such common sense requirements are omitted here (as is the requirement that the computer be plugged in and actually turned on). The process of configuring TCP/IP on a client is a staple in the repertoire of administrators. Because it is such a common undertaking in any Windows networking environment (and installed by default on Windows 2000), its process won't be explained here.

However, installation of the Packet Scheduler isn't done as often. As a new feature of Windows 2000 (specific to Windows 2000 QOS), the installation of the Packet Scheduler can be done during the initial installation of Windows 2000 or it can be done after Windows 2000 is installed. The following steps explain the process of installing the Packet Scheduler once Windows 2000 is installed. If you're going through the setup of Windows 2000, you will recognize many of the following figures (they're the same as the screens you see during setup), so you can apply this process of installing the Packet Scheduler after the Windows 2000 installation to your setup process.

In the Control Panel, launch the Network and Dial-Up Connections applet, as shown in Figure 9.1. Note that there are many ways to get to the Network and Dial-Up Connections applet; this is just one of them.

Right-click Local Area Connection, and then select Properties from the pop-up menu, as shown in Figure 9.2.

The Local Area Connection Properties window, shown in Figure 9.3, appears. If you are performing the initial installation of Windows 2000 on a computer, this is the window that displays during the networking setup portion of Windows 2000 setup. You can install the Packet Scheduler during setup with the same steps outlined from this point on.

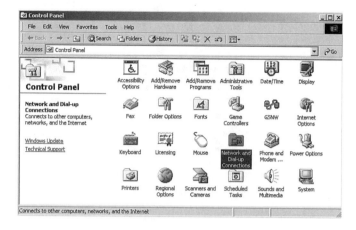

Figure 9.1   *The Network and Dial-Up Connections applet in the Control Panel.*

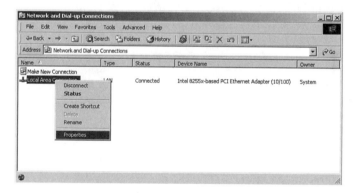

Figure 9.2   *The Network and Dial-Up Connections window.*

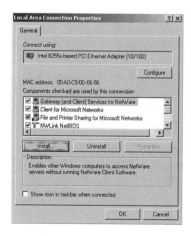

Figure 9.3   *The Local Area Connection Properties window.*

Click the Install button to install a new network component. The Select Network Component Type window appears, as shown in Figure 9.4.

Figure 9.4   *The Select Network Component Type window.*

Choose Service from the choice of network component types, and then click the Add button. The Select Network Service window appears, as shown in Figure 9.5.

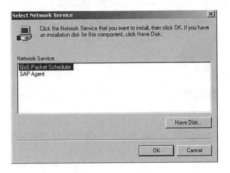

Figure 9.5   *The Select Network Service window.*

Select QoS Packet Scheduler, and then select OK to install the Packet Scheduler. You are returned to the Local Area Connection Properties window. The Packet Scheduler is now displayed in the listing of installed network components, as shown in Figure 9.6.

That's it—the Packet Scheduler is installed on the client. Note that there are hardware requirements that a client must meet (such as an 802.1p-capable NIC) in order to take advantage of all Windows 2000 QOS capabilities. However, with the combination of RSVP signaling capabilities (which are installed with TCP/IP) and the traffic control-enabling Packet Scheduler, the Windows 2000 client is configured to be capable of requesting and maintaining QOS-enabled connections across the Windows network.

Figure 9.6 *The Local Area Connection Properties window, with the QoS Packet Scheduler installed.*

Another important fact to remember is that all current TCP connections are terminated when the Packet Scheduler is installed. Therefore, even though a reboot of the machine is not required when the Packet Scheduler is installed, current TCP connections are terminated, so you should not install the Packet Scheduler if important connections are in progress.

Installing QOS ACS On the Server

The other aspect of Windows 2000 QOS, where its installation (and subsequent configuration) is visible in the operating system, is with QOS ACS. With the Windows 2000 clients' Packet Scheduler installed and the QOS ACS Servers installed in appropriate LAN segments across the network, the Windows 2000 components that QOS-enable your network will be in place. The process of installing the QOS ACS on a Windows 2000 Server is a bit more involved than installing the Packet Scheduler on Windows 2000 clients. As was the case with the installation of the Packet Scheduler, QOS ACS can be installed during the computer's initial installation of Windows 2000 Server, or afterward—once Windows 2000 Server is already installed. This section explains the process of installing QOS ACS after Windows 2000 Server has been installed, but the process is similar during the initial installation of Windows 2000 Server. The following steps outline the process necessary to get the QOS ACS installed on an existing installation of Windows 2000 Server.

The QOS ACS is installed as any other program or Windows component is installed: through the use of the Add/Remove Programs applet in the Control Panel. Launching the Add/Remove Programs applet brings up the Add/Remove Programs window, as shown in Figure 9.7.

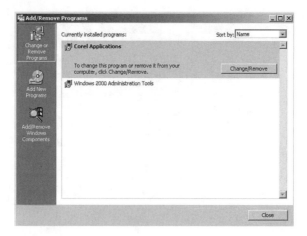

Figure 9.7   *The Add/Remove Programs window.*

The QOS ACS is considered to be a Windows component. Click the Add/Remove Windows Components button in the bottom-left portion of the window, and the window changes to reflect the choice, as shown in Figure 9.8.

Figure 9.8   *The Add/Remove Programs window, when the Add/Remove Windows Components button is selected.*

Notice that the upper portion of the window has also changed, and now displays a section titled Add or remove Windows components, with a corresponding Components button. Click the Components button to begin the process of adding a Windows component (in this case, QOS ACS). Figure 9.9 displays the first screen of the Windows Component Wizard.

Figure 9.9   *The Windows Component Wizard welcome screen.*

Clicking the Next button brings up the screen that enables the installation (or removal) of the various Windows components that are available to a Windows 2000 Server, as shown in Figure 9.10.

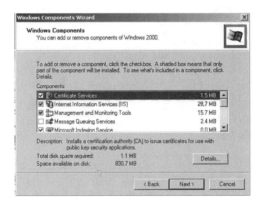

Figure 9.10   *The Windows Components window.*

QOS ACS is considered to be a networking service. Scrolling down through the list of available components brings us to a component called Networking Services, as shown in Figure 9.11.

Clicking the Details button enables you to choose which networking service or services you want to install or remove, as shown in Figure 9.12.

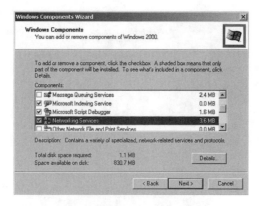

Figure 9.11   *Networking Services in the Windows Components window.*

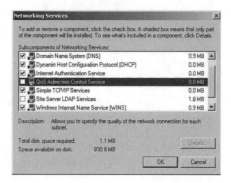

Figure 9.12   *The list of available networking services.*

We're interested in QOS ACS, so the installation of the service is as easy as ensuring that a checkmark is placed next to the service. Once QOS ACS is selected (it has a check in the QOS Admission Control Service box), click OK to continue with the installation. The Windows Components window returns, at which point you click Next to continue with the installation process. When you do so, QOS ACS is installed, and the progress of the installation is displayed in a window, as shown in Figure 9.13. Note that Windows configures all of the selected components, and informs you which component it's working on at any given time. For example, Figure 9.13 shows that Windows is working on the configuration of IIS (which was one of the components that was already selected when QOS ACS was installed).

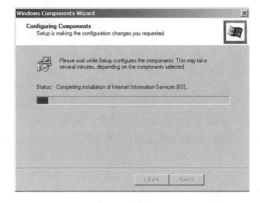

Figure 9.13   *Windows 2000 displays the progress of installing QOS ACS and configuring other Windows components.*

When the configuration of Windows Components is finished, the Windows Component Wizard displays a window that informs you that the configuration has completed, as shown in Figure 9.14. You can click Finish to complete the installation.

Figure 9.14   *Windows lets you know when the configuration of your selected Windows components is complete.*

That's it—QOS ACS is installed.

Summary

With the installation of the Packet Scheduler on Windows 2000 clients, and QOS ACS on Windows 2000 Servers, the Windows 2000-specific software installations for QOS-enabling your network are complete. However, there's more to a QOS implementation than the installation of client and server software.

For the integrator or administrator, there is the issue of non-Windows network devices. Other network devices that Windows 2000 QOS must interoperate with to provide an end-to-end solution must be configured in accordance with your Windows 2000 implementation. Their configuration is specific to their software implementation of RSVP or DSCP or 802.1p, however, rather than on Windows 2000. Thus, the installation of QOS ACS on the Windows 2000 Servers doesn't complete the integrator's job of QOS-enabling your network. There's more work getting QOS running the way you want it to run on your network; the job of the integrator at this point switches from installation of the Packet Scheduler and QOS ACS to that of configuration (in which most of the work rests in configuring QOS ACS).

Implied in such implementation and configuration is the assessment of the integrator (or administrator or IT manager) about how—or whether—to implement QOS in the organization. Even the QOS-enabling part of the network is an undertaking, and the integrator or IT manager would do well to understand the challenges and risks involved in making such decisions. Better yet, having some sort of idea about where to start with such implementations would be helpful, even if it were simply suggestions for different approaches to staging a QOS implementation.

The job of the programmers, of course, is to implement the programmatic capabilities of Windows 2000 into their applications. Such programming requires an understanding of how QOS operates, but it also requires some insight into how to get basic QOS capability built into a given application...and perhaps includes doing some advanced QOS-enabling development work, as well.

The following chapters discuss each of these challenges in detail, and provide guidance on how such challenges can be met.

10

QOS for the Integrator and Administrator

Somewhere along the road to a QOS-enabled network, there must be the actual implementation of QOS capabilities on the network. That's where integrators and administrators come into the QOS picture. If your client has considered deploying QOS in one of its environments, and the consideration ended with a nod of approval and the award (to you) of an implementation contract, welcome—you're the integrator. If you are responsible for ensuring that the ongoing operation of your QOS-enabled network (or its QOS-enabled parts) continues smoothly, welcome—you're the QOS administrator. If you fall somewhere between those two, or if you just want to find out what's involved in getting Windows 2000 QOS running in a network environment, this chapter is where you'll find much of the Windows 2000-specific information you need.

For integrators or administrators, getting QOS running on a network means getting the infrastructure configured and ready to service QOS requests. As explained in the previous chapter, the first steps for such a deployment are almost certainly to get the QOS Packet Scheduler installed on the Windows 2000 clients participating in QOS and to get QOS ACS installed on each IP subnet on which QOS clients reside. Finishing that, however, doesn't complete the integrator or administrator's job—you must now make policies, enforce group policies, or even set enterprise-wide standards. In a word, you must configure.

Planning for QOS on the Network

Because QOS requires the cooperation of network devices across the entire network, there are some items you should ensure are in place...or at least considered...during the course of planning for your QOS implementation. This part of the planning for QOS in the network is simply the logical application of the way QOS works in a network. For example, QOS provisioning requires routers that are either RSVP- or DSCP-enabled; so to provide end-to-end QOS provisioning, the routers in the path between QOS-enabled end nodes should be RSVP- or DSCP-enabled. Or, you can ensure that your routers are over-provisioned to a point at which data transmission delays won't occur.

Note

You can always over-provision network devices in the path where QOS-enabling is desired, and thereby circumvent the need for QOS on those devices. This is simply an application of the definition of QOS—loosely, data transmission quality through network devices that equates to unloaded network conditions. If you over-provision network devices (routers, WAN connections, and switches), they are essentially unloaded. This isn't a better use of network resources (as QOS provides), it's simply a partial or reduced use of network resources. ✦

As we know from reading through much of this book, there is a diverse collection of network devices that contribute to the creation of an end-to-end QOS-enabled connection. Windows 2000 computers on either end of that connection certainly get the connection going (or respond to requests), but the gamut of network devices that may interact with RSVP messages that move across the network can be from any network vendor out there. Thus, their specific implementations can't be covered here. What can be covered in this chapter, however, are the steps you need to take (or to ensure that are taken) in your network to provide end-to-end network connectivity, and the Windows 2000-specific configuring that can get you most of the way to "QOS-enabled-dom." Most of that configuration is done with the QOS ACS and its associated policies.

Despite the seemingly sizeable undertaking that QOS-enabling a network can appear to be, part of any QOS implementation plan should be to keep in perspective the implementation plan and the QOS capability of the overall network. The perspective I'm suggesting is simply that you don't have to have every single network device QOS-capable before going ahead with QOS implementations. This can be a relief for budget-conscious or workload-conscious integrators and administrators.

QOS Implementation Checklist

Any implementation needs a plan. Even something as simple as installing a printer needs a plan—lest you end up with a printer that's fifty feet away from the servicing computer, requiring holes in walls to run an extremely long cable between printer and computer, and a printer that's right under the coffee pot (and *not* more perky with its morning cup of coffee).

Whether simple or complex, you need a plan, and a plan should have some sort of checklist from which you can work.

The following sections provide lists of items you need to consider when planning for a QOS implementation in your network environment. When reviewing these lists, keep in mind that you can implement QOS capabilities in stages (perhaps based on a budget or on available IT personnel resources). In order to create a complete set of lists, however, you'll find a comprehensive set of must-do items in the following sections. When reading these must-do items, just remember that many of them can be tempered or reduced, based on mitigating circumstances (such as budgets).

Some list items are required, even to get basic QOS capabilities. Such list items are suffixed with the term required. *Make sure that these items are completed, even in staged QOS implementations.* ✦

On Clients

Clients include both the sender and receiver of QOS-enabled connections (often, a given QOS client is *both* sender and receiver).

- Install QOS Packet Scheduler on participating Windows 2000 clients— *required.*
- Implement QOS-enabled applications—*required.*
- Install 802.1p-capable NICs in QOS-enabled clients (Windows 2000 or other).

In the Network

The network is generally where you find the diversity of network devices, and many of the following list items require that you consult the installation guide for your given network device (such as a Cisco router) for proper configuration and, if appropriate, additional software packages to enable QOS.

- Install 802.1p-capable switches on LAN segments hosting QOS-enabled clients, and coordinate their installation with 802.1p-capable NICs on clients.
- Configure 802.1p-capable switches, and coordinate their configuration with QOS ACS/SBM configuration settings.
- Install QOS ACS/SBM on Windows 2000 Server computers on each subnet that hosts QOS-enabled clients, and ensure that the server is a member of the same domain as the subnet it intends to manage.

- Install QOS ACS/RRAS on Windows 2000 Server computers and on RRAS Servers hosting WAN connections.

- On each QOS ACS Server, create a user account called *AcsService* and add the account to the local Administrators group. (You can also create the account on a domain-wide basis.) In its Log On property sheet, set the Admission Control (RSVP) Service to log on with the AcsService account. Restart the service to put the change into effect—*required.*

- Install and configure RSVP or DSCP capabilities on routers.

- Ensure that boundary routers (those connected to external networks, which include any such WAN connections) are configured to properly tag (or re-tag) QOS-provisioned packets, according to the SLAs (Service Level Agreements) negotiated with external network service providers.

Service Level Agreements (SLAs) are agreements that your organization secures with networks to which your organization is attached (often an ISP). They specify how your QOS-enabled packets are treated as they cross that (ISP's) network. Generally, such SLAs require that packets coming from your network are tagged (such as with a specific DSCP value) according to the agreement, with charges associated with the transmission of better-than-best-effort traffic. The IETF has recommendations for SLAs, but the specifics of such agreements are, of course, based on the service provider to which your network is attached.

SLAs will be familiar to integrators who know ATM or Frame Relay provisioning (at least, the idea of such service-level guarantees), and associated service-level charges will be familiar. For more information on SLAs, check out the DiffServ working group's page on the IETF Website: www.ietf.org/html.charters/diffserv-charter.html.

Another item you should consider with network devices is the initiative to make network devices capable of interacting with Active Directory. As an LDAP-compliant directory service, Active Directory has the capability to centrally store configuration information for all sorts of software or devices. If network devices are capable of retrieving such information, your configuration effort might be considerably easier in a "store once, apply many" environment, such as an Active Directory-stored configuration profile. Cisco, for example, is working on efforts to enable interoperation with Active Directory. Before you spend too much time configuring your non-Windows network devices one-by-one, check your network device vendor's Web site to see whether it's Active Directory-ready.

Policies

Creating and applying policies are at the heart of the Windows 2000 QOS deployment, and they are often the most difficult tasks for an organization to complete. Despite the fact that the Policies list is short, policies are central to ensuring that your QOS deployment behaves the way you intend it to behave.

- Create enterprise-based QOS ACS policies, and augment them with subnet-specific or user-specific policies only as necessary—*required.*

More information on policy creation for QOS ACS, as well as a detailed step-by-step explanation of how to create policies, are provided in the "Creating Policies" section, later in this chapter.

Gauging Network Usage

Throughout the previous section on staging the implementation of QOS in your organization, there has been an underlying assumption—that you, the integrator or administrator, have knowledge about network usage in your organization. You must apply your knowledge of the use of your network infrastructure to the QOS staging that you do. For instance, if you have a FDDI or ATM backbone that's at 30% capacity and LAN segments that are nearing maximum capacity, you are better off replacing your LAN switches with 802.1p-capable switches and upgrading those segments' clients' NICs, rather than spending money on the backbone. Why? Because your backbone isn't at capacity, but your LAN segments are; you'd get more bang for your budgetary buck by upgrading the LAN segments first. Because the backbone can handle a lot more traffic, it's likely to behave somewhat similar to an "unloaded device." Thus, it isn't in as dire a need for QOS provisioning as your LAN segments are. (You can also apply this logic to WAN connections, individual router connections, and LAN segments.)

In fact, making decisions about which staging approach to take (or whether you need to stage the QOS implementation at all) requires that you have knowledge of network usage and capacity in your network. If you don't, your planning will be filled with gut-level guesses, and that's no way to implement a network. Educated guesses are much better, and educated guesses that are based on gathered data are better yet.

Part of your planning and implementation process must be to get a handle on network usage and capacity. But how do you get information about network usage? How are you supposed to have an education about network usage when those packets are too fast and slippery for you to get your hands on? There are a number of ways to do this, and some are more expensive and involved than others are. But there's one approach that can get you at least 90% of the way without spending an additional dime for expensive network-monitoring equipment: *System Performance Monitor* (formerly called Performance Monitor).

Note

System Performance Monitor enables you to monitor the activity—including the network activity—of any Windows NT or Windows 2000 computer. However, it won't help you monitor or gather data about the network activity of non-Windows (NT or 2000) network devices such as (non-Windows) routers or switches, or WAN interfaces. Therefore, you may need to get creative in the way you use System Performance Monitor to gather your performance data. For example, you may choose to monitor one particular Windows 2000 Server that houses an SQL server that is a candidate for QOS-enabled connections (in addition to the routers between that server and its clients). Other mechanisms are available for non-Windows devices, such as SNMP-based utilities and hardware-based monitors. System Performance Monitor will get you part of the way—a large part of the way, if you're creative—but there are limitations to its capabilities and to the network devices it can assess. ◆

Using System Performance Monitor

System Performance Monitor, a tool that's included in Windows 2000 Server and Professional, enables administrators or integrators to track (in real-time, also known as current activity) the performance of almost every Windows 2000 node, component, feature, or capability that you can imagine (and some that you can't). System Performance Monitor has the capability to monitor everything on your Windows 2000 computer (or other Windows NT or Windows 2000 computers) that you might want to chart, monitor, track, log, report, or be alerted about. Included in that list of interrogating capabilities is extensive network monitoring information—the likes of which you can use to create a well-rounded vision of your network environment...provided that you use it wisely.

System Performance Monitor gets its data by gathering information from *counters*, all of which belong to associated *objects*. Counters are simply tick marks that monitor the activity of different software and hardware components, such as the percentage of time a CPU spends in privileged (kernel) mode or a given network interface's bytes/received per second. Objects gather counters into logical groups. For example, the counters titled % User Time and % Privileged Time (among others) are part of the Processor object. Counters are processed logically by Windows 2000, and their information is then displayed or gathered through System Performance Monitor's collection of data-gathering formats, which consist of the following System Performance Monitor views:

- Chart view
- Histogram view
- Report view

From any of those views, you can view either of the following types of data:
- Current Activity
- Log File Data

For gathering data that you can use to determine the best QOS deployment approach for your network, you'll be most interested in gathering data in the form of *performance log files*. After you save network usage data in the form of a log file, you can view that log file data in any of the three formats listed earlier (Chart, Histogram, or Report view).

Gathering Network Usage Data

Performance measurement is the process of gathering and analyzing data to find out where bottlenecks are located. In the case of gathering data about your network infrastructure, you need to choose a Windows NT or Windows 2000 computer of particular interest (or, more likely, choose a collection of them to get a more complete view of network usage for a particular part of your network). You then choose the appropriate counters from the list of available counters and begin to gather data.

With System Performance Monitor, you can gather data centrally from computers that are scattered about the network, as long as you have proper permissions to do so. To direct System Performance Monitor to gather data from a computer other than the computer you're using, simply tell it to do so in the Add Counters window, as shown in Figure 10.1.

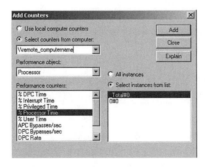

Figure 10.1   *Adding counters from a remote computer.*

The process for gathering data for log files used to be slightly different from viewing current activity. In Windows NT 4 (and earlier), you could choose individual counters and view their activity in any of the three view formats listed previously. With log files, however, you had to choose objects to include in the saved log file, and all counters associated with that object were saved during the course of saving the log file data. With System Performance Monitor, all that has changed. You now can choose individual counters to include in the logs, thereby reducing the size of the overall file. This avoids the previous requirement of having to choose all counters for a given object, even if you were only interested in one of its counters.

To create a log file, take the following steps:

1. In the System Performance Monitor snap-in, select the Counter Logs node, found beneath the Performance Logs and Alerts parent node. Figure 10.2 shows where this can be found.

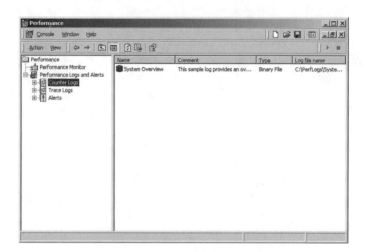

Figure 10.2   *The Counter Logs node in the System Performance Monitor snap-in.*

2. In the right pane, right-click somewhere in the pane, *but not on an existing log file*. You get a fly-out menu similar to the menu shown in Figure 10.3. Choose New, and then select Create New Log Settings from the menu.

3. You are presented with a window that prompts you to name the file. After you provide an appropriate name, you are presented with a tabbed window, in which you can customize the log file to a detailed extent.

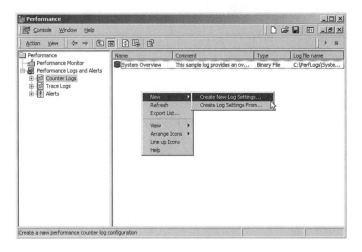

Figure 10.3   *Creating a new log file from the Counter Logs node of the System Performance Monitor snap-in.*

By creating a set of log files (or one log file that gets executed on different computers), you can gather network utilization data that can help you figure out network usage in different areas throughout your network. However, there are some considerations to be given to the data you gather—because making sweeping decisions (or making judgments) based on a snapshot of data can get you in trouble. The next section explains how to take an appropriate approach to sorting through and making sense out of the network utilization data that you gather with System Performance Monitor.

Making Sense of Network Usage Data
A little bit of information can be a dangerous thing. This section is aimed at helping you make the safest use possible of the information you gather from System Performance Monitor. Perhaps most importantly, when analyzing the network data on which you plan to base your QOS implementation, you must take some steps to ensure that the data is as accurate *and pertinent* as possible.

• **Be smart about your measurement period.** If you're attempting to measure the network utilization of an RRAS Server during peak times, don't get a ten-second measurement at 12:00 pm and decide that the server has plenty of resources to service the link...and deem that it can be second-seat in your staged QOS implementation. Along those lines, don't get a ten-second measurement at 10:00 am (perhaps its peak time) and believe that it's indicative of the work in general. Short measurement periods can skew the results and make analysis work inconsequential. A better approach might be to monitor the RRAS Server over a couple of days during two hours of its peak period. Such a sample would be more indicative of actual usage and provide better insights to the actual network utilization that it's experiencing.

- **Get a baseline.** If you have nothing against which you can measure, how will you know whether network utilization is increasing, decreasing, or staying steady? This is also a good idea for ongoing usage because, as you'll notice when you start using System Performance Monitor, QOS has a number of counters associated with QOS ACS as well as other QOS components.

- **Be wary of averages.** In the earlier example, in which you're taking samples over a couple of hours, be careful not to simply take an average over the two hours and decide that network utilization is low or high. Although there may be some useful information in the generalities that you can derive from such averages, making the average your deciding factor for QOS implementation would be tantamount to ignoring important details. Look closely; there may be times of low activity (such as a break time that you weren't aware of) that are skewing a highly utilized or oversubscribed interface.

- **Gather representative data.** You need to make sure that the data you're gathering in the System Performance Monitor logs are representative of the conditions in the network area that you're interested in. If you're determining whether subnet A should be QOS-enabled, make sure that you aren't gathering data from a computer on subnet A that's unused most of the time. If you do, your data probably won't be representative of the actual network usage on subnet A. This goes for servers as well (for example, ensure that you aren't gathering data for a database server that houses only legacy data that's hardly used anymore).

With the data you can gather with System Performance Monitor (and other utilities, such as router logs or similar resources, if available), you can get a view of the network that is better than guesswork. Although it's difficult to get all-encompassing measurements of network activity, you can use available tools to at least make your guesses educated and thus more accurate.

If you're proactive and want to get QOS capabilities into your organization, you can gather this analysis data and present it to the decision-makers in your organization. Thus (if the data supports it), you provide a compelling set of real, hard data to back up your allegation that the network could really benefit from the implementation of QOS—and maybe you could even make some staging suggestions, as well.

Staging QOS Implementations

You don't have to implement QOS in every corner of your network to begin reaping the benefits of QOS. In fact, depending on your QOS requirements and as your resources allow, you can get significant QOS capabilities by staging the implementation of QOS in certain areas of your network. Then, as resources become available, you can implement additional QOS capabilities in your network until you have as much QOS functionality as your network deployment requires.

> **Note**
>
> *If you need to achieve delay-sensitive data transmissions, such as those associated with Guaranteed Service, you need an end-to-end QOS-enabled connection (and you, therefore, probably need more than incremental QOS deployments in your organization). Such traffic is often called real-time traffic. Compare it to traffic that adapts easily to delays, such as best-effort traffic, which is sometimes also called elastic traffic. However, one approach to staging QOS implementations— point-to-point staging—can even help you get around the need for real-time traffic transmissions.* ◆

There are a number of different approaches that you could take in staging QOS in your network, but the most telling point that should be considered is this: Where can you get the most out of QOS? Different networks suffer from congestion in different areas: some in certain subnets, some in the backbone, and others have problems only in the path between two (or more) highly used resources. The following sections provide some guidance on how to partially implement QOS and reap significant benefit from its partial implementation (and perhaps extend QOS to the rest of the network later on). Regardless of whether you stage in subnets, in the backbone, or between a few points on the network, it's important to realize that even partial QOS capability in your network can get results.

LAN Segment Staging

One of the most overt abusers of network efficiency is the IP protocol suite itself. By its very nature, UDP (and TCP, to a certain extent) sends out data as fast as it can, clogging network interfaces and capacities with bursts. It would be better for the network if they would smooth themselves out a bit. The remedy is traffic control, which includes the smoothing of bursts and the shaping of traffic over time (among other things). Even if you only get traffic control going in heavily used subnets, you can immediately reap the benefits of QOS. Perhaps the simplest and quickest ways to gain the benefit of traffic control, as well as other QOS benefits in the subnet, is to start the implementation of QOS by staging its first deployment in the LAN segment.

To take the first step in LAN segment QOS staging, you need only to do the following:

- Install QOS Packet Scheduler on participating Windows 2000 clients.

- Install QOS ACS/SBM on Windows 2000 Server computers on each subnet that hosts QOS-enabled clients, and ensure that the server is a member of the same domain as the subnet it intends to manage.

- On each QOS ACS Server, create a user account called AcsService and add the account to the local Administrators group (you can also create the account on a domain-wide basis). In its Log On property sheet, set the Admission Control (RSVP) Service to log on with the AcsService account. Restart the service to put the change into effect.

- Create enterprise-based QOS ACS policies, and augment them with subnet-specific or user-specific policies only as necessary.

- Implement QOS-enabled applications.

This is a reasonably inexpensive, cost-effective approach to getting significant QOS capabilities into your network environment. Your only costs are those of the QOS ACS Servers, and they can be doing double- or triple-duty (or more). That is, you can have them act as a departmental file server and QOS ACS Server, thereby avoiding the need to deploy a dedicated Windows 2000 Server to QOS ACS. As with any Windows server, you should ensure that the server in question has enough resource capacity to service all of its required duties. You don't want to pick a file server that has its %CPU Time at 95% for your QOS ACS Server.

If you have more available resources for your LAN segment QOS staging or if want to increase the effectiveness of a LAN segment's staged implementation, you can also implement the following:

- Install 802.1p-capable NICs in QOS-enabled clients (Windows 2000 or other).

- Install 802.1p-capable switches on the LAN segment.

- Configure 802.1p-capable switches and coordinate their configuration with QOS ACS/SBM configuration settings.

Implementing these 802.1p capabilities is particularly effective for applications with small amounts of delay-sensitive traffic on LAN segments with large amounts of traffic. Remember that you must also use QOS-enabled applications to take advantage of QOS. So, if you're part of the department or IT management structure that determines which applications are used on the corporate desktop or if you have some input as to design guides for such implementations, ensure that QOS-enabling is part of the design requirements for your important (or QOS-needing) applications. Programmers can also impose traffic control (only) on a given application programmatically, without the need for RSVP signaling. See the QOS section on the Platform SDK at MSDN Online (msdn.microsoft.com) for specifics on how to do so.

Note

Remember from earlier chapters that if you have applications that are not QOS-enabled, their data will get treated by 802.1p as default data. Only applications that are QOS-enabled can potentially transmit data across a LAN segment at better-than-best-effort. ◆

Network Infrastructure Staging

Some networks have sufficient bandwidth availability in their LAN segments. When it gets to the backbone, however, the traffic backs up, and (because the backbone is like the freeway system of the network) if you have to transmit data across the backbone and you're clogged up in the backbone, it doesn't matter that your LAN segments are below capacity. The data transmission will be slow. In such circumstances, you can take the following steps to help make better use of the clogged area in your network infrastructure:

- Install QOS Packet Scheduler on participating Windows 2000 clients.

- Install QOS ACS/SBM on Windows 2000 Server computers on each congested network segment, and ensure that the server is a member of the same domain as the subnet it intends to manage.

- On each QOS ACS Server, create a user account called AcsService and add the account to the local Administrators group (you can also create the account on a domain-wide basis). In its Log On property sheet, set the Admission Control (RSVP) Service to log on with the AcsService account. Restart the service to put the change into effect.

- Create enterprise-based QOS ACS policies, and augment them with subnet-specific or user-specific policies only as necessary.

- Install and configure RSVP or DSCP capabilities on affected routers.

- Implement QOS-enabled applications.

Note

Make sure that you read that second point correctly because it's different from its earlier versions. The need to install and configure QOS ACS on the subnets is due to its "gatekeeper" nature. However, the LAN segment on which you install the QOS ACS can be your congested network backbone, rather than client subnets. In doing so, you regulate QOS-enabled traffic on that segment, and enable the application of QOS policies for traffic crossing that particular subnet. ◆

Point-to-Point Staging

There are other QOS-enabling circumstances that can easily be imagined, among those the need to have QOS provisioning between specific end nodes or specific LAN segments on the network. In such a situation, you can stage QOS implementation so that all network devices and subnets in the path between certain sets of end nodes (such as those on segment A and segment K) are QOS-enabled. The rest of the network comes online with QOS capabilities as budgetary or workload constraints allow.

For a quick point-to-point example, suppose that you have a training department that is connected to a certain part of the network, with video servers that reside in another (centrally located) building. Three routers sit between the training department and the video servers. With point-to-point staging, you can QOS-enable the point-to-point connection (the affected network devices and subnets) between the two locations and get the QOS you need for the training department.

For point-to-point staging, you need to take the following steps:

1. Install QOS Packet Scheduler on participating Windows 2000 clients.

2. Install 802.1p-capable NICs in QOS-enabled clients (Windows 2000 or other) that require point-to-point QOS capabilities.

3. Install 802.1p-capable switches on LAN segments hosting QOS-enabled clients that require point-to-point.

4. Configure 802.1p-capable switches and coordinate their configuration with QOS ACS/SBM configuration settings.

5. Install QOS ACS/SBM on Windows 2000 Servers on each subnet with clients requiring point-to-point QOS capabilities, and on each subnet over which data will need to be transmitted between end points. Ensure that the QOS ACS Server is a member of the same domain as the subnet it intends to manage.

6. On each QOS ACS Server, create a user account called AcsService and add the account to the local Administrators group (you can also create the account on a domain-wide basis). In its Log On property sheet, set the Admission Control (RSVP) Service to log on with the AcsService account. Restart the service to put the change into effect.

7. Create enterprise-based QOS ACS policies, and augment them with subnet-specific or user-specific policies only as necessary.

8. Install and configure RSVP or DSCP capabilities on routers in the point-to-point path.

9. Install QOS ACS/RRAS on Windows 2000 Server computers on RRAS Servers hosting WAN connections.

10. Implement QOS-enabled applications.

After you have a point-to-point QOS stage implemented, bringing other point-to-point stages online can become less resource-intensive because some of your subnets or backbones may already be QOS-enabled. To extend the previous example, if the sales department needs to use the video servers, you can QOS-enable the sales department's point-to-point connection by QOS-enabling the sales subnets and any routers between their subnet(s). You can also QOS-enable the video servers that weren't already QOS-enabled in the first point-to-point stage, and they will be QOS-enabled. Because the video servers and their subnets were already QOS-enabled, a portion of the work necessary to QOS-enable the sales department subnet was already complete.

Other Must-Read Staging Considerations

Which of the QOS staging techniques is best? The answer depends on your network's needs, your resources, and your general disposition about QOS-enabling your network. By approaching QOS in stages, you can minimize the resource impact of QOS deployments while still reaping the benefits of partial QOS provisioning. Each of these staging ideas is flexible and should be molded to your own needs.

These approaches to staging QOS deployments were derived by applying the QOS mechanism logic to the ways you can go about staging QOS implementations. There are other approaches to staging, and some of them might be much better than any of the suggestions that are provided here. You might, in fact, come up with an approach that's better than any of them; if so, use it! While you're at it, share it with others, so they can benefit as well. These suggestions aren't meant to be hard-and-fast rules; they're meant to help get QOS running on your network without having to flip your entire network (or your budget) upside down. The suggestions also illustrate that you can get imaginative with QOS deployment and get some use out of the technology without buying 20 new $200,000 routers.

The must-read part of this section is twofold: These staging ideas should be tailored to your network needs and they are simply applications of QOS implementation logic. If you come up with a different approach to getting QOS incrementally deployed in your network that fits your network needs more closely than any of these staging approaches, you have probably found the best staging approach for your network.

Also, remember that you don't have to stage QOS implementations. You can go ahead with a plan that converts the entire network to QOS in one large undertaking, but that's probably less common than planning incremental stages. With this section, you've been provided with a handful of ideas to get that QOS implementation plan moving ahead.

Configuring QOS ACS on the Windows 2000 Server

When we consider discussions from earlier in the book—discussions that explain the logical path that RSVP messages take in their journey between end nodes—we remember that the first step in a Windows 2000 client's request process (and the last step in the granting process) is QOS ACS. QOS ACS acts as a sort of gatekeeper, through which QOS-enabled clients on its LAN segment must pass before any QOS provisioning can occur. This provides it with the unique opportunity to be gatekeeper and keymaster (in loose, "ghostbusterish" terms). It can be the point at which QOS requests from cooperative Windows 2000 clients can be rejected or approved.

As a result of QOS ACS's pivotal role in QOS provisioning, almost all the configuration-associated Windows 2000 QOS is achieved through configuring the QOS ACS with policies that reflect the configuration that your organization wants to implement for a given enterprise, with additional policies created for individual users or groups.

Creating Policies

The approach to creating policies for QOS ACS is simple: Create wide-reaching enterprise-level policies and augment those policies on an as-needed basis by creating specific policies for user, groups, or particular subnets. This approach enables administrators to get the most results from the least amount of work; rather than requiring all users or groups to have their own policy configurations, administrators can cover everyone (in a blanket policy) and deal with the exceptions.

The creation of policies fall into the following categories:

- Enterprise-wide policies
- Subnet-specific policies

Within each category, two default policies are always available, and should be specified on an enterprise-wide basis:

- Any Authenticated User
- Un-Authenticated User

There are a couple of definitions that need to be explained regarding the two default policies. You need to pay special attention to these explanations because there can be some provision-limiting effects of misinterpreting these default policies.

- **Any Authenticated User:** This policy applies to any user who has been authenticated in a trusted domain *and* who is requesting QOS provisioning from a Windows 2000 client.

- **Un-Authenticated User:** This policy applies to any user who doesn't fall under the previous policy. This includes users who are authenticated to a trusted domain, but who are not running on a Windows 2000 computer. The policy also applies to clients on Windows 2000 computers who are not authenticated to a trusted domain (they could be authenticated to a Windows 2000 domain, but to an untrusted domain).

Because there is a collection of different policies that could apply to a given user (or group), QOS ACS has a progression by which it authenticates users or groups, and to which the policy or policies that their QOS provisioning request applies. The following list describes the steps through which QOS ACS applies policies:

1. User-specific policies in the given subnet
2. Group-specific policies in the given subnet
3. Any Authenticated User policies in the given subnet
4. User-specific policies defined for the enterprise
5. Group-specific policies defined for the enterprise
6. Any Authenticated User policies defined for the enterprise

To paraphrase this hierarchical list of policy implementation, it goes from the most specific for a given locale (subnet), to the least specific for the entire enterprise. The application of this hierarchy and its implications for the creation of subnet-specific policies are discussed further in the next few sections.

Creating Enterprise-Wide Policies

The best approach to creating policies for QOS ACS is to start with a general all-encompassing policy and to add exceptions to that policy as needed. With QOS ACS, that means starting with enterprise-wide policies.

In order to create enterprise-wide policies, you need to have properly installed QOS ACS as a member of the same domain that you intend it to manage. You must have created the AcsService user account, added it to the local Administrators group, and then configured the Admission Control (RSVP) Service to log on with that AcsService account. As long and drawn-out as that process is, it's necessary to get QOS running on the Windows 2000 Server (and it's a security issue as well, so it could be considered a benefit). Once those requisite steps have been taken, you can create enterprise-wide policies by taking the following steps:

1. Launch the QOS Admission Control snap-in. This is generally found by clicking the Start button, and choosing Programs, Administrative Tools, QOS Admission Control. As always, there is more than one way

to do just about everything in Windows, so you can launch the QOS Admission control snap-in from a number of different locations (including the Control Panel). The window that appears looks similar to Figure 10.4.

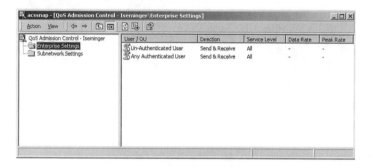

Figure 10.4   *The QOS Admission Control snap-in.*

2. Select the Enterprise Settings node (folder) to display its contents. Included are the two default policies: Any authenticated user and Un-authenticated user. Choose the first policy you want to define; and either double-click on it, or right-click on it and choose Properties from the fly-out menu that appears.

3. You are presented with a window that has multiple property sheets, as seen in Figures 10.5, 10.6, and 10.7. By defining the settings on these property sheets, you set the enterprise-wide policy for the users that fit that policy's description.

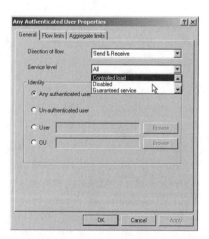

Figure 10.5   *The General property sheet, associated with setting enterprise-wide policies.*

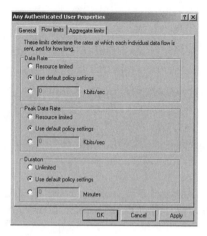

Figure 10.6 *The Flow limits property sheet, associated with setting enterprise-wide policies.*

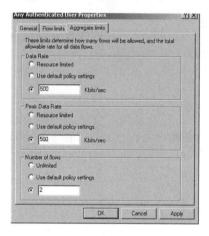

Figure 10.7 *The Aggregate limits sheet, associated with setting enterprise-wide policies.*

4. After these policies are filled in, you have officially created an enterprise-wide policy. Remember to configure both of the default enterprise-wide policies.

Note

It's important to remember that some Windows 2000 domain-authenticated users can fall into the Un-Authenticated Users policy. This policy applies not only to unauthenticated users (users who are not members of a trusted domain), but also to users who may be members of a downlevel domain. It can also include non-Windows 2000 clients that are actually authenticated in a trusted domain. ◆

Creating Subnet-Specific Policies

If specific needs within a subnet differ from policies made on the enterprise level, such exceptions can be specified for specific subnets. To define specific policies within a given subnet, take the following steps:

1. Launch the QOS Admission Control snap-in. This is generally found by clicking the Start button and selecting Programs, Administrative Tools, QOS Admission Control.

2. Select the subnet for which you want to create the specific setting (creating subnets is explained later in this chapter). Similar to the Enterprise Settings folder, the specific subnet includes two default policies: Any Authenticated User and Un-Authenticated User. Choose the policy you want to define, and either double-click it, or right-click it and choose Properties from the fly-out menu that appears. The window that appears looks similar to Figure 10.8.

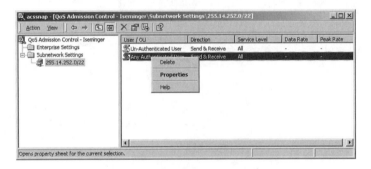

Figure 10.8   *The QOS Admission Control snap-in, with the subnet-based Any Authenticated User fly-out menu displayed.*

3. You are presented with the same policy configuration window that was displayed when you created enterprise-wide policies, along with its accompanying property sheets. By defining the particular setting that you want to modify on the appropriate property sheet and leaving the remaining settings as Use Default Policy Setting, you implement the subnet-particular setting without having to redefine the policy settings that apply to the entire enterprise (thus saving your work).

That's all there is to making subnet-specific changes to the two default policies found in each subnet: the Any Authenticated User policy and the Un-Authenticated Users policy.

If there is one piece of information that you should remember about creating specific policies (instead of using default enterprise-wide policies), it should be this: You need only to define specific variations from the enterprise-wide policies—you don't have to define all aspects of the policy.

In other words, if you only need to increase the peak data rate for a given subnet, then you can define that particular field in the subnet-specific policy (such as the Any Authenticated User policy in a specific subnet). You can let the rest of the fields remain set to Use Default Policy Settings.

Creating User-Specific or Group-Specific Policies

The guidelines for creating user- or group-specific policies are similar to the guidelines for creating subnet-specific policies. Only create them if you need to, and only change the particular settings that deviate from the enterprise-based or subnet-based policies, as appropriate. For example, if you only need to modify a particular user's data rate for guaranteed service on a given subnet, then make only those changes and leave the rest of the parameters in the policy configuration sheets set to Use Default Policy Settings.

There are a couple of points, really clarifications, to keep in mind when you create user- or group-specific policies:

- User- or group-specific policies that are created as enterprise-wide policies apply throughout the entire network (the enterprise). That's pretty straightforward.

- If you create user- or group-specific policies in a subnet node, those policies apply only to that specific subnet and only to traffic traversing that subnet.

- If possible, limit these user- and group-specific variations to each subnet.

If the guidelines are similar to creating subnet-specific policies (and they are), then the steps you need to take are essentially identical, with one exception: you create a new policy, rather than modifying the properties of an existing (provided-by-default) policy. The steps to doing so are as follows:

1. Launch the QOS Admission Control snap-in. This is generally found by clicking the Start button, and selecting Programs, Administrative Tools, QOS Admission Control.

2. Select the scope in which you want your specific setting to apply (enterprise-wide or subnet-specific), and right-click on its node (the Enterprise Settings folder or the particular subnet in which you want the policy to be created). A fly-out menu appears, at the top of which js the Add Policy menu item, as seen in Figure 10.9. Choose the Add Policy menu item.

3. You are presented with the same policy configuration window that was displayed when you created other policies, along with its accompanying property sheets. By defining the particular setting that you want to modify on the appropriate property sheet and leaving the remaining settings as Use Default Policy Setting, you implement the user- or group-specific settings that you want. You don't have to redefine the policy settings that apply to the subnet or the entire enterprise (again, saving you work).

Figure 10.9   *The Add Policy menu item in a particular subnet's folder.*

Managing Subnets

With policies defined or created, the piece of the configuration puzzle that remains is associating the QOS ACS Server with its managed subnet. Specifying the subnet that a given QOS ACS Server is going to manage is fairly straightforward, but it requires a little explanation to clarify the bounds within which it must operate.

As mentioned previously in this chapter, the QOS ACS must be a member of the same domain as the subnet it intends to manage. This requirement is due to the interaction of QOS (and everything else in Windows 2000) with Active Directory (as the "Deleting Managed Subnets" section, later in this chapter, evinces).

There are two primary activities associated with QOS ACS management of subnets:

- Creation of a managed subnet
- Assignment of servers eligible to manage the subnet

For those of you who occasionally make a mistake during the course of preliminary configurations (who doesn't?), there is a third activity that is a little less than intuitive. To save you the grief of trying to find out how to do this by trial-and-error, I'll include it in this chapter as well:

- Deletion of a (created) subnet

Creating Managed Subnets

In order to manage a given subnet, the subnet must be created. One way of doing this is through the QOS Admission Control snap-in. Take the following steps to create a subnet for QOS ACS management:

1. Launch the QOS Admission Control snap-in. This is generally found by clicking the Start button, and selecting Programs, Administrative Tools, QOS Admission Control.

2. Right-click the Subnetwork Settings node. A fly-out menu appears, at the top of which is the Add subnetwork menu item, as seen in Figure 10.10. Choose the Add subnetwork menu item.

Figure 10.10   *The Add subnetwork menu item from the Subnetwork Settings node.*

3. When you select the Add subnetwork menu item, you are prompted to enter the IP address of the subnet you want to add. Then, unless you've done it a number of times, you are confronted with the dialog box seen in Figure 10.11. Once you get it right, the subnet is added to the Subnetwork Settings node, and you can set management options on it.

Figure 10.11   *You put in the IP address of the subnet incorrectly. So does everyone else.*

Reading Binary

Rather than doing a hit-and-miss with the input of the subnet name, take a few steps to help you get it right as quickly as possible:

- *Ensure that the slash (/) is going the right way.*
- *Translate the subnet address into binary, translate the mask into binary, and derive the appropriate input for the IP address window from that combination.*

continues ▶

▶ *continued*

Here's an example taken right from the dialog box. If you have a subnet with an IP address (when masked) of 255.14.252.0, then the subnet has the following binary IP address:

11111110.00001110.11111100.00000000

The confusing sin of omission that is being committed here is that the IP address of your subnet should be discussed in conjunction with your subnet mask. In this example (and in the dialog box), the foregone conclusion is that you have the following network mask:

11111111.11111111.11111100.00000000

That means, in more common (decimal) terms, you have a network mask of 255.255.252.0.

For a quick translation from decimal into binary, the binary version is derived from adding the following values for each bit position (based on whether the bit is set to 1) for each octet (an octet is the period-delimited set of eight bits):

```
  0       0      0      0      0      0      0      0
[128]   [64]   [32]   [16]   [8]    [4]    [2]    [1]
```

In our example, the first octet is the following:

11111110

So, we add the values for the bit positions as follows:

128 + 64 + 32 + 16 + 8 + 4 + 2

The last value is decimal 1, which happens to be the decimal addition value as well as the binary value to which the bit is set (in this case, we're looking at its decimal addition value). It isn't added because the bit in that position of the octet is set to zero. When we add all those together, we get 255, which is the value of the first octet in the 255.14.252.0 address. Other numbers can be generated similarly; in fact (or of course, depending on your level of experience with reading binary) any value between zero and 255 can be generated by a combination of eight bits. Add one more bit, and you double the numbers that can be generated by the combination of bits (nine bits have 512 different combinations, 10 bits have 1024, and so on).

Therefore, if your subnet mask is 255.255.252.0, your mask (of ones) is the following:

11111111.11111111.11111100.00000000

Because the 252 equates to the setting of the first six bits in its octet to one (or in decimal terms, equates to 128+64+32+16+8+4).

How does this apply to the WWW.XXX.YYY.ZZZ/MM format that QOS ACS is looking for? Simple: You have to count the number of bits set to 1 in your subnet mask (starting from the front, or, more intuitively, from the LEFT of the series of octets). That number is the MM that QOS ACS wants after the / (that's a forward slash, remember, not a backslash). In our example's case, that means 8 (the first octet is all 1s), plus 8 (so is the second), plus 6 (in the third octet, 6 bits are set to 1)—for a grand total of 22.

Clear as mud, right? ◆

Assigning Servers to a Subnet

Once you have created a subnet, you can assign one or more servers to manage it. The designation of QOS ACS Servers permitted to manage a given subnet is done from within the subnet's Servers property sheet. Take the following steps to bring up a given subnet's Servers property sheet:

1. Launch the QOS Admission Control snap-in. This is found by clicking the Start button; then selecting Programs, Administrative Tools, QOS Admission Control.

2. Right-click on the Subnetwork Settings node. A fly-out menu appears and the Properties menu item appears in bold. Choose the Properties menu item.

3. When you select the Properties menu item, a window with five property sheets appears, as seen in Figure 10.12. Choose the Servers property sheet, choose Add, and select the Windows 2000 QOS ACS Servers you want enabled to manage the subnet.

Figure 10.12 *The Servers property sheet from a subnet Properties window.*

It's a good idea to provide redundancy for QOS ACS within a given subnet, which can be done by enabling more than one QOS ACS Server to manage any given subnet. You can then install (and have running) a second QOS ACS Server; if the primary QOS ACS Server fails, the backup QOS

ACS Server can automatically take its place until the failed server is brought back online. Because subnet policies are stored centrally in Active Directory, the secondary QOS ACS Server can simply retrieve any subnet-specific policies (as well as enterprise policies) and provide seamless QOS ACS service to the subnet.

Each QOS ACS Server manages each subnet for which it has a local IP address. If a QOS ACS Server has a single NIC with two IP addresses (each logically connected to different IP subnets residing on the same physical wire), the QOS ACS Server will manage each of those IP subnets. If the QOS ACS Server has multiple NICs connected to different physical wires (a multi-homed computer), the same rule applies. The QOS ACS Server will manage each IP subnet for which it has an IP address. The rule, then, is as follows: QOS ACS Server manages each IP subnet to which it is logically connected.

Deleting Managed Subnets

Because you could sprain a finger trying relentlessly to delete a subnet that you created in the QOS Admission Control snap-in, without success, a quick explanation here is aimed at preventing weeks of finger-casts. You can't delete a subnet from the QOS Admission Control snap-in. Because the creation of the subnet is something that Active Directory apparently holds dear, you must go into the Active Directory Sites and Services snap-in to do so, as the following steps explain:

1. Launch the Active Directory Sites and Services snap-in. This is found by clicking the Start button; then choosing Programs, Administrative Tools, QOS Admission Control.

2. Expand the Sites node, expand its Subnets node, and choose the subnet you want to delete.

3. From the keyboard, toolbar, or Action menu, choose delete. You will be prompted that your action is going to delete all the items in its container (including any subnet-specific policies you created). If you're sure, click okay to delete the subnet.

QOS for Non-Windows 2000 Clients

Much of Windows 2000 is based on open standards, and QOS ACS is no exception. QOS ACS is an implementation of the IETF SBM recommendation. Because it is standards-compliant, non-Windows clients that adhere to the SBM standard can also take advantage of QOS ACS capabilities. Note that these non-Windows clients will be seen as Un-Authenticated Users to QOS ACS, as will Windows clients that are not Windows 2000 clients.

QOS for the Programmer

Because most of the Windows 2000 QOS capabilities are made available "under the hood," it means that someone has to get under the Windows 2000 hood and enable applications to take advantage of the QOS capabilities built into Windows 2000. That someone, of course, is you—the applications programmer or developer. If you aren't a developer, this chapter may still be interesting because it gets into the nitty-gritty of how Windows 2000 QOS works in operating system terms. Those terms (operating system implementation terms, that is) can provide insight to an implementation of QOS that is otherwise difficult to find.

This chapter is decidedly geared toward developers interested in enabling their new or existing applications to become QOS-enabled.

How to QOS-Enable Your Application

Developers will find that most of the work that is done to QOS-enable their application is done within the RSVP SP. As explained in Chapter 6, "Network-Driven QOS," the RSVP SP is the primary enabler of QOS signaling for applications. It sits between applications that want QOS provisioning capabilities and the actual Windows 2000 QOS that provide such services. This service layer that the RSVP SP provides has the following intent: to hide the complexities and overhead of programming to the underlying QOS component implementations from developers. If you, as a developer, want to endure such complexities or overhead, the section "How to Program Windows 2000 QOS On a Granular Level," later in this chapter, explains how to do just that.

In overall terms, the process of QOS-enabling an application requires that a given application be able to receive QOS-enabled data, send QOS-enabled data, and close QOS connections. Of course, once a connection is established, an application must be capable of managing the connection as well, which includes such activities as changing QOS provisioning parameters.

Those basic capabilities QOS-enable an application, but, as mentioned throughout this book, the establishment and maintenance of an end-to-end QOS connection also requires that other QOS-enabled network devices—such as routers, switches, WAN devices, and other hops along the path between end nodes—allow such end-to-end communication to take place. That disclaimer aside, the details of QOS-enabling your applications can commence.

QOS Programming Overview

The provisioning of QOS in Windows 2000 is done by using specific Windows Sockets functions, as well as functions and structures created specifically for use with QOS. Taking advantage of Windows 2000 QOS requires creating a connection between end points by using Windows Sockets 2.2 functions, in conjunction with QOS functions and structures, to create a connection and provide QOS parameters that articulate directional QOS provisioning requirements. QOS functions and structures also maintain or change settings associated with a particular QOS session.

The call sequence involved in establishing and maintaining a QOS-enabled connection generally includes preparation calls, such as enumerating protocols and querying available protocols for QOS capability.

Opening a QOS Socket

A QOS-enabled socket is required to create a QOS-enabled connection, which in turn requires finding a QOS-enabled protocol. The process of finding a QOS-enabled protocol involves the following steps:

1 Call WSAEnumProtocols() to enumerate existing protocols.

2 Loop through the enumerated protocols to find a protocol that supports QOS. QOS support is indicated by the setting of the XP1_QOS_SUPPORTED flag in *dwServiceFlags1* in the WSAPROTOCOL_INFO structure.

3 Call WSASocket() and pass a pointer to the WSAPROTOCOL_INFO structure corresponding to the QOS-enabled protocol. The RSVP SP requires an overlapped socket; create the socket in overlapped mode by setting the WSA_FLAG_OVERLAPPED flag in the *dwFlags* parameter of the WSASocket() function.

Note

Don't attempt to use WSADuplicateSocket() *to create QOS-enabled sockets; the* WSADuplicateSocket() *function can't be used on a QOS-enabled socket. Attempting to do so will result in the return of a* WSAEINVAL *error.* ◆

Invoking the RSVP SP

Although a socket can send or receive data in either direction (bidirectional), a QOS-enabled flow is unidirectional. To enable a connection with service guarantees for both sending and receiving from a host, two individual QOS-enabled flows are required. Whether the QOS-enabled flow is for sending or receiving, the initial process of invoking the RSVP SP usually includes the use of one of the following Windows Sockets 2 functions:

- WSAConnect()
- WSAJoinLeaf()
- WSAAccept()
- WSAIoctl(SIO_SET_QOS)

Each of these functions invokes the RSVP SP on the application's or service's behalf, and begins the process of establishing QOS provisioning between end nodes. Each of these functions includes a parameter that provides the application or service with the capability of providing QOS-specific parameters. These QOS-specific parameters are provided through the FLOWSPEC structure, which is included as a parameter of each of the three preceding functions. (WSAAccept() generally implements FLOWSPEC through the callback function provided in its *lpfnCondition* parameter.)

Whenever an application or service calls WSAConnect(), WSAJoinLeaf(), or WSAAccept() with a non-NULL pointer to the QUALITYOFSERVICE structure, QOS functionality is implicitly invoked, which includes the enlistment of any other QOS components (such as Traffic Control or RSVP signaling) that the RSVP SP may need to carry out the necessary QOS provisioning.

Because Windows 2000 QOS flows are unidirectional, different transmission parameters for sender and receiver can be set. In other words, if one socket has two associated flows (one for sending and one for receiving, from the perspective of either end node), the QOS parameters associated with each of those individual flows are set independently of the other flow. Additionally, RSVP semantics are receiver-centric, which means that hosts that want to receive data generally initiate the QOS-enabling RSVP sequence (the host computer that is the sender simply replies to requests). In order for the RSVP SP to act on behalf of an application, the RSVP SP must have QOS-specific parameters associated with each flow. These parameters come in the form of the FLOWSPEC and QUALITYOFSERVICE structures.

The QUALITYOFSERVICE structure is the all-encompassing structure for QOS-specific parameters. It is comprised of three parameters, two of which are FLOWSPEC structures (one for sending, one for receiving).

The FLOWSPEC structure includes configurable parameters, which are as follows:

- *TokenRate*
- *TokenBucketSize*

- *PeakBandwidth*
- *Latency*
- *DelayVariation*
- *ServiceType*
- *MaxSduSize* (maximum packet size permitted in the traffic flow)
- *MinimumPolicedSize*

When the application or service provides values for these parameters, the RSVP SP can characterize the service quality being requested, which in turn enables the RSVP SP to make appropriate requests to corresponding components of QOS.

Further details of the QUALITYOFSERVICE structure and the FLOWSPEC structure can be found on MSDN or MSDN Online (msdn.microsoft.com), or in a reference set that is specifically geared toward providing reference material for Windows networking technologies.

The third parameter of the QUALITYOFSERVICE structure is the ProviderSpecific buffer, which is used for additional provider-specific QOS parameters that are not available in the FLOWSPEC structures. Information about how to use the ProviderSpecific buffer is provided in the section "How to Program Windows 2000 QOS On a Granular Level."

Receiving and Sending Data

Applications can begin receiving data over QOS-enabled flows before the QOS provisioning for the socket is in place (has been admitted). The result of receiving data before the QOS flow is established is the same as receiving data over a non-QOS connection. However, once the QOS-enabled flow is established, the receiver can receive data that conforms to the established QOS-parameters for the flow.

Inherent in the occurrence of events (such as the establishment of the QOS-enabled connection) is the need for an application or service to query for events. The RSVP SP provides mechanisms that enable event notification. These mechanisms differ, depending on whether the host is receiving or sending data.

As a *receiver* on a QOS-enabled flow, a host may initiate some or all of the following actions:

1. To streamline the establishment of existing common settings for the QUALITYOFSERVICE structure, an application or service can use GetQosByName() to enumerate and then retrieve an existing QOS template. It can then apply the values in that template (in the form of a QUALITYOFSERVICE structure) to the connection. Details on this approach are provided later in this chapter.

2. As mentioned previously, a receiver *must* provide QOS-specific parameters to the RSVP SP. These parameters are provided in the *ReceivingFlowSpec* parameter of the QUALITYOFSERVICE structure, which is provided through the use of WSAConnect(), WSAJoinLeaf(), WSAAccept(), or through the Windows Sockets 2 SIO_SET_QOS ioctl opcode, as done in a call to WSAIoctl(SIO_SET_QOS).

Your application may then receive data. Data transmitted by the sender per the constraints of the established QOS-specific parameters is considered conforming data; data that falls outside those parameters, or nonconforming data, is handled differently, based on the QOS_OBJECT_SD_MODE setting, which is particular to Traffic Control. Options for nonconforming data range from relegating it to a best-effort transmission to discarding nonconforming packets.

3. Your application may want to monitor RSVP SP events in order to provide for the QOS-enabled connection. For example, the application may want to monitor the status information and error codes provided with FD_QOS events. (FD_QOS events are requested by using RSVP_RESERVE_INFO in a call to the WSAIoctl() function.) Other RSVP SP events that an application or service may want to monitor include using an RSVP_RESERVE_INFO object to request arrival notification of a RESV message.

4. When the application receives notification of certain events, it may want to take appropriate action to modify its settings or parameters. For example, if an application is notified of the arrival of a PATH message, it may want to use the Windows Sockets 2 SIO_GET_QOS ioctl opcode to retrieve and examine pertinent information, such as the sender's Tspec and the path's ADspec. Information provided in the PATH message may require the application or service to modify its initial QOS-specific parameters to match transmission constraints.

For a *sender* on a QOS-enabled flow, the events differ somewhat from the receiver's collection of available actions. Whereas receivers initiate connections and request certain QOS-specific parameters, senders respond to such requests (note that network devices between the receiver and sender also react to receiver requests, and may reject requests before they ever reach the sender). As a sender, a host may initiate some or all of the following actions:

1. Sending hosts must inform the RSVP SP of QOS-specific parameters in order to enable the RSVP SP to interact with other QOS components on the sending host's behalf. QOS-specific parameters are provided to the RSVP SP through the *SendingFlowspec* parameter of the FLOWSPEC structure, which itself is a parameter of WSAConnect(), WSAAccept(), and WSAJoinLeaf(). The *SendingFlowspec* parameter can also be provided through the use of the SIO_SET_QOS ioctl opcode, as done in a call to WSAIoctl(SIO_SET_QOS).

2. The QOS-specific parameters (*SendingFlowspec*) are based on the application or service's knowledge of the transmission characteristics appropriate for the application or service. For example, bandwidth requirements for database queries of a mission-critical application may be different from bandwidth requirements for high-quality training videos. Latency boundaries may also be different for those types of applications (note that latency boundaries are available only with Guaranteed Service). Therefore, the application is best equipped to provide appropriate QOS-specific transmission parameters, perhaps through the use of a QOS template.

3. Senders may use WSAGetQosByName() to enumerate and then retrieve preinstalled QOS templates that include QOS-specific parameters with appropriate transmission characteristics, based on the type of application. For example, there may be a template called VIDEOBCAST associated with a QUALITYOFSERVICE structure that automatically applies the most appropriate QOS-centric settings for video broadcast senders. The options represented in this step and the previous are either/or; applications either request specific QOS parameters (as in step 2), or apply the QOS parameters associated with a particular QOS template (as in this step).

4. Senders may configure Traffic Control parameters appropriately, based on characteristics of the transmission, such as nonconforming packets (those that exceed the transmission limitations imposed on the sender by its *SendingFlowspec*).

5. The sender may monitor RSVP SP events to maintain the QOS-enabled connection, such as the arrival of RESV messages. Often, the sender will want to monitor status information and error codes provided with FD_QOS events. For example, the sender may choose to stop transmission when the FD_QOS event WSA_QOS_NO_RECEIVER occurs, indicating that there are no longer any receivers for the transmission.

6. The sender may want to use the Windows Sockets 2 SIO_GET_QOS ioctl opcode to look up QOS-specific parameters associated with the arrival of a RESV message.

7. The sender should use the Windows Sockets 2 SIO_CHK_QOS ioctl opcode to query parameters that provide information about the QOS connection, such as allowed sending rate, line rate, and others. Doing so enables the application to ensure that its transmission parameters are consistent with configurations that the network administrator has set up.

Closing the QOS Connection

As you might imagine, closing a QOS connection is much easier than opening and provisioning a connection. Generally, any event that closes a socket also ends RSVP SP servicing on the socket. Examples of events that cause the RSVP SP to stop providing QOS functionality on a socket include the following:

- Using `closesocket()` to close the socket.

- Using `shutdown()` to disable sends or receives on a socket. Note, however, that shutting down only the receive capabilities leaves the QOS-enabled send capabilities for the socket intact. Shutting down only the send capabilities of a socket leaves the QOS-enabled receive capabilities for the socket intact, as well.

- Using `WSAConnect()` with the name parameter set to NULL.

- Using `WSAIoctl(SIO_SET_QOS)` with the parameter corresponding to the *SendingFlowspec* or *ReceivingFlowspec* (both of which are of FLOWSPEC structures) parameter set to SERVICETYPE_NOTRAFFIC or SERVICETYPE_BESTEFFORT. Setting SERVICETYPE_NOTRAFFIC or SERVICETYPE_BESTEFFORT selectively can disable RSVP SP service for sending or receiving, independently of RSVP SP servicing on the opposite direction.

Using QOS Templates

Often, QOS parameters for the FLOWSPEC structure are common among application types, especially multimedia applications and other transmission-sensitive applications such as IP telephones or video software. Such commonality lends itself to the establishment of standardized QOS parameters for a given type of transmission. The RSVP SP provides such standardization and the ease of implementation that comes with prescribed service types, through the use of QOS templates.

The RSVP SP provides three functions that facilitate the enumeration, use, creation, and deletion of QOS templates:

- WSAGetQOSByName()
- WSCInstallQOSTemplate()
- WSCRemoveQOSTemplate()

The QOS templates that are available with Windows 2000 QOS were explained in Chapter 5, "Application-Driven QOS," but I've included them again here for comvenience. The steps necessary to use these and other convenient templates are explained in the following sections.

Template G711
Services packets sized at 340 bytes; suited for up to 27 packets/second; provides Guaranteed Service.

Sending FLOWSPEC Values:

ServiceType	3
TokenRate	9250
PeakBandwidth	13875
TokenBucketSize	680
MaxSduSize	340
MinimumPolicedSize	340
DelayVariation	-1
Latency	-1

Receiving FLOWSPEC Values:

ServiceType	3
TokenRate	9250
PeakBandwidth	13875
TokenBucketSize	680
MaxSduSize	340
MinimumPolicedSize	340
DelayVariation	-1
Latency	-1

Template G723.1

Services packets sized at 68 bytes; suited for approximately 32 packets/second; provides Guaranteed Service.

Sending FLOWSPEC Values:

ServiceType	3
TokenRate	2200
PeakBandwidth	3300
TokenBucketSize	136
MaxSduSize	68
MinimumPolicedSize	68
DelayVariation	-1
Latency	-1

Receiving FLOWSPEC Values:

ServiceType	3
TokenRate	2200
PeakBandwidth	3300

TokenBucketSize	136
MaxSduSize	68
MinimumPolicedSize	68
DelayVariation	-1
Latency	-1

Template G729
Services packets sized at 40 bytes; suited for up to 50 packets/second; provides Guaranteed Service.

Sending FLOWSPEC Values:

ServiceType	3
TokenRate	2000
PeakBandwidth	4000
TokenBucketSize	80
MaxSduSize	40
MinimumPolicedSize	40
DelayVariation	-1
Latency	-1

Receiving FLOWSPEC Values:

ServiceType	3
TokenRate	2000
PeakBandwidth	4000
TokenBucketSize	80
MaxSduSize	40
MinimumPolicedSize	40
DelayVariation	-1
Latency	-1

Template H263QCIF
Service packets sized between 80 and 2500 bytes; accrues transmission tokens at 12,000 bytes/second; provides Controlled Load Service.

Sending FLOWSPEC Values:

ServiceType	2
TokenRate	12000
PeakBandwidth	-1
TokenBucketSize	6000

MaxSduSize	2500
MinimumPolicedSize	80
DelayVariation	-1
Latency	-1

Receiving FLOWSPEC Values:

ServiceType	2
TokenRate	12000
PeakBandwidth	-1
TokenBucketSize	6000
MaxSduSize	2500
MinimumPolicedSize	80
DelayVariation	-1
Latency	-1

Template H263CIF

Services packets sized between 80 and 8192 bytes; accrues transmission tokens at 16,000 bytes/second; PeakBandwidth (burst rate) is not specified; provides Controlled Load Service.

Sending FLOWSPEC Values:

ServiceType	2
TokenRate	16000
PeakBandwidth	-1
TokenBucketSize	8192
MaxSduSize	8192
MinimumPolicedSize	80
DelayVariation	-1
Latency	-1

Receiving FLOWSPEC Values:

ServiceType	2
TokenRate	16000
PeakBandwidth	-1
TokenBucketSize	8192
MaxSduSize	8192
MinimumPolicedSize	80
DelayVariation	-1
Latency	-1

Template H261QCIF

Services packets sized between 80 and 2500 bytes; accrues transmission
tokens at 12,000 bytes/second; PeakBandwidth (burst rate) is not specified;
provides Controlled Load Service.

Sending FLOWSPEC Values:

ServiceType	2
TokenRate	12000
PeakBandwidth	-1
TokenBucketSize	6000
MaxSduSize	2500
MinimumPolicedSize	80
DelayVariation	-1
Latency	-1

Receiving FLOWSPEC Values:

ServiceType	2
TokenRate	12000
PeakBandwidth	-1
TokenBucketSize	6000
MaxSduSize	2500
MinimumPolicedSize	80
DelayVariation	-1
Latency	-1

Template GSM6.10

Services packets sized at 86; suited for approximately 25 packets/second;
accrues transmission tokens at 2,150 bytes/second; provides Guaranteed
Service.

Sending FLOWSPEC Values:

ServiceType	3
TokenRate	2150
PeakBandwidth	4300
TokenBucketSize	172
MaxSduSize	86
MinimumPolicedSize	86
DelayVariation	-1
Latency	-1

Receiving FLOWSPEC Values:

ServiceType	3
TokenRate	2150
PeakBandwidth	4300
TokenBucketSize	172
MaxSduSize	86
MinimumPolicedSize	86
DelayVariation	-1
Latency	-1

Finding and Using QOS Templates

Discovering which templates are available on a system entails enumerating the available QOS templates, which is done by using WSAGetQOSByName(). QOS templates also may be stored in the registry, in the following location:

```
HKEY_LOCAL_MACHINE\SYSTEM\CurrentControlSet\Services\WinSock2\QOS\
GlobalQosTemplates
```

Use the following steps in your application to enumerate available QOS templates:

1. Call WSAGetQOSByName() with the *lpQOS* parameter set to NULL and a pointer to a structure of type WSABUF provided for the *lpQOSName* parameter.

2. A list of available QOS template names is returned in the WSABUF structure pointed to by *lpQOSName*.

3. Peruse the available templates and select an appropriate template, based on the template's name (codec), to service your application's required QOS parameters.

Once your application knows the name of the QOS template that it wants to use, applying the QOS template is achieved by the following steps:

1. Call WSAGetQOSByName(), passing the template name in the *lpQOSName* parameter. In the call, provide a pointer in the *lpQOS* parameter to a QUALITYOFSERVICE structure to be filled with the template's settings. The RSVP SP fills the QUALITYOFSERVICE structure pointed to in *lpQOS* with the parameters from the selected QOS template.

2. Set the *ServiceType* member of the *SendingFlowspec* and *ReceivingFlowspec* parameters of the QUALITYOFSERVICE structure with values that correspond to the requested Service Type. (*SendingFlowspec* and *ReceivingFlowspec* are parameters of the QUALITYOFSERVICE structure, and both are of type FLOWSPEC; *ServiceType* is a member of the FLOWSPEC structure.)

3. Make a QOS-enabled connection request; by using the QUALITYOFSERVICE structure filled in Step 1, your application implements the QOS template's QOS parameters as part of the request.

Installing and Removing QOS Templates

When none of the available QOS templates fit the QOS parameters that your application wants or needs, you may want to install a QOS template of your own. By installing a QOS template that is tailored specifically to your application's needs, the application can benefit from easier and more consistent implementation of QOS parameter requests. The best approach for installing a template of your (application's) own is to make the installation of template part of the application's installation process.

The installation of a QOS template requires administrative privilege. The process of installing a QOS template is as easy as using the WSCInstallQOSTemplate() function, the specifics of which can be found in the reference pages of the function on MSDN or MSDN Online, or your favorite Windows Networking reference book.

Essentially, a successful call to the WSCInstallQOSTemplate() function installs a QOS template and associates the template with the name provided in the function's lpQOSName parameter. Once the QOS template is installed with the WSCInstallQOSTemplate() function, it can be applied to a connection through the calling of WSAGetQOSByName().

Removing a QOS template is even easier than installing one. The details of removing a QOS template are contained in the WSCRemoveQOSTemplate() function reference, again found on MSDN, MSDN Online, or your favorite Windows Networking resource book. As with the installation of a QOS template, removal of a QOS template requires administrative privilege.

QOS Error Codes and Error Values

Errors are a part of programming life. Knowing what happened when the error occurred goes a long way toward fixing the error, so this section contains the error codes that you may run into (hopefully, you won't) during the course of QOS-enabling your application. Errors are returned through the use of the WSAIoctl() function; you can check out the process of using WSAIoctl() with your MSDN subscription content, or over the Internet at MSDN Online (msdn.microsoft.com). Table 11.1 lists the error codes you might run into during the course of developing your QOS-enabled application.

Table 11.1   RSVP SP error codes

Error Code	Description	Application Response
GQOS_NO_ERRORCODE	No error occurred or the error code is unavailable.	
GQOS_GENERIC_ERRORCODE	An error occurred, but the specific error code is unavailable.	
GQOS_RSVP	The error occurred in the local RSVP engine.	Check the QOS call sequence.
GQOS_KERNEL_TC	The error occurred in local traffic control.	Depending on the specific error value, the application or service may retry the operation with reduced QOS requirements.
GQOS_NET_ADMISSION	Admission failure due to the Subnet Bandwidth Manager (part of the ACS).	Stop the operation or retry with reduced QOS requirements.
GQOS_NET_POLICY	A policy-related error occurred.	Stop or retry with reduced QOS requirements (depending on the specific error value).

Windows 2000 QOS also provides a rich set of error codes to help QOS-enabling developers to deal with errors when they occur (see Table 11.2). Also, Microsoft has provided suggestions (found in the far-right column) for dealing with many errors when they occur.

Table 11.2   QOS error codes.

Error value	Description	Application Response
GQOS_NO_ERRORVALUE	No error occurred, or the error value is unavailable.	
GQOS_GENERIC_ERRORVALUE	An error occurred, but the specific error value is unavailable.	
GQOS_BAD_SEND	Bad local address for a receive session.	Check the QOS call sequence.
GQOS_BAD_RECV	Bad local address for a send session.	Check the QOS call sequence.
GQOS_PREEMPTED	Service preempted due to local bandwidth resources.	Try to invoke QOS again at a later time.

`GQOS_CONFLICT_SERV`	Conflicting Traffic Control filters.	Check the QOS specifications.
`GQOS_NO_SERV`	The service is unknown to local Traffic Control.	Check the Service Type parameter.
`GQOS_DELAYBND`	Local Traffic Control cannot meet the specified delay-bound requirement.	Retry the operation with a more relaxed delay-bound requirement.
`GQOS_BANDWIDTH`	Local Traffic Control cannot meet bandwidth requirement.	Retry the operation with a more relaxed bandwidth requirement.
`GQOS_MTU`	The Maximum Transmission Unit (MTU) in `FLOWSPEC` is too large.	Adjust the packet size and retry the operation.
`GQOS_NO_SENDER`	No sender information for the reservation request.	Check the QOS call sequence.
`GQOS_NO_PATH`	No Path State for the reservation request.	Check the QOS call sequence.
`GQOS_BAD_STYLE`	Mismatch in filter style.	Check the `RESV` filter specifications.
`GQOS_UNKNOWN_STYLE`	The filter style is unknown.	Check the `RESV` filter specifications.
`GQOS_BAD_DSTPORT`	Conflicting or invalid destination port.	Check the QOS call sequence.
`GQOS_BAD_SNDPORT`	Conflicting or invalid source port.	Check the QOS call sequence.
`GQOS_AMBIG_FILTER`	Ambiguous filter specification in `RESV`.	Check the `RESV` filter specifications.
`GQOS_INVALID`	Invalid operation or parameters.	
`GQOS_INTERNAL_API`	RSVP API logic error.	
`GQOS_WOULDBLOCK`	RSVP/Traffic Control operation would block.	Retry at a later time.
`GQOS_NO_MEMEORY`	Not enough memory available to execute the requested RSVP/Traffic Control operation	Abort the operation or retry at a later time.
`GQOS_BAD_SERVICETYPE`	Traffic Control error: invalid Service Type.	Check the service type.
`GQOS_BAD_TOKENRATE`	Traffic Control error: invalid token rate.	Check the token rate.
`GQOS_BAD_PEAK_RATE`	Traffic Control error: invalid peak rate.	Check the peak rate.
`GQOS_BAD_QOSPRIORITY`	Traffic Control error: invalid internal priority.	Check the Traffic Control Priority object.

continues ▶

Table 11.2   continued

Error value	Description	Application Response
GQOS_BAD_ADDRESSTYPE	Traffic Control error: invalid address type.	Check the address type.
GQOS_NO_SYS_RESOURCES	Traffic Control error: out of system resources.	Abort or retry at a later time.
GQOS_INCOMPATIBLE_QOS	Traffic Control error: incompatible QOS requirements.	Check the QOS requirements.
GQOS_POLICY_ERROR_UNKNOWN	A policy error occurred for an unknown reason.	
GQOS_POLICY_GLOBAL_DEF _FLOW_COUNT	Policy error: the operation would exceed the global default-policy flow count.	Abort or retry at a later time.
GQOS_POLICY_GLOBAL_GRP _FLOW_COUNT	Policy error: the operation would exceed the global group-policy flow count.	Abort or retry at a later time.
GQOS_POLICY_GLOBAL_USER _FLOW_COUNT	Policy error: the operation would exceed the global user-policy flow count.	Abort or retry at a later time.
GQOS_POLICY_SUBNET_DEF _FLOW_COUNT	Policy error: the operation would exceed the subnet default-policy flow count.	Abort or retry at a later time.
GQOS_POLICY_SUBNET_GRP _FLOW_COUNT	Policy error: the operation would exceed the subnet default-policy flow count.	Abort or retry at a later time.
GQOS_POLICY_SUBNET_USER _FLOW_COUNT	Policy error: the operation would exceed the subnet default-policy flow count.	Abort or retry at a later time.
GQOS_POLICY_GLOBAL_DEF _FLOW_DURATION	Policy error: the operation would exceed the global default-policy flow duration.	Abort.
GQOS_POLICY_GLOBAL_GRP _FLOW_DURATION	Policy error: the operation would exceed the global group-policy flow duration.	Abort.
GQOS_POLICY_GLOBAL_USER _FLOW_DURATION	Policy error: the operation would exceed the global user-policy flow duration.	Abort.
GQOS_POLICY_SUBNET_DEF _FLOW_DURATION	Policy error: the operation would exceed the subnet default-policy flow duration.	Abort.
GQOS_POLICY_SUBNET_GRP _FLOW_DURATION	Policy error: the operation would exceed the subnet group-policy flow duration.	Abort.
GQOS_POLICY_SUBNET_USER _FLOW_DURATION	Policy error: the operation would exceed the subnet user-policy flow duration.	Abort.

Error value	Description	Application Response
GQOS_POLICY_GLOBAL_DEF _FLOW_RATE	Policy error: the operation would exceed the global default-policy flow rate.	Abort or retry with reduced QOS requirements.
GQOS_POLICY_GLOBAL_GRP _FLOW_RATE	Policy error: the operation would exceed the global group-policy flow rate.	Abort or retry with reduced QOS requirements.
GQOS_POLICY_GLOBAL_USER _FLOW_RATE	Policy error: the operation would exceed the global user-policy flow rate.	Abort or retry with reduced QOS requirements.
GQOS_POLICY_SUBNET_DEF _FLOW_RATE	Policy error: the operation would exceed the subnet default-policy flow rate.	Abort or retry with reduced QOS requirements.
GQOS_POLICY_SUBNET_GRP _FLOW_RATE	Policy error: the operation would exceed the subnet group-policy flow rate.	Abort or retry with reduced QOS requirements.
GQOS_POLICY_SUBNET_USER _FLOW_RATE	Policy error: the operation would exceed the subnet user-policy flow rate.	Abort or retry with reduced QOS requirements.
GQOS_POLICY_GLOBAL_DEF _PEAK_RATE	Policy error: the operation would exceed the global default-policy peak rate.	Abort or retry with reduced QOS requirements.
GQOS_POLICY_GLOBAL_GRP _PEAK_RATE	Policy error: the operation would exceed the global group-policy peak rate.	Abort or retry with reduced QOS requirements.
GQOS_POLICY_GLOBAL_USER _PEAK_RATE	Policy error: the operation would exceed the global user-policy peak rate.	Abort or retry with reduced QOS requirements.
GQOS_POLICY_SUBNET_DEF _PEAK_RATE	Policy error: the operation would exceed the subnet default-policy peak rate.	Abort or retry with reduced QOS requirements.
GQOS_POLICY_SUBNET_GRP _PEAK_RATE	Policy error: the operation would exceed the subnet default-policy peak rate.	Abort or retry with reduced QOS requirements.
GQOS_POLICY_SUBNET_USER _PEAK_RATE	Policy error: the operation would exceed the subnet default-policy peak rate.	Abort or retry with reduced QOS requirements.
GQOS_POLICY_GLOBAL_DEF _SUM_FLOW_RATE	Policy error: the operation would exceed the global default-policy total flow rate.	Abort or retry with reduced QOS requirements.
GQOS_POLICY_GLOBAL_GRP _SUM_FLOW_RATE	Policy error: the operation would exceed the global group-policy total flow rate.	Abort or retry with reduced QOS requirements.
GQOS_POLICY_GLOBAL_USER _SUM_FLOW_RATE	Policy error: the operation would exceed the global user-policy total flow rate.	Abort or retry with reduced QOS requirements.

continues ▶

Table 11.2   *continued*

Error value	Description	Application Response
GQOS_POLICY_SUBNET_DEF _SUM_FLOW_RATE	Policy error: the operation would exceed the subnet default-policy total flow rate.	Abort or retry with reduced QOS requirements.
GQOS_POLICY_SUBNET_GRP _SUM_FLOW_RATE	Policy error: the operation would exceed the subnet group-policy total flow rate.	Abort or retry with reduced QOS requirements.
GQOS_POLICY_SUBNET_USER _SUM_FLOW_RATE	Policy error: the operation would exceed the subnet user-policy total flow rate.	Abort or retry with reduced QOS requirements.
GQOS_POLICY_GLOBAL_DEF _SUM_PEAK_RATE	Policy error: the operation would exceed the global default-policy total peak rate.	Abort or retry with reduced QOS requirements.
GQOS_POLICY_GLOBAL_GRP _SUM_PEAK_RATE	Policy error: the operation would exceed the global default-policy total peak rate.	Abort or retry with reduced QOS requirements.
GQOS_POLICY_GLOBAL_USER _SUM_PEAK_RATE	Policy error: the operation would exceed the global default-policy total peak rate.	Abort or retry with reduced QOS requirements.
GQOS_POLICY_SUBNET_DEF _SUM_PEAK_RATE	Policy error: the operation would exceed the subnet default-policy total peak rate.	Abort or retry with reduced QOS requirements.
GQOS_POLICY_SUBNET_GRP _SUM_PEAK_RATE	Policy error: the operation would exceed the subnet default-policy total peak rate.	Abort or retry with reduced QOS requirements.
GQOS_POLICY_SUBNET_USER _SUM_PEAK_RATE	Policy error: the operation would exceed the subnet default-policy total peak rate.	Abort or retry with reduced QOS requirements.
GQOS_POLICY_UNKNOWN_USER	Policy error: the user is unknown.	Check the user's identification and security attributes.
GQOS_POLICY_NO_PRIVILEGES	Policy error: the user has no privilege.	Check the user's identification and security attributes.
GQOS_POLICY_EXPIRED_USER _TOKEN	Policy error: the user identification token has expired.	Abort or retry.
GQOS_POLICY_NO_RESOURCES	Policy error: out of resources.	Abort or retry at a later time.
GQOS_POLICY_PRE_EMPTED	Policy error: the operation was pre-empted.	Abort or retry at a later time.
GQOS_POLICY_USER_CHANGED	Policy error: user identification has changed.	Abort.
GQOS_POLICY_NO_ACCEPTS	Policy error: the operation was rejected by all policy modules.	Abort.

Error value	Description	Application Response
GQOS_POLICY_NO_MEMORY	Policy error: out of memory.	Abort or retry at a later time.
GQOS_POLICY_CRAZY_FLOWSPEC	Policy error: invalid FLOWSPEC.	Check the FLOWSPEC structure.

How to Program Windows 2000 QOS On a Granular Level

Most developers will find that the RSVP SP and its functions provide all the QOS-enabling capabilities that they need to let their applications take advantage of Windows 2000 QOS. For those who need more finite, granular control over how Windows 2000 implements its various QOS capabilities within their application (or service), this section is where you'll find such information.

The ProviderSpecific Buffer

The *ProviderSpecific* buffer is a member of the QUALITYOFSERVICE structure, and is of type WSABUF. The *ProviderSpecific* buffer enables developers to provide special QOS information, such as RSVP or Traffic Control parameters and settings.

The *ProviderSpecific* buffer includes a length field, and a pointer to a buffer. The buffer may include multiple objects, and each object must contain the following, in the following order:

1 A type field that identifies the object.

2 A length field that contains the length of the object, excluding the header.

3 The object data itself.

All objects referenced in the *ProviderSpecific* buffer must be contained within the same piece of contiguous buffer memory.

Receivers can use the *ProviderSpecific* buffer to do the following:

- Specify nondefault RSVP Filter Style, *FlowDescriptors*, and *filterspecs*.
- Request RESERVE_CONFIRMATION.
- Specify one or more policy elements to RSVP.
- Retrieve QOS and RESV_CONFIRM events.

Senders can use the *ProviderSpecific* buffer to do the following:

- Specify Traffic Control parameters such as shape/discard mode and set internal-priority objects.
- Retrieve QOS events.
- Retrieve or specify policy elements.

Controlling RSVP Signaling

As you know, RSVP is an IETF-standardized protocol that ferries QOS requests between end nodes and interacts with all RSVP-enabled network devices in the path between end nodes. RSVP signaling is automatically initiated whenever the RSVP SP determines that basic QOS provisioning requests (through standard RSVP SP functions, as described in the first half of this chapter) merit doing so. Through the use of the *ProviderSpecific* buffer, however, RSVP SP lets developers directly interact with RSVP, enabling fine-tuning or special service requests to be made without depending on the RSVP SP to interpret conventional QOS requests (as done through parameters in the QUALI-TYOFSERVICE structure) and pass such requests down to RSVP.

Using *RSVP_RESERVE_INFO*

The RSVP_RESERVE_INFO object enables applications to specify granular QOS parameters directly to RSVP, facilitating the fine-tuning of RSVP reservations. To implement the RSVP_RESERVE_INFO object, you must pass a filled RSVP_RESERVE_INFO object through the RSVP SP to RSVP by using the *ProviderSpecific* buffer. The following parameters can be fine-tuned with the RSVP_RESERVE_INFO object:

- RESV Confirmation Requests
- RSVP Filter Style

Getting *RESV* Confirmation Requests

The RSVP_RESERVE_INFO object enables a receiving application to be notified of the outcome of an RSVP reservation request by setting the *ConfirmRequest* member of the RSVP_RESERVE_INFO object to a nonzero value. The setting of this parameter is necessary because RSVP network nodes are not required to automatically generate RSVP CONFIRMATION messages, per the RSVP specification.

Because data for a given QOS flow is treated as BEST_EFFORT traffic until the reservation is in place, developers have a compelling reason to enable RSVP confirmation immediately after a WSAConnect(), WSAJoinLeaf() function call, or use of the SIO_SET_QOS ioctl. Data sent on the connection before the arrival of the RSVP confirmation notification shouldn't exceed the permitted send rate (which is discovered by querying with the SIO_CHK_QOS ioctl) because nonconforming traffic is discarded. After the RESV message arrives (triggering the RSVP confirmation), the RSVP SP modifies Traffic Control service to match the RESV state.

> **Note**
>
> *Note that no more than one confirmation notification is received for each QOS-enabled function call (or direct RSVP call) made on a receiving socket. Also, note that RSVP confirmation requests are only useful for receiving applications.* ◆

Fine-Tuning RSVP Filter Style

As we know from previous chapters, RSVP recognizes three filter styles that define how RSVP-enabled network devices treat packets that are transmitted along the path between an end-to-end QOS-enabled connection. RSVP's three filter styles are as follows:

- Fixed Filter (FF)
- Wildcard Filter (WF)
- Shared Explicit (SE)

RSVP SP Service Types (Guaranteed Service, Controlled Load, and Best Effort) are associated with RSVP filter styles. Because of this association, RSVP SP automatically translates its Service Types into the appropriate RSVP filter style as part of its RSVP invocation. With RSVP_RESERVE_INFO, however, developers can override the default setting that the RSVP SP assigns by using the *Style* field of the RSVP_RESERVE_INFO object.

Default RSVP filter style settings can be overridden through the use of the RSVP_RESERVE_INFO object by specifying one of the following values in the *Style* parameter of the RSVP_RESERVE_INFO object, along with required *flowdescriptors*:

- The RSVP_FIXED_FILTER_STYLE Object—Overrides default settings of the WF RSVP filter style setting for multicast or unconnected UDP unicast receivers. This is useful when attempting to generate multiple FF reservations for connected unicast receivers, which otherwise would connect only a single FF reservation. Note that *flowdescriptors* must be specified when using the RSVP_FIXED_FILTER_STYLE object, so that the *NumFlowDesc* parameter of RSVP_RESERVE_INFO is set to 1 and the *FlowDescList* of RSVP_RESERVE_INFO is set to the sender's address/port.

- The RSVP_WILDCARD_STYLE Object—Overrides default settings of the FF RSVP filter style setting for unicast receivers. Note that *flowdescriptors* must not be specified when using the RSVP_WILDCARD_STYLE object, so that the *NumFlowDesc* parameter of RSVP_RESERVE_INFO is set to 1 and the *FlowDescList* of RSVP_RESERVE_INFO is set to the sender's address/port.

- The RSVP_SHARED_EXPLICIT_STYLE Object—Overrides default RSVP filter style settings. The RSVP_SHARED_EXPLICIT_STYLE object is used to create an RSVP SE reservation. Note that the *only* way to create connections that use the SE RSVP filter style is through this mechanism. The RSVP_SHARED_EXPLICIT_STYLE cannot be applied to TCP receivers or to connected UDP receivers. When the RSVP_SHARED_EXPLICIT_STYLE is used, the flow's resources are shared between all sources. Also, when using the RSVP_SHARED_EXPLICIT_STYLE object, *flowdescriptors* must be specified, so that the *NumFlowDesc* parameter of RSVP_RESERVE_INFO is set to 0 and the *FlowDescList* of RSVP_RESERVE_INFO is set to NULL.

Disabling RSVP Signaling

Receiving applications can have RSVP signaling on a per-flow basis by using the bit-wise OR operator, the SERVICE_NO_QOS_SIGNALING flag with the value in the *ServiceType* field of the *ReceivingFlowspec* parameter of the QUALITYOFSERVICE structure.

A registry variable may also be used to disable RSVP signaling, but this approach disables all RSVP signaling on the entire interface. The registry variable that disables RSVP signaling for the entire interface is the following:

```
\hkeylocalmachine\system\currentcontrolset\services\tcpip\parameters\
➥interfaces\<interface>\qos\EnableRSVP
```

Setting the registry entry to 0 disables RSVP signaling for all flows passing through the interface. Setting the registry entry to 1 enables it.

Joining RSVP Sessions

Joining an RSVP session requires making appropriate function calls that are particular to the type of RSVP session that an application or service wants to join. However, due to the inherent differences between unicast (both TCP and UDP) and multicast sessions, each has to be discussed separately. To generalize, however, the following are usually true:

- Unicast sessions usually use WSAConnect().
- Multicast sessions use WSAJoinLeaf() (and sendto() for multicast senders).
- Both unicast and multicast can use the WSAIoctl(SIO_SET_QOS) function/opcode pair.

Using *WSAConnect()* to Join Unicast RSVP Sessions

The use of WSAConnect() function with RSVP-enabled TCP sessions is straightforward because parameters match quite well between parameters associated with WSAConnect() and parameters necessary for RSVP to operate. Table 11.3 illustrates which conditions of a TCP socket (left column) correspond to RSVP conditions (right column), which enable the TCP socket to join the session.

Table 11.3   Associating TCP socket conditions with RSVP sessions.

TCP Socket Is	RSVP Session Is Joined
Not bound, or is bound and not connected (the WSAConnect() function is not issued)	Never
Bound and connected	If both of the following conditions are true: The port and address specified in any session match the socket's bound port and address. *SenderTemplate*, which is specified in PATH state associated with the session, matches the connected peer's port and address.

The use of WSAConnect() with RSVP-enabled UDP unicast sessions is less stringent than its use with TCP sessions, largely due to the fact that it is not always possible to determine unique addresses associated with a UDP socket. Table 11.4 illustrates which conditions of a UDP unicast socket (left column) correspond to RSVP conditions (right column), which enable the UDP unicast socket to join the session. These mappings do not apply to UDP multicast sessions.

Table 11.4   Associating UDP socket conditions with RSVP sessions.

UDP Unicast Socket Is	RSVP Session Is Joined
Not bound and not connected	Never
Bound using INADDR_ANY, and not connected (the WSAConnect() function is not issued)	If the port specified in any session matches the socket's bound port.
Bound using a specific address and not connected	If the port and address specified in any session match the socket's bound port and address.
Bound using INADDR_ANY, and connected	If both of the following conditions are true: The port specified in any session matches the socket's bound port. *SenderTemplate*, which is specified in PATH state associated with the session, matches the connected peer's port and address.
Bound using a specific address and connected	If both of the following conditions are true: The port and address specified in any session matches the socket's bound port and address. *SenderTemplate*, which is specified in PATH state associated with the session, matches the connected peer's port and address.

Using *WSAJoinLeaf* to Join Multicast RSVP Sessions

Multicast UDP sockets are expected to create the multicast UDP socket using WSASocket(), and to indicate that they are multicast receivers in the accompanying (WSASocket) flags. If multicast UDP sockets don't use WSASocket() (and associated multicast flags), the RSVP SP may not be able to determine that the socket is multicast, and therefore may send undesired RESV messages. Table 11.5 illustrates which conditions of a UDP multicast socket (left column) correspond to RSVP conditions (right column), which enable the UDP multicast socket to join the session (note that these mappings do not apply to UDP unicast sessions).

Table 11.5   Associating Multicast socket conditions with RSVP sessions.

UDP Multicast Socket Is	RSVP Session Is Joined
Not joined to a specific multicast group (the WSAJoinLeaf() function is not issued)	Never

continues ▶

Table 11.5   Associating Multicast socket conditions with RSVP sessions.

UDP Multicast Socket Is	RSVP Session Is Joined
Joined to a specific multicast group (using the WSAJoinLeaf() function)	The multicast port and address specified in any session match the multicast port and address specified in the WSAJoinLeaf() function call.

Applications are required to use WSAJoinLeaf() to send and/or receive multicast traffic, and are required to set the *dwFlags* parameter of WSAJoinLeaf() to JL_SENDER_ONLY, JL_RECEIVER_ONLY or JL_BOTH, to indicate the direction in which QOS service is requested.

> **Note**
>
> Note *that alternate multicast semantics, such as simply calling* sendto() *with a multicast address (for sending) or using* IP_ADD_MEMBERSHIP *(for receiving) do not invoke QOS service.* ◆

Using *sendto()* and *WSASendTo()* by Multicast Senders

Senders that join multicast sessions using WSAJoinLeaf() are required to call sendto() or WSASendTo() with the correct multicast session address to send data to the multicast session (even though the multicast session address is already provided with the WSAJoinLeaf() function call). If the sending application calls sendto() or WSASendTo(), specifying a multicast session address other than the address specified with the WSAJoinLeaf() function call, the data will not receive QOS provisioning.

Also note that QOS-enabled applications should only call sendto() or WSASendTo() when acting as a multicast sender. Unicast (UDP or TCP) sender applications must specify their destination address using WSAConnect(), and it is sufficient for that application to use send() or WSASend() calls, rather than sendto() or WSASendTo().

Using *WSAIoctl(SIO_SET_QOS)* during RSVP Sessions

The use of WSAIoctl(SIO_SET_QOS) generally isn't necessary; the use of connection-oriented Windows Sockets function calls (such as WSAConnect()) is usually sufficient for providing the RSVP SP (and therefore RSVP) with requisite QOS and address parameters.

> **Note**
>
> *Using additional error information (such as that returned using FD_QOS) can make the QOS-enabling part of application development easier.* ◆❑

One exception is when a UDP application receives from multiple senders, in which case the WSAIoctl(SIO_SET_QOS) function/opcode pair must be used to specify QOS parameters to avoid limiting the socket to receive traffic from a single sender (as the use of a connection-oriented function call such as WSAConnect() would do).

Another exception is when a UDP transmit uses sendto() to transmit data to one or more receivers through an unconnected socket (NetMeeting 2.1 is an example of such an application). In this circumstance, the sending application must do the following in order to invoke QOS provisioning:

- Supply the RSVP SP with one or more appropriate *SendingFlowspec*(s) by issuing one or more SIO_SET_QOS ioctls.
- Provide the RSVP SP with the destination address(es) by issuing one or more QOS_DEST_ADDR object(s) in the *ProviderSpecific* buffer.

The WSAIoctl(SIO_SET_QOS) function/opcode pair is also useful for modifying QOS parameters subsequent to the establishment of the connection with a connection-oriented function call. This functionality also enables an application to separate the specification of QOS parameters from the determination of local and peer addresses that are implicit in making a connection-oriented function call.

Programming Traffic Control

Windows 2000 QOS enabled developers to specifically program different aspects of traffic control (such as enabling shaping, smoothing and flow regulation) without the involvement of RSVP or the Windows 2000 RSVP SP. Such programmatic capabilities provide more flexibility for developers and their applications. These capabilities remove the dependency on RSVP for the implementation of service quality provisioning.

Developers can use TC API to go about programming traffic control, and the definitions of the functions and structures within the TC API are the best resource for providing guidance (and definitions) of how to go about doing so. The TC API function and structure definitions can be found on MSDN, MSDN Online, or in a comprehensive reference set on Windows Network Programming.

Index

Symbols

New Riders Professional Library

Michael Masterson, Herman Kneif, Scott Vinick, and Eric Roul:
Windows NT DNS
(ISBN: 1-56205-943-2)

Sandra Osborne: *Windows NT Registry*
(ISBN: 1-56205-941-6)

Mark Edmead and Paul Hinsburg: *Windows NT Performance Monitoring, Benchmarking, and Tuning*
(ISBN: 1-56205-942-4)

Karanjit Siyan: *Windows NT TCP/IP*
(ISBN 1-56205-887-8)

Ted Harwood: *Windows NT Terminal Server and Citrix MetaFrame*
(ISBN: 1-56205-944-0)

Anil Desai: *Windows NT Network Management: Reducing Total Cost of Ownership*
(ISBN: 1-56205-946-7)

Eric K. Cone, Jon Boggs, and Sergio Perez: *Planning for Windows 2000*
(ISBN: 0-7357-0048-6)

Doug Hauger, Marywynne Leon, and William C. Wade III:
Implementing Exchange Server
(ISBN: 1-56205-931-9)

Janice Rice Howd: *Exchange System Administration*
(ISBN: 0-7357-0081-8)

Sean Baird and Chris Miller: *SQL Server Administration*
(ISBN: 1-56205-955-6)